KEEPING
YOUR SANITY
(In An Insane World)

KEEPING YOUR SANITY

(In An Insane World)

Practical essays for your
psychological well-being

Second Edition

Edward A. Dreyfus, Ph.D.

CONTENTS

*This volume is dedicated to the hundreds of patients
who have privileged me with their trust and have allowed me
to participate in their journey of self-discovery and transformation.
They have enhanced my life and made it more meaningful.
I am grateful for having had the opportunity to have been of service.*

INTRODUCTION

Keeping Your Sanity (Second Edition) is a series of essays designed to give people an opportunity to explore themselves as they come to terms with the various trials and tribulations of everyday life. This second edition has several new chapters in addition to revising some of the previous chapters.

We live in a complex, uncertain, sometimes crazy world where things just don't seem to make sense. Stuff happens. We often feel out of control. We all face these concerns almost daily. Most of us, however, do not recognize that we have a lot more control over how the issues we face affect us. We have a lot more power than we give ourselves credit for. Life in the twenty-first century is complex. Relationship issues, social issues, addictions, environmental crises, personal tragedies, illness, depression, spiritual issues, sexuality, and more, all have an impact on how we feel about ourselves and how we cope with life.

Mental health practitioners receive training in the science and art of psychotherapy, which for many individuals, is the treatment sought for trying to come to terms with many of these issues. Most people, however, do it alone. Sometimes we are successful in our attempts; often we are not.

These essays are based on almost four decades of practice as a clinical psychologist and psychotherapist. People seek psychological help for many reasons. While each person brings a unique set of experiences, concerns, and issues, the general areas with which people struggle are similar. The majority of these issues fall into several categories: compulsive behaviors, relationships, social issues, problems in living, and taking charge of one's life. I have grouped the essays that fall into these categories.

Compulsive behaviors include rigid behaviors that, while designed to be helpful in coping with the stresses of living, become dysfunctional over time. Perfectionism, workaholism, alcohol and substance abuse, compulsive eating or other food-related disorders are attempts on an individual's part to gain control over some aspect of his or her life. The solution, however, becomes worse than the problem it was designed to alleviate.

Relationship issues dominate our lives. We want better marriages, better family relationships, and more friends. We want to find a mate and begin a family. We struggle with the challenges of having two careers while raising a family.

Social issues greatly affect our lives. Real issues such as the economy, natural disasters, and gender roles are among a few of the issues that confront us. Traditionally psychotherapists only focus on internal struggles. We now recognize that real events in our lives can affect our psychological adjustment.

There are a host of *problems in living* that can make dealing with day-to-day issues more difficult. Sometimes the stimulus for the difficulties we experience originate outside of ourselves such as the in the case of a natural disaster or a downturn in the economy. Other times the origin lies within ourselves as is the case in sexual dysfunction, some depressions, anxiety and panic, and shyness and guilt, to name a few.

The last section of the book focuses on *taking charge* of our lives. These chapters deal with how we can empower ourselves to become more impervious to the trials and tribulations of daily life. These essays try to teach you how you can strengthen your psychological immune system and feel empowered. The last chapter, "Designing Your Life," presents a new paradigm for looking at one's entire life, stressing the importance of planning one's life rather than simply falling into a life.

The essays can be read in any order depending on the issues which are of most concern to you at any given moment. In the course of my practice I found that sometimes people found it easier to integrate new ideas when they were able to see them in print, in the privacy of their own home. These essays helped them integrate these ideas into their everyday life. In some cases the essays raised questions that were then explored in treatment. In other cases, people felt that they were reading about themselves and sought treatment. I have tried to take some of the most common concerns and present them in a way that the layperson could understand and utilize.

Compulsive Behaviors

1

COMPULSIVE BEHAVIOR: DISEASE OR SYMPTOM?

Many mental health practitioners are promoting the notion that alcohol abuse, drug abuse, overeating, gambling, anorexia, bulimia, and smoking are diseases. By using the disease model, its proponents believe that people are more apt to seek help because having an "illness" is more acceptable than having psychological or behavior disorder. I am reminded of the effects of saying that people with emotional difficulties were "sick," and suffering from a "disease." Psychology and psychiatry moved a long way forward when we listened to Thomas Szasz[1] declare that mental illness was a myth, to Karl Menninger[2] discussing degrees of personality organization, and to Benjamin Rush when he spoke of problems in living. Now it appears we are moving backwards. What will be the next "disease" to appear in the news media?

The disease model states that alcoholism and compulsive overeating, for example, are diseases and can be compared to diabetes in that diabetics react to sugar in a similar way that overeaters have a reaction to food and alcoholics to liquor. Therefore, in both instances the individuals must carefully monitor their intake. If they do not rigidly adhere to their respective diets there will be dire consequences. The compulsive overeater, for example, maintains that if he/she does not monitor food intake, there is a chemical imbalance that takes over and control over one's eating is no longer possible. So, the theory maintains, the compulsive overeater is not "normal" insofar as eating is concerned, but rather he or she has a "disease" and is "sick."

The question that this thesis does not address, however, is: Why do compulsive overeaters and alcoholics, knowing that they are not able to control their substance abuse once it is started, persist in breaking their diet? The diabetic's disease is the failure of the body to produce sufficient insulin; the disease is not the individual's failure to stay on a diabetic diet. It is not the *behavior* that is the disease; it is the manner in which the body metabolizes alcohol that may be the disease, leading to the necessity for dietary control, or in the case of the substance abuser and alcoholic, abstinence. While there may be a biological or chemical basis for some compulsions, the disease model does not account for the compulsive *behavior* itself; it only accounts for the specific substance.

HISTORICAL PERSPECTIVE

Many years ago mentally disturbed persons were considered to be inhabited by the devil; they were ostracized from their communities and families and were treated with disdain. They were locked up, deprived of their human rights, and often killed. Pinel, in the eighteenth century, cut the chains of the inmates of the insane asylum at Bicitre and freed them, declaring that they were not possessed of evil spirits, but rather that they were medically ill. This was the beginning of a movement which sought to achieve humane treatment for the mentally disturbed. It was an extremely important step forward. By declaring these people ill, the indignities they suffered were reduced. It was *necessary* to call them "sick" in order to obtain humane treatment.

As the theories of Sigmund Freud were made available and became acceptable, it was discovered that many of these individuals were not ill in the medical sense, but rather they were psychologically disturbed. The "talking cure," as psychoanalysis was then called, demonstrated that mental "illness" could be cured through words. This was another very important step, for now, people with psychological disorders could be viewed with some dignity and could potentially be treated by non-medical practitioners. Unfortunately, neither the patients nor the practitioners were accorded the same respect as those with physical ailments being treated by physicians. In fact, many people still believe it is much more acceptable to be physically ill than it is to be psychologically disturbed.

So, instead of being chained in dungeons and be forgotten, the mentally ill were locked in hospitals and treated. However, it gradually became obvious that they were still ostracized from the community, and were being treated as second-class citizens. Though they were treated better physically, they still carried the stigma of being "sick," which was almost as dehumanizing as being thought of as "inhabited by the devil." Now they were pitied, but they still lost their freedom, their dignity, and their human rights.

The movement away from the disease model toward a psychological model helped pave the way toward integrating the "mentally ill" into the community rather than segregating them. It had the effect of gaining more respect, understanding, and dignity for all people with emotional difficulties. Instead of seeing these people as "sick," we began seeing them as having "problems in living," which could be understood and resolved. Such a psychological model permitted greater numbers of non-medical practitioners to "treat" these individuals and has made such treatment more available and more affordable to more people. People began to feel more comfortable treating troubled people humanly without having to see them as "sick." (In fact, they found that the disease model interfered with effective treatment.) People trying to cope with internal or external stress may do so in maladaptive ways. This does not make them "sick."

CONSEQUENCES OF A DISEASE MODEL

When it came to compulsive behaviors, however, even the most compassionate individuals had difficulty accepting that people did not seem able to control their own behavior. Hence, they treated alcoholics as "bums," overeaters as "fatsos," gamblers as "stupid," etc. And these people viewed themselves similarly. So, the concept of illness was invoked once again. And once again people were treated for their "illness" and others viewed them more compassionately as, "Don't laugh at your overweight Aunt Mary, she has an illness," or "Your drunk Uncle Charley is sick." I think it is pitiful that a society has to resort to seeing people as sick in order to be compassionate towards them. And I believe it adversely affects people's self-esteem to have to consider themselves sick in order to be related to humanly. I find it sad that people, so hungry for acceptance, either self-acceptance or acceptance from others, will accept the appellation "sick."

The advocates for various self-help and other groups that deal with compulsive substance abuse view these compulsions as diseases. They promote the concept of disease in order to entice substance abusers into treatment. If they can convince these people that they are "sick" and they are suffering from a "disease" then it is believed that more people will accept treatment.

We live in a society that loves labels—whether on clothes or on people. We tend to relate to the clothes people, with the labels on the outside, just as we treat the labels we pin on people: schizophrenic, alcoholic, ACA, incest survivor, borderline personality, etc. And people seem to need to view themselves as "sick" in order to be treated humanly (and in order to treat themselves with care.)

Psychology strove for years to move away from the medical/disease model so that healers would relate to people as people not as labels, not as "sick." This was called the humanistic movement and eschewed the medical model and sought a psychological model. I see a reversal of this effort and find it regressive. And I think, in this context, that 12-step programs, with their emphasis on disease and "sickness," foster this regressive type of thinking.

While I do not object to the results or even some of the methods employed, I do object to the use of the terms "disease" and "sick" as a means for achieving these results. There are consequences to using a disease model, which extend beyond merely controlling substance abuse. In our quest for expediency, we are often shortsighted.

Social Consequences

I object to the idea that compulsive *behavior* is a disease. It does not matter whether there is a chemical imbalance that leaves these people vulnerable to gaining weight and drinking, the disease concept is not appropriate for the compulsive behaviors. Society decides on what is compulsive, and using the disease concept, any one of us could be viewed as "sick" for any behavior that people deem compulsive. Thus, someone who is a workaholic, a smoker, or a nail-biter could be considered "sick." Don't people have the right to engage in activities, even unhealthy activities, without being considered "sick"?

Compulsive behavior is rewarded in our society. Indeed, people are taught to be compulsive; that is, we are taught to be punctual, orderly, committed, organized, etc. We are taught to hide our feelings through activity. We are taught to keep busy when we are feeling badly. We are even taught to eat when we are "blue." All compulsive individuals are taught at an early age to deny feelings through some form of activity. And if you learn your lessons well, you could be considered "sick."

Psychological Consequences

Some psychological consequences of the disease model are:

1. Individuals tend to give up responsibility for their life; they can see themselves as victims because the "disease" is not their fault.
2. Individuals seek someone to "fix" them without examining the causes or issues, which may produce the compulsion; only the symptom is examined.
3. There is a loss of dignity and self-esteem in believing that one is "bad" or "sick" for having gone off a diet, or drinking, etc.
4. Individuals often use "illness" or "disease" to avoid taking responsibility for their behavior just as they might have gotten "sick" to avoid going to school.
5. This kind of infantilizing has long-term consequences to one's self-esteem and self-confidence, though it may have immediate results. Patronizing others does not enhance one's self-concept.
6. By seeing oneself as "sick," one invites compassion and pity; and one then begins to see oneself as pitiful, hoping

for a magical cure that someday will be discovered if one is "good."

Because we live in a society that also looks askew at individuals with psychological problems, especially compulsive disorders (they tend to be viewed as lacking in willpower or lacking in moral fiber), it is much more palatable to talk in terms of the "disease" which needs to be treated than it is to deal with mal-adaptive coping behaviors. It is more acceptable to go to the medical doctor's office than it is to go to the psychotherapist's office. So the disease model has much more appeal for the majority of our society.

Thus, what started out as a humane approach to a problem has become in itself a problem. Originally, calling compulsive behaviors a disease was for the purpose of increasing compassion toward the obese, the alcoholic, or the gambler. Gradually the solution has produced the very effect it sought to eliminate—namely, reducing human dignity and reinforcing the notion that one is not a responsible adult. Rather, the compulsive substance abuser is viewed as a helpless child who is "sick" and needs to be told what to do. (In fact, in some of these self-help programs, members are referred to as "babies.")

There is no doubt that were we to promote a psychological model of abuse rather than a disease model, many individuals would not seek treatment; that would be their choice. However, in my opinion, there is greater harm to many more people from the potential loss of responsibility, choice, and dignity by invoking a disease model. What will be the next "sickness" for which treatment will be given? When do we have the right to behave differently than society dictates without being labeled "sick"?

Political Consequences

If we accept a disease model for compulsive behavior, then what will stop people from thinking about other psychological disorders as diseases? And if this happens, we will be back where we were fifty years ago, believing that all people with emotional problems are "sick." Who will treat these "sick" people? Clearly the medical profession has a vested interest in promoting a disease model, for it is physicians who treat the "sick." It does not matter to the public that the "disease model" was only a *metaphor* used to encourage people to seek help. Over time the metaphor is lost and we are left with a model that is inappropriate. While the idea of using a disease model as a metaphor to make it more palatable for some people to accept treatment has some short-range appeal, the long-range consequences may be less attractive.

Many people do not comprehend the use of the disease model as a metaphor or as a theoretical model for generating hypotheses. Metaphors and models often become functionally autonomous; they take on a reality of their own. Yesterday's metaphors become today's reality. As the use of the term "disease" increases, and with more public acceptance of the notion that compulsive behaviors are diseases, we must become concerned with the long-term consequences on our thinking about the relationship between emotional disorders and disease.

Are we heading toward a time when, once again, people with problems in living and emotionally disturbed human beings will be viewed as "sick" and in need of medical, not psychological, treatment?

AN ALTERNATIVE MODEL

I think that a model based on integrating psychological,

biological, and social factors for understanding and treating chemical dependency, addictions, and compulsive behaviors is more appropriate than a disease model. Such a model takes into account biological (including genetics, physiological predisposition, and chemical components), social, and psychological factors in understanding compulsive behaviors without invoking "sickness" or disease as causative. The individual, in this model, remains responsible for how she/he deals with their life without the loss in dignity.

This model accepts that there may be genetic, chemical, biological, etc., factors involved in some addictions (for not being able to metabolize alcohol, for example), but this does not account for why an individual continues to rely upon their addiction for dealing with problems in the living. It recognizes that there are social issues involved in compulsive behaviors, which have nothing to do with biology or chemistry. It further states that psychological, not medical, factors are the most powerful in understanding and controlling human behavior. It accepts the basic principle that human beings are fundamentally responsible for their own behavior and have the power to choose how they will conduct their lives. It accepts that people are free to choose how they will live their life; even if that choice is self-destructive, it is still their choice. People can choose to play the game of life differently than most without being labeled "sick." They must, however, accept full responsibility for the consequences of that behavior.

2

IN SEARCH OF PERFECTION

The belief that perfection can be achieved affects the lives of countless numbers of people. Many people are obsessed with achieving perfection to the point that it affects their physical and psychological well-being. These individuals are commonly referred to as perfectionists. They seek the perfect mate, the perfect job, the perfect body, and they are often unhappy in their quest. Even the most mundane task can become an ordeal since the task must be performed to an exacting standard. These people experience disappointment and dissatisfaction and are often unable to enjoy the simple pleasures of life. They believe that perfection is attainable; they experience falling short of the goal as failure.

Sam, a successful accountant, wakes up every day with his heart palpitating and his palms sweating. He is anxious even before the day begins. He dreads having to go to work fearing that each action he takes will be criticized; he fears he might make a mistake. He prefers routine tasks so at least he has a reasonable chance of success. He would rather stifle his creativity than take a chance of failing.

Sally, a competent nurse, dreads getting a promotion for fear that she will fail. She must constantly review her work to make certain that she has done everything perfectly. If one thing is out of line she fears that she will be fired. It doesn't matter that she has received commendations over the years; she believes that she is only as good as her last performance.

Mary, a gourmet cook, housewife, and mother, is afraid to make something new for her family's dinner. In spite of her talents and their protests about dinner being too monotonous, she knows that it would take her hours to perfect something new. Though she would like to entertain people in her home, she is reluctant because she knows that it will take her hours if not days to prepare; everything will have to be perfect-clean house, perfect dinner, perfect grooming, etc.

John, a brilliant attorney, reads over legal documents with the precision of a neurosurgeon, as if every word was a life or death decision. He finds himself irritable, short-tempered, impatient, and filled with self-doubt. He is not being either the husband or father he wants to be.

These individuals spend an inordinate amount of time trying to make certain that they will avoid making mistakes. In the process they stifle their creativity, frequently refuse promotions, and often avoid anything new because of their need to have everything they do measure up to a standard of perfection.

Process vs. Outcome

Perfection is meant to be an abstract ideal toward which we strive in an attempt to gain proficiency and to excel. It is a concept designed to spur us on to greater heights. The meaning of the word perfection is illustrated by the phrase "striving toward perfection." Few people who adopt seeking perfection (as opposed to achieving perfection) as a value expect to achieve it. Seeking perfection merely connotes that process of moving closer to an abstract ideal which an individual or group has established.

In most instances, however, the concept of perfection in itself has no meaning in a concrete sense. It only takes on meaning when we ask the question, "Perfect for what?" In other words, it is a relative concept. What may be perfect for one circumstance or one person or group may not be perfect for another. People can agree, by consensus, on what they will establish as the ideal in any given circumstance. And this may change as newer techniques for achieving this end are developed. What is the perfect weather, the perfect fishing rod, or the perfect knife? In each case we would have to ask, "Perfect for what purpose?" Perfect weather for sailing is not the same as perfect weather for ice-skating. The perfect fishing rod when deep-sea fishing for marlin is different from that used when lake fishing for trout. And the perfect knife for hunting is different than the one used for stemming strawberries.

Perfectionists become obsessed with the outcome of any performance. These people feel compelled to complete a project to some arbitrary standard, irrespective of the purpose to be served. In many instances the function of the project gets completely overshadowed by the compulsion to make the outcome meet up to some standard of proficiency, e.g., polishing a pick-up truck used for hauling manure to the same level of perfection as a limousine used for a celebrity. For these individuals, purpose and function is not relevant. Perfection is absolute.

Perfectionists are driven to have everything they do meet some internal standard of perfection. Often these people find it difficult to take on projects because they will spend so much time and energy carrying out the task that they become overwhelmed and often either cannot complete the task or they take so long to do that it no longer matters.

Healthy Striving

A distinction must be made between people who strive for perfection and perfectionists. People who strive for perfection view the pursuit of perfection as the highest ideal. For these individuals it isn't the outcome that is important, but rather it is the process. It is the hunt rather than the kill, the journey rather than the destination that takes priority. Those who strive for perfection attempt to perfect their craft, their skill, and their abilities. Striving rather than achieving is the higher value.

People who pursue perfection with zest, joy, and passion are not to be confused with the perfectionists. These individuals do not respond to less-than-perfect achievement with self-criticism, blame, anger, or anxiety. Rather, they have learned to embrace their mistakes. They view their mistakes as opportunities to grow, to learn, and to discover. These people are more concerned with the adventure and the pursuit than they are with how things turn out.

Yes, they are pleased when they achieve their goals, but this is in addition to the joy they experience in the process. They relish the process as contrasted to perfectionists who view the process as a risk and merely an opportunity to fail. Perfectionists are often relieved when a project is put off, rather than feel a sense of disappointment.

Perfection and Control

Perfectionists need to be in control of their world. Since it is impossible to control the outcome of everything in their life, they narrow their world to one that is manageable. This accounts for why they are more comfortable performing familiar tasks, thereby reducing their anxiety about being out of control.

Perfectionists live in a narrowly defined world in which they feel empowered. It is much easier to control a small confine than a larger one. And in this narrowly defined world, they believe it is more possible to be perfect. The fewer activities they engage in, the greater the possibility of achieving this goal. Waiting for perfectionists to make a never-tried-before-dinner to their perfectionist standards could leave one hungry for a long time. Even perfectionists become frustrated with themselves, often refusing to cook or even eat because they could not prepare it to perfection. Time is often the enemy of perfectionists since they cannot achieve perfection on a schedule.

Perfectionists cannot tolerate mistakes. Even the slightest error is frustrating and can even generate overwhelming anxiety. It is as though each act were a life and death struggle. Each mistake could cause imminent catastrophe. Perfectionists even lose sleep worrying about projects in which they think they may have made a mistake.

Perfectionists live in a world where annihilation, criticism, and chaos lie around every corner. Perfectionists have such difficulty dealing with criticism that they have to protect themselves by every means available. Their narrow world, narrow range of activities, and obsession with perfection all help to ward off the anticipated criticism. Self-rebuke, self-criticism, and self-denial are often characteristics of perfectionists. They would rather criticize themselves than be criticized.

Perfectionism is a symptom of underlying anxiety, fear, and insecurity. Its purpose is to ward off anxiety, stemming from a self-image that is based on performance. Perfectionism is an attempt to master and control the environment.

A positive self-concept is developed by receiving encouragement and support for the person we are rather than for our performances. Since there is the natural tendency to master our environment, receiving positive responses for our efforts and our achievements serves to encourage us to move forward in the world. By contrast, receiving criticism and rebuke for our effort discourages us and places us in a position of jeopardy when confronted with tasks. Thus, the fear of withdrawal of love and approval generates a fear of taking risks, and a subsequent fear of making a mistake.

Roots of Perfectionism

Perfectionists often feel unworthy, guilty for some real or imagined transgression, and anxious. Generally, they simply don't feel "good enough." Perfectionists keep their world at a minimum so that they won't have to become overwhelmed with all of the possible imperfections, be open to criticism from others, and can avoid maintaining their things in perfect order. By keeping the world narrow, perfectionists are not exposed to the threat of criticism.

Societal values, schools, families, and individual interpretations of the world all play a part in the development of the perfectionist behavioral style.

Our society reinforces perfection. Thus, most of us experience some form of perfectionism. Some of us learn that it is the striving for perfection that is important while others learn that it is the outcome that matters. It is this latter position that creates most of the problems.

From childhood we learn that being "good" is very important to our parents. We learn that "good" means being quiet, orderly, clean, and disciplined, where being controlled is rewarded. We learn to delay gratification, put our toys away, not to spill our milk, and to scrub our hands clean.

And the child with the neatest room, cleanest hands, unsoiled clothes gets the gold star. From early on we train our children to function in the world where being compulsive and perfect pays off.

Schools further reinforce these values. We are taught to color within the lines; we are questioned about what happened to the 2 percent on a 98 percent correct paper. We are asked why we received one B in an otherwise straight A report card. Schools make it difficult for a child to make a mistake. There is criticism, punishment, and thwarting of the child's curiosity and desire to explore and take chances. Conformity is the goal and in many schools merely controlling the children takes a higher priority than learning and discovery. Perfect children are quiet children.

When the child lives in a world where there is considerable criticism for errors, mistakes, and omissions, the child feels anxious, fearing loss of approval and love. In order to ward off this anxiety and the anticipated criticism, the child begins to put pressure on him/herself to do better. The child then begins to criticize himself for not performing up to the internalized parental standard.

Some children grow up in a family where there is considerable discord. Often parents divorce, leaving a sense of insecurity, anxiety, and helplessness in a child. In an attempt to cope with these feelings the child focuses on some area of his/her life that she/he can control. By focusing on some narrowly defined area the child can feel less anxious and more in control. Focusing still further and trying to achieve perfect control can even further reduce the anxiety. At least in this one area the child feels in charge.

Even as adults we can all experience this feeling. When we are feeling overwhelmed or anxious we can begin to focus our attention on some project over which we feel some sense of mastery and thus experience an attenuation of the anxiety. When we learn this behavior as children it can become a way of life. Rather than dealing with the feelings of anxiety, helplessness, and chaos the child continues to narrow his/her world. By reducing his/her range of emotions and activities, the child does not to have to experience those feelings again. This pattern becomes a way of life. They avoid feelings of anxiety, fear, guilt, helplessness, and abandonment by constructing their world such that these experiences will never occur to them.

Imperfect and Happy

Perfectionism becomes ingrained in the very fabric of a person's personality. And because it is continuously reinforced in our workplace, and in society generally, it is very difficult to relinquish. The payoffs are considerable. We learn very early in life that mistakes are not acceptable.

So how can we change? It often feels as though the consequences of giving up perfectionism will be worse than dealing with the pain.

First, in order to change you must be willing to endure the short-term agony of giving up your cherished beliefs—which in many instances have helped you to survive in a chaotic world. *Second,* you have to develop a new belief system, one that is more congruent with contemporary information. Most of the beliefs held to by perfectionists are based on data collected during childhood. *Third,* you must be willing to risk changing behavior. Though this is easier once you have changed the beliefs, habitual ways of behaving are difficult to change. *Fourth,* few people are able to accomplish these feats alone. Support from friends and family, along with working with a psychotherapist, is frequently necessary. Remember, these beliefs and behaviors were developed in childhood. They are very resistant to change.

The following are some ideas for you to consider:

1) Mistakes are opportunities in disguise. They offer you the opportunity to look at a situation from a different perspective. Many inventions and discoveries have been the result of a mistake. Columbus discovered America while searching for the West Indies; he simply got lost!

2) Embrace your mistakes and learn to forgive yourself. Most of us grow more from support and affection than from criticism. Criticism causes us to shrink from the world. Mistakes indicate that you have made an attempt— that you have dared to try!

3) People who have been voted into the Hall of Fame or earned an Oscar or received a Pulitzer Prize, have had many a song, book, movie or play bomb or even trashed before (and after) they had a hit. Babe Ruth held the record for the most home runs and the most strikeouts!

4) Intentionally perform a task to less than perfect standards; see what happens. Notice how you feel.

5) Keep your mind on the purpose of your tasks. Be certain that the energy you put into the project is related to the purpose of the task. Remember: perfection is relative.

Be human: make a mistake!

3

EATING DISORDERS

During the last fifteen years there has been an increase in the number of people diagnosed as having an eating disorder. And there has been an increase in the number of eating disorders units in psychiatric hospitals. *The Diagnostic and Statistical Manual* published by the American Psychiatric Association now includes eating disorders as part of its nosology.

While both men and women are susceptible to eating disorders, it is more common among women for whom the quest for thinness has become an obsession. A common saying among women is: "You can never be too rich or too thin."

The increasing number of weight-loss programs and the number of weight-loss products available to the consumer is a testament to the obsession with weight. Billions of dollars a year are spent on the products. Diet books galore have flooded the market. The number of Overeaters Anonymous and meetings available has dramatically increased.

Food and addictions. Whether your habit is cocaine, running, eating, or purging, you are addicted if you cannot control when you start or stop the activity.

People who suffer from an eating disorder are just as addicted to their behavior as drug addicts or alcoholics are addicted to theirs. They use food to cope with the stresses of life. Food can alter one's mood in the same way drugs can. Food can relieve pain, can give a rush, and can soothe. Food can offer temporary relief from loneliness or low self-esteem. While it can give a sense of power and a brief reprieve from conflict or unhappiness, relying on food for coping with life can cause serious physical and social problems.

Some people choose overeating, others purge, others starve themselves, and still others use a combination of these. *In each case there is an underlying depression with which the person is trying to cope.* They are trying to gain some degree of control over a world in which they feel out of control.

Why someone chooses one method over another depends on a combination of personality type, family background, and social factors. The means a person develops relates to their usual way of coping with stress.

I. DESCRIPTION

There are three primary forms that an eating disorder takes: compulsive overeating, anorexia, and bulimia.

Compulsive Overeating refers to a behavior in which people have lost control of their eating habits and feel compelled to eat large quantities of food. These individuals tend to binge on food to the point where they often feel physically ill. Food is perceived not merely as a substance to nourish the body, nor is it viewed as a substance to be savored. *The compulsive overeater uses food in the same way that an addict might use drugs or alcohol.*

Compulsive overeaters feel as though they have little or

no control over the urge to eat or the behaviors that follow; once they have begun, they cannot stop until they have finished all the food they have begun to eat. Sometimes they can finish all the food on hand and then have to go to the store for more; they eat until they are exhausted. They often feel compelled to go for a "food fix" in the middle of the night.

Of course, compulsive overeaters gain a significant amount of weight, the consequences of which are very destructive to the rest of their physical health. They tend to develop high cholesterol, heart disease, hypertension, and other health problems due to forcing the body to work harder because of the excess weight and poor diet.

Anorexia is just the opposite of compulsive overeating. The anorexic compulsively starves herself, often to the point of emaciation. She can make a meal of a single apple, often spreading it throughout the day. She has a distorted sense of her body. The anorexic is preoccupied with thinness, constantly feeling that she is too fat.

She is perfectionistic and, just as the compulsive overeater is out of control with respect to how much she eats, the anorexic feels that she must maintain maximum control for fear of losing control. She is constantly proving that she can maintain complete control only to find that she can never achieve her ideal size. She can focus on a speck of fat around her ankle or elbow and strive to get rid of it at the expense of the rest of her physical health.

The anorexic does not see herself as others see her. Despite her size 2 dress size, when she looks in the mirror she sees a fat person. No amount of convincing will change her mind. Unfortunately, not until she has done some physical damage to herself will she seek help.

Though friends and family are the first persons to notice the problem, they are usually unable to affect the thinking of the anorexic. Physicians are frequently the only persons in a position to make an appropriate intervention. And then, it is often because of the physical damage that has already occurred. They are in the ideal place to make an appropriate referral. However, *the referral must be followed through.* And this is often difficult. It is necessary to encourage anorexics to seek the help they desperately need. *Anorexia is a potentially life-threatening disorder.*

Bulimia is the most recent form of eating disorder. It was unrecognized until ten years ago. Bulimia is often combined with either compulsive overeating or anorexia. The bulimic forces herself to vomit, to rid herself of the feeling of fullness. She equates the feeling of fullness with actually being fat. The most common form of bulimia is purging by inserting the finger into the throat, forcing vomiting. Vomiting also can be induced chemically by using vomiting agents. Some bulimics become addicted to laxatives, while others become "exercise bulimics," exercising many hours a day to shed the calories accumulated by eating.

Frequently bulimics engage in a binge-purge cycle where they may binge on a particular food and then purge immediately afterward. Thus, many bulimics go unnoticed by family or friends since they appear to have a healthy appetite in public, only to disappear into the restroom to purge themselves of the food. Some bulimics have learned to purge merely by concentrating. They have conditioned themselves to induce vomiting.

Force-vomiting has serious physical effects. It can disrupt the electrolyte balance in the blood, destroy the enamel on the teeth, rid the body of valuable nutrients, and create swollen and infected glands.

Some visible signs that someone might be purging are: "chipmunk" cheeks, swollen and painful glands, anemia, poor sleep, hair loss, loss of concentration, depression, irritability, and loss of menstrual cycle. *If you know anyone experienc-*

ing these symptoms, strongly urge them to seek professional help before they do permanent physical damage.

II. ETIOLOGY

The question remains, however, why some people develop eating disorders while others do not. There are three major groups of factors that contribute to eating disorders: social, familial, and psychological.

Social: As the Billy Crystal line goes, "It's not how you feel but how you look." Our society has always been preoccupied with physical beauty at the expense of feelings. One aspect of physical beauty is the shape of the human figure. This ideal shape will vary from generation to generation. At one time the voluptuous Marilyn Monroe look is idolized, while at another time it is the stick-figure, Twiggy look.

Men have always been less concerned with their body shape than women; and men have always been interested in the shape of women. Thus, we find that eating disorders are far more prevalent among women. They are preoccupied with having men find them attractive and admiring of their bodies. They spend billions of dollars a year trying to lose weight; they will have their bodies surgically altered, all to fit the latest "ideal" that often turns out to be some man's conception of physical beauty.

Their preoccupation becomes so great that they become obsessed with trying to live up to some ideal promoted by the media: movies, television, and magazines. The advertisers are constantly promoting some product that women can buy that will give them the "look" or the body they desire.

Even in grade school it is the girls with the best figure that are the most popular. And this preoccupation with image has become an obsession. Clothes, appearance, and figures have become status symbols. And the models for these "teenyboppers" are the older teens who, themselves, were preoccupied with looking "hot" and looking older. The teenager modeled herself after the ultra-thin models in fashion magazines who wore the clothes they coveted.

Boys have similar problems to girls during the early years from grade school through high school or even college. It isn't until after he enters his profession and makes money that his body style takes on less importance. Prior to this, the young boy has to be athletic. It is on the baseball or football field or basketball court that a young boy becomes popular with his mates and with the girls.

Society has played a significant role in the development of eating disorders. Those women who were born with larger bone structure, glandular difficulties, or a genetic predisposition toward being larger than average, or who have metabolisms that do not burn off calories as fast, or who cannot exercise rigorously, are doomed to become pariahs, left out of the "in crowd." Thin is in, fat is out. What does this attitude do to a youngster? She/he finds that no matter what she does she cannot be like the thin group.

Familial: From the time a woman is a little girl she hears her mother, her friends, and the media telling her how she should look. Mother does it by modeling the preoccupation with food and weight. She emphasizes the importance of looking good. Their well-meaning mothers who, after all, wanted their daughters to be part of the "in-crowd" often place their little girls on diets. They want their daughters to reflect positively upon their poor self-image.

The family plays an important part in the development of the individual; it plays an even more important part in the life of someone with an eating disorder. The role of the mother is especially important. Frequently there is incomplete bonding between mother and child. The mother is often involved in her own life, to the exclusion of the child. The child is more of a symbol or fantasy child to the mother than a real person. The mother is perceived as both ungiving and withholding, thinking only of herself, or over indulgent, more concerned with the child's appearance than with how the child feels. Feelings are placed second to intellect and reason.

There is often a failure of empathy with how the child experiences the world. Parents often are too involved with their own lives to attend to the child. They want their children to be well-behaved, perform well, and give them no trouble. The children learn that they should not express their feelings, especially if their feelings are unpleasant. Often these individuals believe that their feelings will be invalidated, that they will be talked out of their feelings.

Psychological: People who develop eating disorders experience their families as placing a high premium on performance. Therefore, they become perfectionistic, always try to please others, have difficulty tolerating criticism, and are terrified of rejection. Even the slightest criticism is experienced as rejection and blame. They often walk through life feeling that they are wrong and cannot do anything right. They believe they must hide their feelings, especially anger and pain. Thus, they tend to turn their anger inward, upon themselves, leaving them feeling depressed, hopeless, and discouraged. They turn their rage toward themselves for being bad; after all, they reason, if my mother couldn't love me, how can anyone else? This leaves them feeling unlovable and without self-esteem.

They spend their life either (a) trying to get someone to care for them, often going from one "perfect" relationship to another or, (b) settling for any relationship just to avoid having to be alone with themselves or, (c) harboring the fantasy that once they find someone to love them then they will finally be happy.

For some, food becomes their best friend. It is always there to nurture and never says "no." For others, food becomes a way for demonstrating control. The person feels as though she does not have control over any part of her life, but at least with food she can take it in, spit it out, or cut it into very small pieces, portioning it out in specific ways. For all persons with an eating disorder, food is a substance to block feelings. The preoccupation with food blocks everything else from consciousness— blocks all pain. And thus, offers some solace.

III. TREATMENT

There are several forms of treatment for eating disorders depending on the severity, length of time that it has been present, age of person, and family history. The approaches can include any of the following:

Individual therapy: patient is seen 1-3 times per week by a mental health professional to examine the underlying feelings connected with food, correct inappropriate belief systems, and to develop new coping strategies;

Group therapy: patient joins a psychotherapy group with others who have an eating disorder or other compulsive behavior, which is led by a therapist, focusing on developing interpersonal skills and learning more effective coping strategies;

Support group: patient participates in a self-help support group with others suffering from an eating disorder; the support of others is necessary to break the dependence on food and the solitary nature of the cycle;

Medication: anti-depressants and/or anti-anxiety medications may be helpful and even necessary to aid in breaking the compulsive behavior patterns *in conjunction with psychotherapy*; **medication should not be the only form of treatment for it could become a substitute for food;**

Family therapy: the patient, along with members of the individual's family, meets with a therapist to work toward resolving family stresses and to learn new ways of communicating;

Hospitalization: in cases where the behavior is so self-destructive that the individual feels unable to cope with life, hospitalization may be necessary; usually, the patient spends 3-6 weeks in an eating disorders program;

Multifamily therapy: this is often part of an eating disorders program where the patient and his/her family meets with a therapist and several other families in which there is a member with an eating disorder, to discuss the difficulties within the family; family members are supported and learn from each other.

In cases where there has been physical damage, medical care may be necessary. Early detection of the problem is important. Most practitioners use a combination of these approaches depending on the particular individual being treated. It is common for patients treated both within and outside of the hospital setting to be seen in individual therapy and to participate in a support group. The support of family and friends is important in the recovery from an eating disorder. It is not something that one can do alone. However, with psychotherapy, the support of family and friends, and participation in a support group, recovery is possible.

4

WORKAHOLISM

AND OTHER ADDICTIONS

When I was a child the term "addict" connoted a sleazy looking character hiding in a back alley somewhere, shooting heroin into his arm. The term "alcoholic" brought images to one's mind of a similar character lying in the gutter somewhere with the stench of cheap booze permeating the air around him. Now we know that neither of these images is appropriate for either the drug addict or the alcoholic. We now know that there are many more drug addicts and alcoholics who are not in alleys or gutters but are in boardrooms and luxury homes. Moreover, there are many more addictions than just alcohol and drugs. One of the most common is the addiction to work.

Addictions and society

We live in an age where addictions seem to be proliferating. People from all walks of life are addicted to food, drugs, alcohol, gambling, cigarettes, coffee, sex, exercise, and work.

Many of these addicts smile and proudly proclaim their addiction: "I am a workaholic" or "I am an exercise junky." In our society many addictions are perceived as "good addictions" while others are perceived as "bad." We used to take pride in proclaiming, "I can drink you under the table," implying that one could drink a great deal without falling flat on his face. We supported the person who could handle his liquor and "really put it away." Now we know better. And during the 1960s and 1970s there were a great many people who would be proud of the number of LSD trips they had taken or how much pot they smoked; a large number of people condoned the use of drugs. And the same was and continues to be true for cigarettes: "I am a two-pack-a-day man."

In each of these instances society supported the behavior. Business supported the behavior. Then we learned of the destructive aspects of these behaviors. Today we have workaholism—and people proudly confess that they are workaholics. And once again, society reinforces this behavior. The workaholic receives the approbation of his/her peers, colleagues, and family. Even those that silently shake their head on hearing how much the workaholic puts into his/her job are also tacitly approving and even subtly envious. Sometimes people will question themselves as to why they are not working harder despite their belief that one ought to live a more balanced life.

Work as a value and a defense

Compulsive behavior, especially when it applies to work, has been a value of our society since Martin Luther proclaimed that work was the way to salvation. At the same time that work was exalted, the expression of feelings was admonished. People were taught that stoicism was the preferred manner in which to deal with one's emotions. This made for a grand combination; people quickly found that they could suppress feelings by keeping busy. The harder people worked, the less they felt, and the greater the external reward. These rewards came in the form of social approval and relief from pain. And the external reward had to be fairly intense in order to reduce the internal pain. Addicts are always looking outside of themselves for satisfaction. They have considerable difficulty feeling good about their accomplishments. The world may view them as successful, but addicts seldom feel satisfied. Self-satisfaction is virtually unknown to them.

People also discovered that they could obtain an adrenaline rush either by working very hard or by experiencing the anxiety that goes with believing one is not performing well enough. This type of anxiety blocks other feelings. If you are preoccupied with performance, you have no time to think about such issues as the meaning of life, the health of your marriage, or whether you are happy. Or even the pain in your chest or stomach. You can just work right through your body's signal that something is wrong.

When you hold onto the belief that work is the most important value and expressing and/or experiencing emotions is perceived as either bad, negative, or inappropriate, the stage is set for addictive behavior. If you are not able to reach the level of achievement expected, you feel anxious or bad about yourself. In order to cope with these feelings, you can turn to a substance in order to eliminate the pain. If, on the other hand, you are able to achieve the desired standard, you will continue to do so. However, in both of these instances, the initial relief from discomfort obtained from the substance or from the work, does not last. A feeling of dysphoria or letdown soon follows, which leads to a hunger for either the substance or more work. As this process progresses, the yearnings increase and the amount of substance or work needed to quell the feeling increases. Many workaholics have expressed the feeling that they get from working as a rush and have stated that they feel let down when the work stops. Seldom, however, do they have a sustained feeling of satisfaction from the work they perform. *The addictive process* begins with engagement in the behavior that brings relief from some feeling of anxiety, depression, or worthlessness. Just as depression is reduced by exciting activity, work offers workaholics relief from loneliness or low self-esteem in their jobs. These activities are effective as a brief reprieve from conflict or unhappiness.

Compulsive behavior can be defined as any behavior over which you experience yourself as having no control. Addicts rely upon their compulsive behavior to cope with life. And this behavior, in turn, causes problems in living. It is obvious to most of us that the behavior of alcoholics is detrimental to their health and damaging to their family as well. Workaholics' behavior is no less destructive, but not quite as apparent.

Workaholics restrict the range of their emotions, leaving themselves susceptible to headaches, insomnia, agitation, temper outbursts, backaches, ulcers, hypertension, etc. They often are running one step ahead of depression and feelings of worthlessness. Family and social life suffers by the workaholic's preoccupation with work. Spouses, children, and friends often feel that they are neglected.

When spouses of workaholics feel neglected, they are likely to seek other avenues for their satisfaction. Some manage to sublimate their needs by developing other interests; others have extra-marital affairs in order to get their need for affection met.

Workaholics are so preoccupied with their work that they often are not aware of the problems within the family. Crises snap them out of their world, but only briefly. As soon as the crisis passes, business goes on as usual, until the next crisis.

Family, friends, and hobbies are perceived as interruptions to work.

Am I a workaholic?

With the increasing awareness that work can become an addiction, as one might have expected, there has evolved a Workaholics Anonymous movement complete with a twelve-step program for those who feel that their lives have gotten out of control.

According to this movement, you are a workaholic if you answer yes to three or more of the following questions:

1. Do you get more excited about your work than about anything else?
2. Are there times when you can charge through your work and times when you can't get anything done?
3. Do you take work to bed with you? On weekends? On vacation?
4. Do you work more than forty hours a week?
5. Is work the activity you like to do best and talk about most?
6. Do you turn your hobbies into moneymaking ventures?
7. Do you take complete responsibility for the outcome of your work efforts?
8. Have your family and friends given up on expecting you on time?
9. Do you take on extra work because you are concerned that it otherwise won't be done?
10. Do you underestimate how long a project will take to get done and then rush to complete it?
11. Do you believe that it is OK to work long hours if you love what you are doing?
12. Do you get impatient with people who have other priorities besides work?

13. Are you afraid that if you don't work hard you will lose your job or be a failure?
14. Is the future a constant worry for you even when things are going very well?
15. Do you do things energetically and competitively including play?
16. Do you get irritated when people ask you to stop doing your work to do something else?
17. Have your long hours hurt your family and other relationships?
18. Do you think about work while driving, while falling asleep, or when others are talking?
19. If you are eating alone, do you work or read during your meal?
20. Do you believe that money will solve the other problems in your life?

Perhaps the standards of Workaholics Anonymous are too high. Nevertheless, they serve as a useful index of how much of a priority work has become in your life. Even if you were to raise the number of *yeses* to five, or twenty-five percent, a great many people would be considered workaholics.

Workaholism and gender

From the time a man is a young boy he is taught that his self-worth would be derived from his work. As early as five years of age a boy hears parents asking what he will be when he grows up. And he learns rather quickly that saying "a bird" is not the right answer. Young men are not reinforced for their sensitivities, their interest in art, music, and dance. They are not reinforced for expressing their feelings, for being warm and caring, or for just being themselves. They are taught that their self-worth, their value as people, will be determined by what they do, how much they earn, and whether they win. Young men are taught that their value is derived through power and money. They are warriors who must win in battle (sports are just practice for war with someone the victor and someone the vanquished).

In short, men learn virtually from birth, first that they should not express their feelings—"big boys don't cry." Second, that their self-worth will be derived from what they do and how well they do it. And third, that the approval from others is gained through winning. Thus, a man's job becomes the center of his very existence. Through it he is able to suppress his feelings, achieve a sense of self-worth, and gain the approval of his peers. The more intense the suppressed feelings, the lower the self-esteem; and the greater the need for approval, the more important work becomes.

As women have gained equality in corporate America, they have become increasingly like men insofar as how they approach their work. With this equality there has been an increase in heart attacks, hypertension, and a decrease in their life expectancy. More and more women are becoming workaholics with all of the rights and symptoms that go with it.

Historically, women were far better than men in pacing their life. They would take time to socialize; talking on the phone and keeping in touch with friends was characteristic of women. They had many hobbies—knitting, crocheting, handicrafts, etc. As women gained equality, they began to emulate men. They gave up their hobbies, reduced their social contacts to those that are work related, and spent more time working. Rather than teaching men an alternative way of relating to work, women have lent their support to the male model of work. They, too, have become workaholics.

Even women who are full-time caretakers believe that

they should be "supermom" capable of doing everything. They have learned to put aside their own feelings in order to achieve supermom status and believe that they are failures if they cannot do so. So we have workaholics even in the home.

Co-dependency and enablers

Co-dependents have been described as those people whose lives have become unmanageable as a result of living in a committed relationship with someone who is addicted. These people become so involved with the addicted person's addiction that they do not adequately care for themselves. They often become addicted to the caretaking of the addict and thus, do not deal with their own feelings, letting their own life disintegrate.

Co-dependents also become enablers. Without being aware of it, the co-dependent often makes it possible for addicts to continue their destructive behavior. For example, the co-dependent of an alcoholic may make excuses for the alcoholic's behavior. Or even tell the alcoholic that is OK to drink a little on certain occasions.

In the case of the workaholic, the co-dependent may want the income that the workaholic can only achieve by being addicted to his/her work. The co-dependent may make excuses for the workaholic's lateness by saying, "He's preparing for a very important business meeting." Or by praising her for getting a bonus that could only be achieved by overworking.

Thus, the co-dependent becomes an integral part of the problem. If the co-dependent does not want to continue this behavior, it is necessary to change his/her own behavior so as not to support or encourage the addictive behavior.

Co-dependents inadvertently give messages to the

workaholic that the behavior is acceptable and even admired. At least they give conflicting messages to the addict. Furthermore, there is considerable satisfaction to be gained by perpetuating the behavior. One of the most common forms of secondary gain derived from the addictive behavior is the sense of power co-dependents feel with respect to the addict. Co-dependents get to feel needed, superior, or righteous. Other people perceive the co-dependent as a martyr or people may feel sympathy for him/her. The addict is so busy feeling guilty, anxious, and depressed that she/he cannot see the investment the co-dependent has in maintaining the addictive behavior.

The dance between the workaholic and the co-dependent partner is often very complicated. Co-dependents will swear that they want the behavior to change. Yet when asked whether they would be willing to change their own behavior in order to produce the results they say they want, there is resistance. There is comfort in the familiar. If the addict changes, the entire family system changes.

What can be done to change?

Giving up an addiction is very difficult. The addict must recognize that the behavior is destructive and must have sufficient motivation to want to change. One cannot go on with business as usual if one is going to effect lasting change. There must be a behavioral change. The addictive behavior serves as a defense against dealing with emotions and feelings about oneself. Once there is behavior change, those feelings will begin to emerge. And these feelings can be very uncomfortable. There is a tendency to want to return to old behaviors to reduce the discomfort rather than to work through the feelings that emerge. In order to do this, the addict needs support from family and friends. The family is very important since it is the family that will feel the effects of the behavioral change. And sometimes the changes are not comfortable. Remember, the family has learned to cope with the addict in familiar ways as well.

With addictions such as drugs, cigarettes, coffee, and alcohol it is rather easy to see what behavior has to change. What makes these addictions difficult is the compounding effects of physiological dependency. However, substance abusers (those addicted to alcohol, drugs, cigarettes, coffee, etc.) can quit the substance and can commit to a life without the substance. Once on the road to recovery, they can avoid taking the first drink. Even the gambler can stay away from betting.

But workaholics cannot stay away from working. And this is what makes it so difficult to change. In order to effect change, the workaholics must still engage in the very activity that promotes the addiction. In this way workaholics are similar to people with eating disorders. They must continue the activity in order to survive.

Workaholics must: (1) change their beliefs about themselves and their relationship to work. (2) They must be willing to alter their lifestyle. (3) They must restructure their values. (4) They must be willing to work through the feelings that emerge as their addictive behavior changes. And all of this must be done on the basis of the belief that life can be different, more fulfilling, and more satisfying some other way.

Workaholics imagine that their life would collapse if they changed. Their fantasies are catastrophic. Thus, is it necessary to proceed slowly.

As you begin these changes, being in psychotherapy and having a support group and/or group therapy can be invaluable. These changes are difficult and rarely can be done alone, especially if there is no immediate crisis such as a heart attack or impending divorce. These changes often result in considerable anxiety and resistance being generated. When old beliefs are challenged, feelings that you have tried to avoid experiencing will begin to surface. The support of a group and the assistance of a trained professional exploring these feelings with you will help you continue through the process of change.

Baby steps. When workaholics attempt to change, they often try to accomplish the fete all at once. Hence, they set themselves up for defeat. By taking small steps you can increase the probability of continuing to change and reduce the frustration that occurs when expectations are set too high. It is necessary to try one change at a time. Such a change might be leaving the office one hour earlier one day a week on a regular basis. Or taking an extra half hour for lunch one day a week. Or deciding to take one day of vacation time when it is not a vacation or holiday.

Developing and maintaining friendships is important. Workaholics tend to isolate themselves from everyone except business associates or clients. *Regular exercise preferably with other people is necessary.* Exercise gives a sense of accomplishment and your body secretes natural relaxers and stimulants. *Develop and maintain a hobby* to re-focus your attention to a non-competitive, non-money making activity. These baby steps collectively will add up. It is not always necessary to make big changes (except in urgent situations); changes occur one step at a time.

Becoming a workaholic didn't occur overnight. Change will take time. These suggestions form the foundation for a lasting change. Build on it.

5

ALCOHOL AND SUBSTANCE ABUSE

I have been alarmed by the increasing incidence of alcohol and drug abuse, especially among teenagers. Users are getting younger; even children as young as eight years old have been found using various mind-altering substances. Drug, alcohol, and tobacco use is the cause of more deaths, illnesses, and disabilities than any other preventable health condition and seriously undermines America's family life, economy, and public safety[3]. For the past few decades, national surveys have consistently shown that about 10 percent of American adults have significant problems related to their own use of alcohol. In addition, about 25 percent of adults have reported that they use tobacco on a regular basis and about 7 percent use illegal drugs. The following are some additional alarming statistics[1]:

In the 1960s, 7 percent of new female drinkers were ages 10 to 14. Today the figure is at 31 percent.

Inhalant use is most prevalent among young children and usually entails inhaling household items such as shoe polish or paint thinner.

More than 1,000 products widely available in households can be used as inhalants.

There is a direct connection to the use of methamphetamine and the American work ethic. As many as 9.4 million Americans have used the drug at least once.

Everyday 3,000 kids start smoking and a third of them will eventually die of tobacco-related causes. Two of three 12-to 17-year-olds who smoked cigarettes in the last year show signs of addiction.

A survey of American teens found that one in four said they had a friend or classmate who had used Ecstasy; 17 percent said they knew more than one user.

Two-thirds of Americans with serious substance abuse treatment needs are not being treated.

6.4 percent of Americans age 12 and older used illicit drugs or misused prescription drugs.

15.3 percent reported that they had engaged in binge drinking in the past month and 5.4 percent drank alcoholic beverages heavily.

Difference between Abuse, Dependence, and Addiction

Alcohol and drug use ranges on a continuum from use to dependence, characterized by increasing loss of control and increasing functional impairment. The term *abuse* is a broad term that refers to any maladaptive use of a psychoactive substance. There comes a point where the use of the alcohol or drug is no longer voluntary and becomes involuntary and beyond the individual's control. When it reaches the stage where alcohol or drug use is no longer voluntary and interferes with daily functioning, we call it an *addiction*. Dr. Alan Leshner, director of the National Institute on Drug Abuse, stated that the condition of addiction is a "biobehavioral phenomenon" characterized by a movement from a state in which use is at least under some degree of voluntary control to a state in which use is both compulsive and uncontrollable. He characterized *addiction* as a different state from abuse. Leshner states that with addiction there are fundamental brain changes that occur with increased use. These brain changes create a need in the individual for increased, compulsive use of the substance. In addiction there is a loss of control and increasing use despite negative consequences. The term *dependence* refers to a more severe form of abuse characterized by habitual use of a substance that is taken more frequently and in larger amounts over time, leading to increasingly negative consequences.

Historically, there have been two camps regarding the understanding of drug and alcohol addiction. One camp, dominated by physicians, holds to the belief that addiction was based on a disease model. It states that there is a genetic and/or biochemical basis for addictions and that the individuals cannot consistently control their drug-alcohol behavior without total abstinence. They claim that there is no cure because addicts cannot escape the biochemical predisposition. The other camp, dominated by psychologists, believes that alcohol and drug abuse is a learned behavior and, as such, can be unlearned, changed, or controlled through behavioral-learning models of treatment.

Increasingly, addiction workers in the field are coming to the realization that neither approach alone may be sufficient for treating a large number of addicts. For some individuals there may be a biochemical basis for their addiction, for some a behavioral basis, and for still others, both may be involved. Furthermore, these workers are recognizing that treatment isn't based on a "one size fits all" model. While the abstinence model may be appropriate for some individuals, a moderation approach may be effective for others. Addiction is a multivariate disorder with no simple solutions. By offering only one approach, we put addicts in the position of either adopting the only available treatment approach, whether or not it works for them, or not receiving any treatment at all. Most professionals in the field recognize that treatment of addiction must focus on the addictive behavior itself rather than on the cause of the addiction.

Drug Abuse

Nora Volkow, M.D., of the Brookhaven National Laboratory, says:

> "Classically, people thought that drug addiction was a disease that involved the centers of pleasure—that people are taking the drug because it's pleasurable. But that is not the case. In fact, addicted people don't have as strong a pleasure response as people who are not addicted. Recent data are showing us that addiction entails a basic disruption of motivational circuits."

Not only does drug abuse affect the emotional centers of the brain, but also recent research shows that drug abuse alters cognitive activities such as decision-making, planning, and memory. The evidence is clear that cocaine and marijuana use affect the frontal cortex, which is located at the center of the brain governing cognitive activity. Such disruption in the frontal cortex might be responsible for the poor decision-making. Recent research with a gambling task tested drug abuser's decision-making ability. Not surprisingly it was found that drug abusers made poorer decisions on the gambling task than participants in a control group."

The research is mounting that the long-term affects of drug abuse are much greater than most people believe. It is not just that these affects occur while actively using the drugs. Rather, these affects continue after drug use is discontinued. It takes a long time for most drugs to clear one's system and there may be residual physical and psychological affects long after that.

Alcohol Abuse

Alcohol abuse is more insidious than drug abuse. Since having a drink is socially sanctioned, there is no overt reminder that the behavior may lead to trouble down the road. With illicit drugs, merely using the substance is a reminder because it is illegal. Having a cocktail at dinner, drinking a beer at a ballgame, and celebrating a wedding with champagne are all socially supported and even encouraged. One can receive accolades for being able to hold one's liquor. Becoming "shit-faced" in college is a right of passage. There are many models of respected people enjoying alcohol. This is not true for other substances. Hence, it is easy to rationalize moving from the occasional beer, cocktail, or glass of wine to daily use.

It is easy to go from the meal-enhancing drink to using alcohol to self-medicate for social inhibition, depression, loneliness, anxiety, and other discomforting affects. Because some people can develop a tolerance for higher levels of alcohol in their system, they may need higher doses in order to experience the same effects. One drink becomes two, two becomes three. Where one beer was good, for some people it can easily become three, four, or more during the week with a few extras on the weekend.

Unfortunately, most alcoholics are not aware that they are alcoholics until they get into some difficulty. And when there is some warning, they often deny it. Often, the early signs are related to work performance, health problems, social problems, legal difficulties, financial problems, or marital difficulties.

Some people are born with a genetic and biochemical predisposition that leaves them more vulnerable to abusing alcohol. They do not receive a signal from their brain that they have had enough or too much. Rather than producing sleep, nausea, or other obvious physiological effect, they develop a tolerance for large amounts of alcohol. In fact, with continued abuse they begin to crave the substance. In addition, these people find that the alcohol temporarily comforts them by reducing shyness, anxiety, depression, and inhibition. In a world where alcohol use is approved of and even encouraged, it becomes part of the culture. Alcoholics do not want to think of themselves as not able to control their drinking. They want to keep up with and be part of their social group. Declining a drink in many situations is difficult for these people. It is not until they have developed a dependence that interferes with work, family life, and social life that they begin to recognize that they have a problem. But by then, it is often too late. The physiological craving for alcohol becomes so great that giving it up does not seem like an option. The centers of the brain that regulate judgment have been so affected that it takes a crisis to motivate these individuals to seek treatment.

Signs of Abuse

The very nature of substance abuse is such that people do not want to admit that they have a problem. People around them do not want to admit that there is a problem, and healthcare practitioners tend to either overlook or fail to investigate the possible existence of substance abuse. Hence, the individual goes diagnosed and untreated. There are several areas in which signs of abuse may appear.

Problems in living: financial problems including poor financial decision-making; poor judgment; legal problems including traffic tickets (e.g., DUI) and accidents; occupational difficulties such as poor performance, absence, conflict; social problems such as inappropriate behavior, missed appointments, chronic lateness.

Physical effects: increased incidence of health problems, poor dietary changes, and higher tolerance for substance causing increased quantity and frequency of use; experiencing withdrawal when not using; higher incidence of nausea, dizziness, and vomiting; disrupted sleep pattern.

Psychological and behavior effects: emotional instability, e.g., irritability, impatience; difficulty in abstaining from use; using substances to regulate affect, i.e., to reduce social inhibition, relieve stress, reduce anxiety or depression; denial and defensiveness when substance use is suggested.

Treatments

Interestingly, the research found that all people are not affected similarly by alcohol or drug abuse. For some the cognitive centers of the brain are more affected, for others the emotional centers. And for some, both centers are affected. This has profound implications for treatment. One treatment does not fit all abusers. There is no magic bullet. In order to determine the best fit for any given individual, a complete psychological history and history of abuse and treatment must be taken. This places the individual into a context in order to decide what approach or approaches may be most beneficial.

Most treatment approaches agree that that the focus of treatment must be on the cessation of substance abuse. Even those experts who believe that it is possible for the alcoholic to learn to drink in moderation suggest that cessation for a period of time in the beginning of treatment is necessary in order for the patient and clinician to develop a clear picture of the role alcohol plays in the individual's life. Most approaches, however, have abstinence as their goal, especially for those individuals who have a family and personal history of chronic abuse.

The following are some of the current treatment approaches for substance abuse:

Individual skill-based treatments: these approaches help clients interact more effectively with others without using alcohol or drugs. These approaches focus on coping and skills training to help clients quit or decrease abusing alcohol and drugs by teaching them strategies to address interpersonal, environmental, and individual "skill deficits" that may provoke substance abuse.

Motivational Enhancement Treatments: this approach is based on a model that encourages patients to explore the consequences of drinking in a supportive, non-threatening environment. One technique, called motivational interviewing, asks patients what about their alcohol or drug use causes them difficulties, enabling clients to examine their habits objectively. Once clients see how substance abuse or dependence affects their lives, they are motivated to change.

Cognitive Behavioral Treatment: CBT states that human behavior is learned through personal experience and cognitive thought patterns. Changing behavior requires learning how to think differently about situations and how to change dysfunctional behaviors that cause problems. Alcohol dependent people have learned to drink in response to specific situations. The treatment task is to identify the "alcohol triggers" and then apply techniques to develop new ways of thinking and new behavioral skills for coping with these triggers.

Environmental and relationship-based treatment: in this approach family members and significant others are taught coping skills and strategies to help influence their loved one's drinking and motivation to change.

Behavioral marital and family treatment: this approach works with both the individual and the spouse or family to decrease or eliminate abusive drinking-related consequence.

Twelve-step programs: these in-patient or out-patient programs are based on the 12-step model of Alcoholics Anonymous except that professionals lead them. Some professionals in private practice also use such a model, while other practitioners use AA to supplement and support the work being done by the patient in individual treatment.

Medications: Two medications–disulfiram and naltrexone—have been approved by the FDA for alcoholism with a third showing promise, acamprosate, which is pending approval.

Naltrexone appears to be most effective with fewer side effects. As mentioned previously, no one treatment is effective for all substance abusers. Several variables must be taken into account in order to find the treatment that is most effective for any given person. Such factors as duration of addiction, family history, degree of substance abuse, extent of disruption in the patient's life, health, and degree of motivation, to mention the most obvious, must be evaluated.

The first step in the treatment of substance abuse, after collecting a complete psychological, health, and substance abuse history, is to focus on harm reduction. If an individual is placing him or herself, or his or her family, in immediate danger, action must be taken to reduce the impending danger. Sometimes this may require in-patient treatment and sometimes it may involve the entire family. It requires developing a plan of action that can be implemented quickly. The focus during the early sessions is on changing the addictive behavior. In order for treatment to be effective, the individual must be sober. That is the first goal. Staying sober is the bulk of the work. Once sobriety has been achieved, treatment can focus on helping the patient restructure his or her thinking, behavior, lifestyle, and focus.

Maintaining sobriety becomes a top priority especially in the early stages of treatment.

Frequently, substance abusers have personality difficulties in addition to their addiction. Such concurrent psychological problems as depression, anxiety, social phobia, low self-esteem and other such personality issues, need to be addressed, as well as the addiction. Alcoholics and drug abusers often use various substances as a form of self-medication to help them cope with these issues. In treatment, however, we first focus on the substance abuse and then work with the personality issues that may co-exist. Sobriety or harm reduction is the immediate goal.

Conclusion

Our typical image of an addict is someone in a back alley shooting up or a drunk tottering on the street. This depiction is grossly misleading. Addicts are often professionals in high-powered positions. They are surgeons, judges, lawyers, dentists, CEOs, business owners. They are making decisions that affect the lives of thousands of individuals and costs millions of dollars in lost productivity and through faulty decisions. Too often, these people are in denial about their abuse and do not recognize the extent to which they are cognitively impaired.

There is no one cause for substance abuse and no one treatment. Substance abuse is a bio-social-psychological problem. Genetic predisposition may be more of a factor in one individual than another. The role of brain chemistry and genetics is different from person to person. Social and psychological influences likewise vary. Hence, treatment must be tailored to each person.

The first priority in treatment should be harm reduction, with eventual sobriety. When the individual is "clean and sober," she/he can collaborate in his or her treatment with full mental acuity. A treatment plan can then be devised and a determination can be made as to what factors are influencing the abuse. Then a decision can be made as to whether moderate drinking, in the case of the problem drinker, is possible. Some approaches, however, such as AA, believe that abstinence must be a lifetime commitment. Other approaches suggest that moderate drinking is possible for some alcoholics. In either case, a thorough evaluation is necessary and a sober brain is required to make that decision.

Relationships

6

SOMEONE RIGHT FOR YOU[4]

I am constantly hearing the lament: "Where have all the good men (women) gone?" The way people talk you would think that mates were an extinct species. In this article I will be discussing the issue of mate selection in human beings and ways in which you can increase the odds of finding a "compatible mate." You do not have to be alone; and there is more than one partner for you if you are willing to change your attitudes and put in a little effort. You must give up certain myths, time-honored beliefs, and begin to take charge of your romantic life. Romance is no different than any other aspect of your life. It requires that you take the responsibility for making it happen. Your perfect partner is not going to materialize out of thin air and appear in your living room. You must develop a plan of action and then act upon it. Many folks are very sincere about their desires to be involved with another person, but are not committed to making it happen. Sincerity is an attitude, while commitment is an action. Sincerity without action does not make anything happen.

Let's take a critical look at some common myths about romance.

Myth I. Luck is the essence of romance. Luck has very little to do with romance other than to maintain the illusion that we are helpless pawns in the game of love. Most folks engage in their search for a partner and then hope for the best. These people have no expectation of winning. Many people approach romance in the same way that they approach a gambling table in Las Vegas. They put their dollar on the crap table, roll the dice, and pray. Professional gamblers, however, do everything in their power to increase the odds in their favor. And professional lovers do everything in their power to increase their possibilities of meeting the person of their dreams.

I am reminded of the story of a young man who regularly prays to God to win the lottery. Day after day, week after week, he prays and prays and nothing happens. Then one day, in the middle of his prayers, he hears thunder and lightning and the voice of God booms down upon him. "Charlie, meet me half way, buy a ticket." People tend to pray, wish, hope, and dream about finding their ideal mate, but they seldom develop a strategy or plan of action. They spend more time and energy planning a dinner party than the most important human relationship of their lives.

Myth 2: Marriages are made in heaven. This myth is similar to the first one in that it assumes that relationships are pre-ordained, out of the hands of ordinary mortals. It assumes that we do not have any control over the mates we end up with and that we must settle for those that we find ourselves involved in. Human beings make choices. And many of them are poor choices.

While this myth has romantic overtones, it denies human beings responsibility for their choices. It leaves us at the mercy of some fictitious master plan governing our lives and the freedom to choose is obviated. If, indeed, marriages were made in heaven, then God made a great many mistakes. Rather than attribute those mistakes to God, we should exercise our God-given right to choose and learn how to make more effective choices. God doesn't provide us with a mate—rather, God provides us with the ability to choose.

Myth 3: *There is only one partner that is perfect for each of us.* If this were the case, then it would not be possible for people to have happiness in a marriage after the death of a spouse. Clearly, since people do indeed find happiness in second and even third marriages, there is more than one potential mate available for each of us. Our job is to increase the probabilities of finding those potential partners.

In order to find these potential mates we must develop a strategy. Just as there is more than one house that we can fall in love with, there is more than one potential mate. If we increase the pool of available partners, we can then fall in love with any one of them. The trick is to set up our criteria, take appropriate actions, and then allow for nature to take its course.

I am reminded of a friend who decided that he wanted to marry a woman who was beautiful, had considerable financial backing, and was of the same religion as he. He only dated women after he checked their family's financial standing with Dunn and Bradstreet, who belonged to his church, and whom he found to be beautiful. By surrounding himself with rich, beautiful women of the same religion as he, he could then allow himself to fall in love with any one of them.

What About Romance?

Romance and love at first sight are integral to our fantasies about mate selection. We love to hear stories about how people fall in love. We love the notion of two people gazing across a crowded room, eyes meeting, and love is in bloom.

More often than not these people are in lust, not love. But this is not to say that this cannot happen. However, it is unlikely.

More often love grows between two people who have a common connection. It is the common connections that bind us, love then blooms in the soil of mutual interest, mutual respect, and friendship. What my strategy will do is increase the odds of this happening.

Think, for example, of the process we go through in selecting our "dream house." First we develop an idea of what we are looking for: one-story, Mediterranean-style, four bedrooms, large yard, in a particular geographic area, near schools, etc., and we establish a price range. We may even get quite specific, because, after all, we will be spending a lot of time and money in this house and we want to insure, as best possible, that we will be happy in it. (Yet when it comes to choosing a mate, we will go to a bar and hope we get lucky.) Next we contact a real estate agent and tell the agent our requirements. We also drive around various neighborhoods on our own, read magazines and newspapers, make inquiries; in short, we do our homework. Then the agent begins to show us around. Not infrequently we may spend many months and view many houses, sometimes hundreds of houses and even years, depending upon our particular preferences. All along the way we are collecting information and fine tuning our choices. Finally, one day, we step out of the agent's car and find ourselves standing in front of our dream house; it's love at first sight! And that's what we will tell people. We eliminate the fact that we spent many hours, months, years, looking, searching, refining before acquiring the "dream house." A similar approach should be used for mate selection. Only with mate selection it is even more difficult since the mate has to choose you as well, whereas the house does not.

Developing a Plan

Now that we have debunked some of our favorite myths, we are ready to move to the next step: developing a strategy. Most people become rather wary at this point. They believe that romance should just happen without any strategizing. I am a firm believer in letting nature take its course. However, I am also interested in empowering people to give nature a helping hand. There is nothing in this plan that is against romance. Developing a plan increases your likelihood of success. We develop plans and strategies for everything in life that we succeed at—careers, a dinner party or wedding, performing surgery, buying a new or used car, planning our estate, designing a house, decorating an apartment, or going on a vacation. You name it. If we are successful, we have made a plan. Yet in spite of this knowledge, when it comes to romance, we prefer to rely on chance and then we wonder why the divorce rate is so high. If our businesses or dinner parties had as high a failure rate we surely would begin to analyze why and try to do something about it. Well, the same is true for romance. It is clear to me that the old way of mate selection has not been working. It is time for a new way.

Step One: What are you looking for? Most of the time when I ask people what they are looking for in a mate they say something like: "Someone attractive, intelligent, and sensitive with a good sense of humor." They try to give the impression that they are not asking for much. However, on closer investigation I usually find that the list is much more extensive. So, in this step, make a complete list of what you are looking for in a mate. Include those characteristics that are important for everyday living on a long-term basis.

We must distinguish between several categories of mate: *roommate, playmate, friend, and permanent mate.* Each of these has its own set of characteristics, with some degree of overlap. Many people have not distinguished between them and therefore, may be stating that they want a permanent mate where in reality they are seeking a playmate. A permanent mate is some combination of roommate, friend, and playmate. Therefore, it might be wise for you to make up three lists of characteristics, one for each of these three types of mate. Once you have developed these lists, merge them. Some characteristics may be eliminated. Intelligence may, for example, be more important in a mate than a playmate; neatness is more important in a roommate than in a friend.

Step Two: Take a personal inventory. Honesty is very important in this step. List all the characteristics that describe you. Pretend that you are describing yourself to someone else; what would you say? Once you have developed this list, ask three of your closest friends to develop a list describing you. Tell them to be brutally honest. Compare their list with your own. Then ask them to look at your list and let them tell you whether they agree with your self-assessment. If there is a discrepancy between how you see yourself and how your friends see you, then you have some work to do. Somehow, you have to reconcile your self-perception with the perception of others.

Step Three: Separate fantasy from reality. Most of us have images of ourselves that often are at odds with reality. We have an idea of who we would like to be and present the image to the world rather than the reality. Sometimes we tell the story so often we tend to believe it ourselves.

When it comes to relationships we cannot present the person we would like to be to others as if it were the person we actually are. This would never fly in business; it is called false advertising. Truth in advertising is very important in developing a relationship. We often deceive ourselves, as well as others. In this step you must assess what you say you want with the reality of who you are. Some men say that they want an independent-thinking, self-directed woman, who has her own career. In reality they want a woman who will take care of them and be the Mom they never had. It is similar to the guy who goes to the horse riding stable and tells the person who rents horses that he wants a frisky thoroughbred because he thinks of himself as a jockey. After he falls off a few times and has to walk back to the stable he realizes that he should have been with a gentle mare.

Step Four: Increase your opportunities. Make a list of the type of activities you enjoy: biking, dancing, cooking, spiritual, self-help, yoga, art, horseback riding, etc. Begin to participate in those activities in an arena where both single men and women can be found. If you are interested in cooking, for example, find a cooking class that is likely to be attended by both men and women. By attending activities that you are interested in, you are able to insure that you will have a good time even if you do not meet someone who is of interest to you. Do not participate in activities where the end result determines whether you enjoy yourself. Do not waste your time going to places where the odds are stacked against you: meat (meet) markets, bars, dance clubs, large gatherings, etc. are not places to meet potential mates. Maximize your use of your time.

Step Five: It pays to advertise. Let all of your friends and relatives know that you are seeking a mate. Make use of business associates. Everyone is a potential agent. And most people love the idea of helping someone find a mate. Tell them about yourself and specifically what you are looking for so they can better represent you. Don't be bashful, be honest. Think of these people as you would a real estate agent; tell them exactly what you are looking for so that you can increase your likelihood of success. The more information they have, the better. Make use of dating services, but check them out first. Make sure they are reputable. Get references. Do the types of people you are looking for participate? If you have a flair for writing, use the personals column, but again do some homework. Check the credibility of the magazine and quality of the ads. Do the types of people you are looking for advertise in the column?

Early Imprinting

The first relationship we observe is that of our parents. This forms a template deep in our unconscious that affects our choice in a mate. Our parents form a model of what relationships are like and what adult males and females are about. As such, these early imprints have a profound effect on our choices of mates and our expectations with respect to a relationship. If this early imprinting was positive, we are likely to have satisfying interpersonal relationships and a positive image of others. However, if it is negative, it may well have the opposite effect. Sometimes the effect was so negative, even though we may not be aware of it, it can severely interfere with our interpersonal satisfaction. Repeated destructive relationships, co-dependence, and generally unhealthy relationships may ensue. In these cases, professional intervention may be necessary before you can proceed with some of the steps indicated above.

7

TWO=CAREER FAMILIES:

CONTRACTING FOR INTIMACY

The days of a single model for marriage are over. Now there are multiple models. No longer is it the rule for the man to bear the sole responsibility for bringing home the proverbial bacon while the woman is responsible for caring for the home and children. In some marriages it is the woman who is the primary wage earner while the man assumes the role of homemaker and primary caregiver. As women's roles change in our society, so does the nature of marriage change. Therefore, alternative models to the traditional one where Dad brings home the bacon and Mom takes care of the home had to evolve.

The most common model alternative is the two-career family. In this model both the husband and wife have committed themselves to the pursuit of a career. Television's *The Cosby Show*, depicting a lawyer/wife and physician/ husband, has replaced *Father Knows Best*. Two-career families are different from the families where women have worked to help with the family finances. In the two-career family it isn't only necessity that places both husband and wife in the market place, but choice. Each partner chooses to follow a career or take a job to achieve both financial rewards and personal fulfillment. In many instances financial necessity has no bearing on this choice.

With the change in models also comes a change in the family structure as well as a host of matrimonial and familial problems that need to be addressed. New "job descriptions" must be developed. It is no longer viable to assume that traditional descriptions of the role of husband and wife will suffice. It is not possible for the woman to assume the role of homemaker, primary caregiver, and cook while trying to hold down an executive or professional position. It is no longer sufficient for the man to bring home a paycheck, take out the trash, and merely help around the house. We need an equal division of labor to make the two-career family work.

When working with couples where there are two careers and/or the merging of two families, I often suggest that the couple spend some time developing an intimate contract or marriage handbook. In developing these handbooks or contracts, **as much attention is paid to the process of communicating and negotiating as to the content of the contract.**

Marital Agreements

All couples can benefit from an intimate contract. Even couples who have been married for many years. After years of marriage, it is often necessary to re-negotiate the marriage to keep it vital and relevant for current circumstances. The same roles may not be appropriate after the children have left the nest or after retirement. After years of marriage, as people grow and change, so do expectations and desires change. The marital contract can revitalize the marriage. It can facilitate dispute resolution and communication, reduce misunderstandings, and free individuals to deal with each other's feelings more directly. More often than not, marital disputes begin as an argument about some issue that can be negotiated. The content of the argument is less important that the feelings being expressed. When couples learn to negotiate disputes, and contract for settlements, they are then free to deal with the underlying feelings and emotions.

Pre-nuptial Agreements. The pre-nuptial agreement can be a very valuable tool for couples. It can provide a vehicle for spelling out the couple's philosophy of marriage. The pre-nuptial agreement is an opportunity to articulate implicit and explicit expectations. Most marital conflicts occur because of the hidden expectations each person brings to the marriage. These expectations often are not met leaving at least one party disappointed, hurt, or resentful. The focus during the negotiating of a pre-nuptial agreement should be on each person's beliefs, expectations, and values regarding marriage, themselves, and their partner. Implicit expectations should be made explicit. Frequently it is not until after marriage that each finds out their partner has a host of unexpressed expectations, often referred to as a "hidden agenda."

I encourage my clients to include all aspects of the relationship in their pre-and post-marital agreements, everything from child rearing and religion to whose responsibility it is to take out the garbage and finances. Particularly when both spouses work full-time, an accord should be reached in advance over such mundane items as: whose job it is to walk the dog, to pay the bills, wash the laundry, cook, grocery shop, etc. It is surprising how emotionally charged these simple issues can be, simply because one *assumed* the other would do this or that; bringing everything out in the open eliminates these assumptions. Financial matters are often the most difficult. Therefore, I suggest that they should be saved until last, when both parties feel a vested interest in the success of the negotiating process.

Family Contracts. The entire family, including children, can be included in the contract. Two-career families need to negotiate a realistic contract based on mutual respect and cooperation in order for the relationship to run smoothly. Therefore, children should be included in the negotiation. This goes beyond the assigning of chores and responsibilities. Children, especially adolescents, can negotiate for privacy, telephone time, transportation, alone time with parents, and so on. When children feel a part of the negotiations, they are more likely to follow through with their agreements. When children can levy consequences against parents for violations (as in failing to pick up a child on time or not showing up at a soccer game) they have more invested in making the contract work.

A Model of Communication

The process of negotiating agreements serves as a model for learning how to negotiate within the relationship; it can be a very intimate process. Indeed, **learning the process of developing an agreement can be the most important outcome.** During the negotiations the couple learns to compromise, listen, communicate, and understand. The agreement can serve to increase the probability that the couple can at least be friends "until death do us part," if not lovers. Through negotiating a contract, various issues that couples have to face can be brought to the surface before the event actually occurs. More importantly, through developing the contract, the couple learns the process of negotiating which can only help them during those periods of conflict.

Attention must be paid to what the underlying concern might be for each item being negotiated. There may be undisclosed reasons for wanting a particular item included in the contract. Frequently, motives are unconscious and require even more skill to uncover. Without such exploration, however, negotiations often fail. There may be a hidden dynamic operating between the couple and unless this dynamic is brought to light, negotiations may come to a halt. Let us consider the couple that is discussing financial issues. Often the concern has more to do with issues of trust, love, independence, power, security, control, and fear than with finance. There may be historical antecedents for wanting a particular arrangement. If the underlying reasons are not explored, negotiations may be hampered.

Everyone enters marriage with hidden expectations— often even hidden from oneself. Consciously or subconsciously, these expectations and beliefs affect every aspect of the relationship, and insofar as they can be made explicit—and communicated—the relationship automatically improves. Each person comes to understand exactly what the other believes about marriage and why a particular item was included in the contract. It is easier to accept a spouse's desires when you understand the importance he or she attaches to them. I guide people through the process with the goal of improving communication, which is the most important component of any successful marriage. With effective communication and listening skills the couple can negotiate out of clarity rather than fear.

A Foundation of Understanding

Each contract has a preamble that sets out the general intent of the agreement rather than plunging into the specifics. The intent of the marital agreement is not for planning a divorce, but rather to smooth the way for future discussions.

It is an opportunity to openly discuss issues in an atmosphere of caring. It is essential to spend considerable time and effort building a foundation of trust and understanding. This phase of the negotiations can serve to set the overall tone and intent of the agreement.

During these negotiations a great deal of information is revealed. Frequently this information would not be revealed until many months or years into the marriage. Often religious values, male and female roles, attitudes toward work, recreational time, and money would not often be discussed until there is a conflict. By that time the argument has already begun. During developing a contract many of these issues are resolved, paving the way for fewer and less intense arguments later.

All close relationships have intimacy and organizational aspects to them. Lovers are primarily concerned with the interpersonal issues while roommates may be concerned with the maintenance issues. Marital relationships involve both sides—business and interpersonal. The business or organizational component of a relationship deals with those everyday issues that give continuity to the relationship without having to spend endless time and energy dealing with the details of living together. Once these issues have been agreed to, the couple is free to spend time and energy into deepening the relationship.

Most of us were taught that love conquers all. It was on this basis that many people married. It was not until afterward that we realized that "love alone is not enough." We found relationships to be hard work not only in developing good communication but also in learning how to live together.

Frequently I have observed that the strain of dealing with the business side often has caused a breach in the relationship. Living with someone in a love relationship is very complex to begin with. Modern life is not simple, particularly when people are trying to balance two careers, child-care, romance, day-to-day home repairs, social life, and some personal time. Therefore, it is necessary that the relationship be given a great deal of attention and planning in all areas.

Often couples argue about concrete issues such as who take out the trash or who is the bigger slob as cover-up for some other emotional issue which one or both parties are unwilling to confront, e.g., not feeling loved or appreciated. Sometimes the underlying issue is obscured by anxiety or is even unconscious at the moment. The concrete issue becomes a convenient focus for letting off steam without directly addressing the real issue.

Similarly many couples find that a "nuts and bolts" issue such as neatness or punctuality or not fulfilling promises can equally affect their feelings of affection. However, since some day-to-day issues appear to be petty, the individuals choose to cover them up rather than confront them. Such covering of apparently petty issues often leads to larger issues that can affect the very core of the relationship. Couples can make significant progress toward resolution of many of these conflicts by approaching them in a direct way, thereby, clearing the path for examining any underlying issues. If couples learned to negotiate the business issues they would then be free to discover and work through the interpersonal issues. It is difficult to feel affectionate toward someone when you are feeling taken advantage of or are angry about the amount of time your lover spends in the gym or on the phone. These issues can be negotiated.

Developing the Contract

These are some of the most important purposes of the contract:

1) Learning how to negotiate
2) Separating business from interpersonal issues
3) Listing responsibilities
4) Defining interpersonal needs
5) Developing child-care philosophy and responsibility
6) Negotiating consequences in case of default

In my work with couples I suggest that they begin by listing all of their expectations of the relationship and of their partner. They are instructed to include their entire wish list in attempt to make all the implicit expectations explicit. The list should include all of the little boy and little girl fantasies that they each had regarding marriage.

During the development of this list it is important for the participants to question (*not* challenge) each other as to the basis of the request. If we can understand the intent of the request, or what the request means to the other person, we are more likely to find various methods of dealing with the issue. It is easier to agree to something if we understand the underlying intent, reason, or motivation.

Once this list is prepared we can begin developing the contract. The intent is to develop an agreement that will serve as a personal manual or guide for dealing with various aspects of the relationship. Its purpose is to make it easier for the relationship to flourish even when difficulties arise. By learning how to negotiate a contract and by having the basic issues articulated, the couple can resolve issues and even prevent discord.

Once the business side of the relationship is negotiated we can examine, and subsequently negotiate interpersonal issues. While we cannot control or contract for feelings, we can negotiate for time and activities that allow for the inter-personal growth and intimacy. Remember: feelings often follow actions as well as precede them. One can negotiate the amount of time spent together. One can negotiate for special time during the week; say a date for dinner alone, mid-week. A decision can be made that each evening the couple will go for a walk together to discuss the day's events or to share feelings. Vacations can be negotiated, whether they are a short camping trip or a longer one. The time that one retires in the evening and how long one spends at work, as well as whether work is brought home, are all open for negotiation. Once these issues are brought to the table and discussed, agreements can be made which, when followed, can appreciably enhance the quality of the relationship.

Consequences of a Breach. All contracts should be entered with good faith. Each party should be committed to fulfilling his or her agreements. However, human beings, being what they are, may violate their agreements. Therefore, consequences should be included in the contract. These consequences become part of the negotiations. Consequences for violations can range from the personal to the financial. For example, one couple included in their contract that if the husband violated a particular clause he would have to wash the wife's car. Another contracted a massage as a consequence. Consequences can include personal favors, chores, or money. One husband "fined" his wife $1.00 for each article of clothing left in the living room. These consequences are greater for more egregious violations ranging to division of household effects, in case of dissolution of the marriage. For the most part, however, consequences serve as reminders that the violation took place and that the contract should be taken seriously. Failing to take the contract and its consequences seriously may portend difficulty ahead.

Negotiating contracts, whether by couples or families, can be challenging, fun, and rewarding. Couples who have experimented with the contract have found that the process of working on the contract brought them and their family closer. With greater intimacy, the dynamic life of the two-career family becomes an exciting adventure. The development of the contract and making it work can become a family project to which all members can commit.

8

DIVORCE: WHAT WENT WRONG?

The "D" word strikes at the heart of all married couples. Pre-nuptial agreements—agreements made even before marriage—all have provisions for what happens in the event of a divorce. Recent statistics suggest that 50 percent of all marriages in the United States will end in divorce. In Southern California the divorce rate is purported to be even higher, somewhere in the neighborhood of 60-75 percent, depending on which study one reads. In this article I will be exploring some of the reasons that people divorce, some of the consequences of divorce, ways to prevent divorce, and, when all else fails, approaches to divorce that can be less stressful to all of the parties involved.

Changing Expectations

The institution of marriage has changed dramatically over the past 100 years. Many factors played a part in this evolution. In the 1890s marriage was often a matter of convenience. Roles for men and women were clearly defined; each knew what was expected of them. Men were expected to work, with their primary responsibility that of being the family provider. Women were to take care of the home and bear children, for whom they would then be the caretaker. Marriages were for the purpose of raising a family—breeding children who would grow up to help with the chores, work the fields, or take over the family business.

With the industrial revolution, the Second World War, and finally the technological revolution, much of this changed. Each of these revolutions provided greater leisure time, greater freedom from chores, and a reduction in the need for progeny to be junior workers—in the field or in the home. Thus, families had fewer children. World War II created a need for women to enter the work force. And when the war was over, they did not want to return to the home. Two-income families became the norm. Today, women work for the same reasons men work, not just to provide a second income. They have their own careers, interests, and activities equal to men.

The family changed from: "Dad wears the pants in the family" to "Mom and Dad are partners in the business of family." The expectations men and women have of one another and subsequently of marriage have changed. Couples expect more of one another and from their marriage. With increased information, leisure time, mobility, and affluence, people have more time to learn about themselves and to experience various lifestyles. They have more contact with how other people live. They also have increased opportunity to learn about themselves. In less affluent times, when roles were clearly defined along gender lines, peoples' self-concept remained static. Today, however, after being continuously bombarded with information and the possibility of change, the concept of self has become more dynamic.

When two people are married and over a period of years at least one person, if not both, undergoes a significant change in self-concept, the marriage will also change. The selves that married are no longer the same. If interests, goals, and values change along with a changing self, you have a different dynamic set up between the two persons. In some cases this dynamic is such that the marriage no longer seems viable. When we combine this change with the awareness that we will be living longer, it appears more probable that people will seek a second or third partner with whom they feel more compatible.

It is no longer sufficient for a man simply to be a terrific provider and for a woman to be an outstanding homemaker. People expect more. Men and women want intimacy, romance, affection, understanding, commonality of interests, conversation, common values, and exciting sex, to mention a few of the more common requirements. They want an equal partnership with one another, where both parties participate equally in all of the decisions pertaining to the home and to child-rearing, regardless of who is earning more money.

Increased longevity, increased affluence, and increased opportunity for personal growth, when combined with significantly changing expectations regarding marriage, suggest that people must learn new or different ways of relating to one another if their marriage is going to survive. When this is not possible, either for lack of desire, capacity, or interest on the part of one or both parties, divorce becomes an option.

Mortality

A magazine article I recently read stated that people, particularly women, who are currently aged 65, are expected to live until 85. Younger people are expected to live longer, into their 90s. More and more people are reaching the age of 100 and beyond. It is becoming commonplace for people to have more than one career in a lifetime. After all, a youngster of 65 still has another 20 or more years in which to begin a new career. Young people today no longer think about a career that they will be in for the rest of their life; they think more about their "first" career, fully expecting a second or perhaps third career to follow.

These same young people are thinking about marriage in a similar vein. Many of them recognize that the concept of marriage "until death do us part" is more a figurative use of the phrase than a literal use. People currently in their 40s who married while in their 20s are realizing that to have one partner for a lifetime may be highly improbable. When you think about it, it is rather a minor miracle that two people, from different backgrounds, with different histories, and different needs, can find each other and live together for 20 or 30 years. But to live together for 50, 60, or 70 years! . . . The likelihood of two people growing in similar directions and similar paces would appear to be small. People in their 20s have different values, expectations, needs, and interests than they may have when in their 40s. And people in their 40s may be different than those in their 60s. Priorities and goals change. People change. As friends may grow apart as people grow and change, so may spouses.

Yet, in spite of the odds, many people are able to make marriage at least tolerable for many decades. Some people grow together, while others grow separately but are sufficiently satisfied with one another to remain together.

Negotiation and Compromise

Contemporary marriages have to rely upon different models than in previous generations. The metamorphosis of marriage has been underway since the 1950s. The models represented by *Father Knows Best, I Love Lucy,* and *Leave It To Beaver,* where the man was the provider and the woman was the housewife, was the model of the day. In the 1980s we began to see a different model of marriage as represented by *The Cosby Show*, where two professional people were married and raising a family.

In previous generations a woman was taught to accommodate—to put aside her needs in favor of the needs of the man. She was to accommodate her needs to him. This model of marriage reduced women to the status of wife, while elevating men to the status of husband. The power lay with the husband.

In a marriage of equals, constant accommodation on the part of one person will eventually cause resentment and subsequently, conflict. Compromise and negotiation, on the other hand, recognizes the equality of both parties as they seek an equitable and mutually satisfying solution to a problem. In compromise neither party may get exactly what they want at any given time. In these marriages, preservation and enhancement of the relationship is more important than getting what one wants. Couples must learn to let go the argument in the service of maintaining an intimate connection. When being right and winning becomes more important than the relationship, the marriage will be in trouble.

One of the most important aspects of contemporary marriage is learning how to negotiate. A successful marriage today has more in common with business negotiations than with *Father Knows Best*. The better able a couple is in learning the skills of negotiation, the less conflict they will experience and the greater their satisfaction.

When either party is more interested in winning, not able or not willing to negotiate, and has poor communication skills, the more likely they will have the kinds of difficulties that will lead them to consider divorce.

Divorce: Failure or Change

Many people inappropriately believe that divorce means that they have failed. Not that the marriage failed, but that they personally failed—hence, they are a failure. It is as though they believe that when people marry it is supposed to last forever, as though it were pre-ordained; thus, if the marriage ends they must have done something wrong to make it happen.

As we can see from the forgoing analysis, many factors contribute in the decision to divorce. No one takes the issue of divorce lightly. Endings, however, are a part of life. Everything has a life expectancy. People are finite, imperfect beings, living in an imperfect, constantly evolving, constantly changing world.

Change is the only constant. Hence, marriage is constantly evolving and imperfect. Sometimes two people are able to grow, change, and evolve in similar directions, sometimes not. Sometimes our expectations remain constant; more often they change. Sometimes our expectations are the same as our partners, and sometimes not. The longer we live, the more possibility for change to be in different directions. "'Til death do us part" is more likely when we live to be 50 than when we live to be 100.

Anger

All too often divorcing couples do so in an atmosphere of hostility. They forget that they once were in love with one another. This is indeed unfortunate. Divorce ranks second only to death of a loved one as the most stressful of life's experiences. The stress in inevitable. But the strife is not.

Usually there are other variables at play that lead to the acrimony accompanying divorce. Frequently the acrimony covers pain and hurt. This is true regardless of who feels like the injured party. Pain is integral to loss. In a divorce there are many losses. The loss of the fantasy of marriage and the magic of the relationship, the loss of the friendship, the loss of friends, a lifestyle, a home, familiarity, children, loss of love, identity, to name but a few of the losses.

When we are angry we do not have to experience the hurt and the loss. We can cover the pain with anger, at least temporarily. Sometimes our anger is directed toward the other person for not being all that we wanted them to be or expected them to be. Sometimes we are angry because they other person did not change; we think, "if only she/he would change then we would not have to divorce."

Sometimes we feel angry because our spouse has victimized us. We feel like the injured party and we want to fight back. We want to hurt the other person in the same way we feel hurt. So what do we do? We hire a lawyer to help us get back at our spouse. We want to hurt our spouse while we are protecting ourselves.

Sometimes we are angry with ourselves for not being a better spouse, for not knowing better, for not paying attention, for not being all that we might have been. Rather than get angry with ourselves, we get angry with our spouse. Sometimes we fight about who gets the dog or the dishes so we can feel empowered.

Sometimes we get depressed, too. We blame ourselves, we feel guilty. We are ashamed. So we hire a lawyer to help us give everything to our spouse in order to make amends for real or imagined hurts that we have inflicted.

Divorce Counseling and Divorce Mediation

One of the reasons that divorce often takes as long as it does is because many issues just mentioned are being acted out during the course of the dissolution. An alternative to the expensive, stressful, and time-consuming approach of a litigated, hotly contested divorce is to try either divorce counseling and/or divorce mediation.

Divorce counseling, when conducted by a licensed mental health practitioner who specializes in working with divorcing couples, can help the couple sort out the emotional from the practical issues of the divorce. As I pointed out earlier, anger over practical issues such as property, is usually a product of lingering resentment with regard to the relationship, not the property itself. Once the couple can resolve or at least clarify the cause of the anger, reasonable negotiations can occur. (Unfortunately, many couples have to learn the hard way that the court will, more often than not, come to the same conclusion regarding the property that the couple could have come to had they not been so angry.)

Divorce counseling is concerned with helping the couple gain some sense of closure regarding their relationship. It can help the parties grieve their loss, preparing them to move into the future, perhaps not as friends, but at least not as enemies.

Divorce mediation is the healthy alternative to a litigated divorce. The focus of a mediated divorce is on reaching an equitable solution to such issues as spousal support, property division, child custody, visitation, etc. The couple meets with a mediator (or in my practice, a mediation team consisting of a lawyer and a psychologist) to resolve each and every item. Without assessing blame or fault, the mediator helps the divorcing parties develop alternative solutions for addressing their specific areas of conflict.

By choosing mediation, the parties talk to each other, rather than through their attorneys. This direct communication resolves conflicts in less time and is less costly than traditional litigation. When children are involved in a dispute, the mediation process encourages parents to focus on their children's best interests and to maintain a relationship with their children while the parties design a parenting plan.

Each party has control in a mutual, decision-making process. Mutual expression of perceptions, values, and emotions are allowed, thereby reducing damage to important family relationships. This enables the parties to tailor a personalized agreement that resolves their individual and unique concerns and reflects the best interests of their children.

An important goal for successful mediation is reaching a fair agreement. The parties decide what is fair, not the attorneys and not a judge.

9

MAKING YOUR MARRIAGE WORK

Half of all the couples marrying today will end in divorce. In previous generations it was not surprising to hear that a couple was celebrating their twenty-fifth, thirtieth, or even fiftieth wedding anniversary. Will any of the current generation celebrate these milestones? What can people do to increase the probability of a long and satisfying marital relationship?

Marriage today is far more complex. In the 1950s and earlier, roles for men and women were clearly defined. Each partner knew what was expected of him or her. People referred to men's work and women's work. If each partner filled those explicit expectations, there was a reasonably good chance that the marriage would endure. Even personality styles were prescribed. Men were supposed to be strong, silent, competent, unemotional, problem-solvers, good providers, handy around the house, and protectors. Women were supposed to be good cooks, competent housekeepers, seamstresses, social, religious, and nurturers. Men and women cut each other a great deal of slack in other areas, so long as each played by the prescribed rules and played their socially defined roles. With the technological evolution, the women's movement, and increased life expectancy, came a profound change in these static, traditional roles.

People began to question what they wanted out of marriage. Families relied more upon hired domestic help in the form of housekeepers, caregivers, and day carers to fulfill many of the customary roles. Marriage began to take on a different meaning and serve a different purpose than was traditionally the case. If we add to this mix the awareness that we simply live longer than in previous generations, it becomes obvious that "until death do us part" means a lot longer than at any time in history. When folks are living well into their 80s and marry in their 20s, the span of time could be over 60 years. It becomes possible for us to consider multiple long-term relationships. People can consider one type of relationship for their childbearing years, and another type of relationship for the years afterwards. We can even consider having more than one family, i.e., raising children with more than one partner.

Despite all of these changes, most people enter marriage carrying with them many of the same beliefs appropriate for the previous traditional marriage. Their consciousness has not caught up with the reality of the times. Hence, when they marry they often find that their traditional beliefs are ineffective, leaving them with few guidelines on how to be in a marriage. Today's marriages, more than any time in history, depend more upon communication, intimacy, relating, compromise, negotiation, and understanding. We must be able to negotiate in the living room and make love in the bedroom, and be skilled at both. Expectations in loving have similarly changed. Since love-making is no longer exclusively for the purpose of procreation, no longer just for a man's pleasure, and it is no longer expected that men be more knowledgeable and experienced than women, then couples expect more from one another, requiring greater communications between them.

Since both sexes are equally able to perform nearly all of the tasks required in a marriage, neither has to depend on the other for these abilities. Even the issue of having children no longer is necessary for marriage. People can choose to have children or not and can have children without having a partner. Even adoption is possible for single individuals. Therefore, the very basis for marriage changes from fulfilling certain functions to fulfilling emotional and psychological needs.

In order to learn more about how people maintain long-term marriages, and what some of the impediments to them might be, psychologists went out into the field to learn more.

Psychologist, Dr. Judith S. Wallerstein, co-author of *The Good Marriage: How and Why Love Lasts*, carried out in-depth interviews with 50 couples who have been married at least nine years, had children together, and who independently regarded their marriage as happy. Dr. Wallerstein identified nine "psychological tasks" as the pillars on which any marital relationship rests. The following are Dr. Wallerstein's nine tasks:

Separate emotionally from one's childhood so as to invest fully in the marriage and, at the same time, to redefine the lines of connection with both families of origin.

Build togetherness based on mutual identification, shared intimacy, and an expanded conscience that includes both partners, while at the same time setting boundaries to protect each partner's autonomy.

Establish a rich and pleasurable sexual relationship and to protect it from the incursions of the workplace and family obligations; it is the second part of this task which must not be overlooked or taken for granted.

(For couples with children) Embrace the daunting roles of parenthood and to absorb the impact of Her Majesty the Baby's

dramatic entrance into the marriage. At the same time the couple must continue the work of protecting their own privacy.

Confront and master the inevitable crises of life and maintain the strength of the marital bond in the face of adversity and create a safe haven within the marriage for the expression of difference, anger, and conflict.

Use humor and laughter to keep things in perspective and to avoid boredom and isolation.

Provide nurturance and comfort to each other, satisfying each partner's need for dependency and offer continuing encouragement and support.

Keep alive the romantic, idealized images of falling in love, while facing the sober realities of the changes wrought by time.

Dr. Wallerstein's tasks are not easy. To accomplish them requires that each spouse be committed to enhancing their marriage and making it work. In addition, they require that each spouse be equally committed to their own personal growth as well as the growth of their partner. The preservation and enhancement of the marriage partnership must be a top priority.

Psychologist Dr. Howard Markman at the University of Denver believes that, "Love and commitment to the relationship are necessary for a good marriage, but they are not enough. What are needed, on top of that, are skills in effective communication and how to handle conflict." Dr. Markman, along with Dr. Clifford Notarius of Catholic University of America, studied 135 about-to-be-married couples. **"How you handle conflict is the single most important predictor of whether your marriage will survive,"** according to Dr. Markman. These researchers found that certain behavior patterns usually signaled an impending collapse in the marriage:

• When either partner—although it is most often the male—withdraws from conflict.

- The tendency to escalate conflict in the face of disagreement and the inability to stop fights before they get ugly.
- The tendency to invalidate the relationship by hurling insults at each other. Dr. Markman says, **"One 'zinger' counteracts 20 positive acts of kindness."**

You should note that neither Wallerstein nor Markman say that we should avoid conflict. Conflict in marriage is inevitable. How we deal with conflict is the important issue.

In addition to the suggestions already made, the following additional ideas have been culled from the literature on what makes for a successful marriage as well my clinical experience with hundreds of couples.

Be Realistic. Couples often go into marriage with idealistic notions of what marriage is all about. These ideas are handed down from generation to generation or gleaned from popular magazines, TV shows, or simply conjured from their own fantasies of what they would like. Each individual should make clear what their explicit and implicit expectations are and clarify these expectations such that they are clearly understood by one another. Where there are discrepancies, a mutually satisfying compromise must be reached.

Do Not Take One Another for Granted. This can be a killer for a relationship. It usually occurs sometime after the honeymoon period. When our partner feels taken for granted, not respected or acknowledged, and feels that others are a higher priority than him/herself, resentment brews. A regular "state of the union" check-in with your spouse as to how s/he is feeling about the relationship can help avert resentment build-up.

Communication Skills. Being able to communicate is one of the greatest assets in any relationship. Being able to articulate our thoughts and being certain that the listener understands what you wish to say take considerable practice.

Often we believe we are saying one thing, while the listener is hearing something entirely different. The listener often is responding to either what they believed you to say or their own interpretation. Communication requires both good transmission skills (articulation) and good receptive skills (listening). Without both, communication will be at best, difficult. The next time you want to discuss something important with your spouse, follow the following steps:

- *Arrange for a convenient meeting time rather than trying to have a discussion on the fly when it is likely to be interrupted.*
- *Find a "talking stick" (any small object will do). So long as one person is holding the stick, that person also holds the floor. Once the stick is passed, it becomes the other person's time to talk. This technique prevents interruptions.*
- *Express your point, and then, passing the stick, ask your spouse to repeat what you said so that you can be certain that you were at least heard. If your partner is not able to repeat what you said or you do not feel understood, repeat your point until you are satisfied.*
- *The listener's job during this exercise is to be certain you understand and communicate that understanding to your spouse before you comment on the content of what you are being told.*
- *Once your partner feels heard, then it becomes your turn to comment and be heard.*
- *Continue this process until resolution, passing the "talking stick" and alternately being in the role of transmitter and receiver.*

This approach, often referred to as "active listening," once learned can prevent misunderstandings and serve to keep emotions under control. It is difficult to react emotionally if you are truly listening and have to communicate understanding before you get a chance to react.

Regular Meetings. There are two types of meetings that can facilitate communication: a business meeting and a date night. Couples often find that scheduling regular business meetings, just as one would do in a business partnership, to discuss the business of the marriage is helpful and indicates that the marriage is a high priority in their life. Date night is one evening each week set aside for the purpose of emotional connecting. No business matters are discussed. Each partner takes responsibility on alternative weeks for planning the date, just as they might have done during courtship. Dates do not have to be elaborate events. A picnic on the bedroom floor or at the park at sunset can be every bit as romantic as a $100 dinner.

Keep the Romance Alive. Maintaining the romance in a relationship is vital to the vibrancy of the relationship. Once folks marry they often become quite lax in this department. They allow business, chores, and children to get the way of their romantic life. In a busy life, especially if there are children, it takes considerable effort to maintain romance. But it is worth it. It takes planning, creativity, and commitment.

Develop Sexual Skills. People believe that having sex is just "doing what comes naturally." Believing this is like thinking that world-class ballroom dancers are simply born—no rehearsals, no practice, no innovation, no experimentation, and no mistakes. No one would believe that Fred Astaire and Ginger Rogers did not practice in order to be graceful as they appeared on screen. The same holds true for sexual activity in the bedroom. **Good lovers are made, not born.** Many times men and women believe that somehow the man is supposed to "know" what to do and be good at it. Fearing failure, they do only what is tried and true. One of the most common problems that couples have is the lack of innovation. Sex becomes boring. Such predictability can lead to staleness and apathy. Communication about sexuality, and the willingness to experiment, will keep the bedroom activities exciting, interesting, and fun.

Be Complimentary. It costs nothing to compliment your partner and it sure feels good to receive them. We are often chary about paying compliments to our mates, letting them know that we think they are pretty/handsome, smart, clever, well-dressed, kind, a good parent, etc. We do not have to wait until some occasion when we purchase a greeting card to let our mates know that we think they are special.

Show Appreciation. Another small thing that feels good. Thanking your partner for making dinner or taking out the trash, picking up clothes from the dry-cleaners, and in general letting him/her know that she/he is appreciated can go a long way in creating a caring environment. Couples are very quick to criticize one another when chores do not get done, but they are very remiss when it comes to showing appreciation.

As you can see from the foregoing, maintaining a contemporary marriage is no easy task. It requires hard work. To think that a successful marriage—that is a relationship between two people that is fulfilling, enhancing of one's sense of self-esteem, emotionally gratifying, nurturing, and supportive—can be achieved by merely living under the same roof without investing effort and time, would be naive thinking. Some individuals believe that marriage should be easy, and if it is not, they think something is wrong.

Marriage, like any other worthwhile endeavor, requires patience and practice. When there is difficulty, it may require outside help. Just as a business may require a consultant, so too might a marriage. Today's marriages are more than just two people living under the same roof. They are complex and dynamic entities that become even more complex as children enter the picture. For then, there are additional dynamics that must be incorporated into the mix. Maintaining a marriage is one of our most significant challenges.

10

ATTACHMENT THEORY AND RELATIONSHIPS

I have been working with couples since the 1970s. During the last thirty plus years I have learned several things about how couples interact. First, when a couple goes to the movies together, even though they are sitting side by side in the theater, they end up seeing two different movies. Second, for most couples there are six people present in the home: the couple and their respective parents. Third, people tend to recreate their early childhood relationships in the context of their marriage. Fourth, couples often recreate their parents' marriages with slight variations. Last, despite their best efforts and promises to do otherwise, people end up becoming similar to the parent they vowed they would never become like.

And if these observations weren't enough to make relationships challenging, recent developments in attachment theory suggests that people interact with their significant other in a style similar to that which they developed in relation to their primary caregiver, most often their mother, during their formative years. These findings have significantly impacted mental health practitioners' understanding of the dynamics of the couples seeking their counsel. By understanding the underlying attachment style of each partner, the counselor is better able to assist the couple in learning more effective ways of communicating and understanding each other. Similarly, as you are better able to understand your own and your partner's attachment style, you may be more effective in negotiating the barriers to intimacy between you.

Attachment Theory. Attachment theorists attempt to understand and explore the ways in which young children form attachments to their mothers. They want to find out what effect various parenting styles have on children and whether these parenting styles can be classified in any meaningful way. Can the parenting style predict how children will subsequently behave in interpersonal relationships?

The early researchers in child development wanted to find out what children needed in order to develop optimally. Subsequently, researchers wanted to make predictions with respect to children's behavior, under the various parenting styles. Later researchers investigated adult attachments to see whether the attachment styles observed in children persisted into adult relationships.

In order to explore these questions, attachment theorists spent countless hours observing large numbers of children as they interacted with their mother in laboratory and home settings. Trained observers sitting in the room with parents and children recorded the parent-child interactions. In addition, the interactions were videotaped for later review. The investigators then scrutinized these observations. In the case of the videotape, such scrutiny was often frame-by-frame. On analyzing the results, the researchers determined that they could classify the various parent-child interactions into three major attachment styles. They are:

Securely attached: these children sought their mother when distressed, were confident of her availability, were upset when she left the room, were eagerly greeting her upon her return, and warmly accepted her and were readily comforted by her embrace. The mothers of these children were empathically tuned into their child, were consistent in their behavior toward the child—offering comfort and support when needed—and allowed the children to explore his/her environment. The mothers were able to soothe their child and anticipate their child's needs. They were sensitively attuned to their child and reliable in their responses.

Avoidantly attached: these children depended less on their mother as a secure base; they sometimes attacked her with a random act of aggression; they were far more clingy and demanding than the secure children; and, though in many case were upset by their mother leaving the room, would ignore her upon her return. The mothers in this category were rejecting as well as somewhat harsh in their treatment of their children.

Anxiously attached: these children were the most overtly anxious. They were clingy, demanding, and upset when their mother left the room. Despite wanting their mother desperately, when she returned, the children would show anger, went limp in her embrace, and generally were not able to be soothed. The mothers in this category were often inconsistent in their behavior toward their children and erratic or chaotic in their responses.

Attachment styles in adulthood. The next question attachment researchers wanted to answer is whether these early childhood attachment styles carried forward into adulthood and into the parenting styles they developed. The following generalizations can be derived from the attachment theory research.

Securely attached people naturally gravitate toward other people. They are comfortable in most social relationships. They easily seek help from others and assume that others will give that help. They generally trust others and can empathize with the feelings of others. They enjoy sharing their feelings, are able to listen to others, and are capable of soothing themselves when they are hurt.

As parents they show little evidence of self-deception, seem willing to depend on others, have a balanced view about their own role in their relationships, recognize that they are similar to their parents in various ways (not all of them positive), and generally seem to accept the importance of relationships in their lives. They then model such acceptance for their children.

Adults who had *avoidant attachment* histories seem unable or unwilling to take attachment issues seriously. They answer questions in a guarded way, without much elaboration, and often have trouble remembering their childhoods. They seem to dislike and distrust looking inward. They seem to ward off crucial parts of their inner feelings through various defensive processes such that that they neither feel the pain of rejection nor do they long for love. In describing their own affectionless childhood they have often been heard saying, "That's what made me the strong person I am today."

As parents, the avoidantly attached tend to be unconnected with the emotional lives of their children. They appear to be distant and uninvolved, often going through the motions of parenting without much emotional engagement. They tend to be unemotional and unsympathetic toward their children's plight or hurt. These parents take a back seat to family life, often appearing to be uninvolved in the daily life of their children or, for that matter, their partners.

Adults with *anxious attachment* styles often speak as if the feelings, hurt, and anger they had as children were as alive in them today as they were twenty or thirty years before. They describe childhoods characterized by intense efforts to please their parents, considerable anger and disappointment, and by role reversals in which they had tried to parent their parents. They still seem so enmeshed with their parents that even as they recall their past, infantile feelings flood and bewilder them.

As parents, the anxiously attached are often anxious in their role as parents. They are overly tuned in to their children's feelings, often looking to their children for validation as parents. They are overly responsive to their children's needs and are overly concerned with what others think of them as parents. Their children become reflections of their own self worth. They are often able to contain their own feelings sufficiently to be adequate parents, but their behavior may take on an intensity that reflects their internal anxiety.

Attachment styles of couples[6]. Now let us explore how these attachment styles play themselves in adults when they enter marriage or are in a relationship.

Securely attached couples, where both partners are securely attached, demonstrate an ability to shift freely between being depended upon by their partner and depending on their partner. There is mutual awareness of the other partner's feelings and thoughts from either vantage point. There is open expression of the need for comfort and contact as well as reception of the contact. Reciprocity and symmetry in the relationship patterns characterize secure couple relationships.

Where both partners are *avoidantly* attached, each partner refuses to acknowledge either dependency in oneself or in the other person. The couple typically lives in parallel, but distant, fashion with each other. There is limited intimacy between the partners. Each partner fulfills her or his respective responsibilities in the relationship with little sense of connection to the other. Their communication style is more pragmatic than emotional. Though they may have many common interests as well as separate interests, it is only through their common interests that the majority of their connection to each other takes place.

In *anxiously attached couples*, where both parties are insecure, there is asymmetry and rigidity in the relationship, with each partner taking a fixed position in emotional transactions. Anxiously attached couples show little awareness of the other's emotional experience and minimal capacity for empathic resonance within the relationship. They are so involved with their own insecurities that empathic listening is at best, difficult. Closeness is difficult for these couples since they are both easily hurt, often holding onto resentments for extended periods of time. They find self-soothing behaviors difficult. Fears of rejection and abandonment make intimacy difficult.

In a relationship where one person is *anxious* and the other is *avoidant*, one partner may seek and demand emotional contact in the relationship, but is dissatisfied and angry about the contact. There is a sense between the individuals that the emotional contact sought from the other is never adequate to fulfill emotional needs. The anxious partner feels chronically deprived and emotionally abandoned, while the avoidant partner expresses disdain for or no understanding of his or her partner's needs for dependency.

In the couple relationship where one person is *securely attached* and the other is *anxiously attached*, there is the possibility, or at least the hope, for attachment change in the insecure partner. During the course of the relationship the anxious partner may develop trust and have an emotionally corrective experience that substantially alters their perception of the relationship.

In relationships where one person is *securely attached* and the other is *avoidantly attached* the secure person tends to seek emotional understanding from people other than the partner. The avoidantly attached partner is often practical, giving through doing rather than by giving by sharing emotional connection. Avoidantly attached people often give the impression of not caring. However, this is not necessarily the case. It's just that they may show their caring in ways that do not leave them feeling vulnerable.

Commentary. When one is thinking about these different attachment styles it is necessary to keep in mind that the four styles represent broad categories. There are many variations on these themes. There is no one-to-one correlation between your attachment style as the child in a relationship to your behavior as a parent in a parent-child relationship or as a partner in a marriage. However, there does seem to be a relationship between these early childhood experiences and how people will interact in a primary relationship. This relationship between childhood experience and contemporary behavior allows us to understand some of the complexities that occur in committed relationships.

There are many factors that affect how we relate to our partners, not all of which stem from our childhood experiences. However, there is no doubt that our early experiences with our first caregivers will influence how we interact with our partners.

In large measure, we will form a relationship that is similar in style to the first relationship imprint that we experienced; namely, that between our parents. The relationship between our parents becomes our first model of an intimate relationship. Not only will we create a relationship that is similar in many ways to our parent's relationship, but we will also emulate the behavior of the same-sexed parent. After all, it is our same-sexed parent that becomes the model with whom we will identify ourselves. The manner in which our primary caregiver interacted with us will have a significant impact on whether we will feel secure in an intimate relationship, avoid intimacy, or feel insecure in an intimate relationship.

Impact on relationships. Is it no wonder that marriage is as complicated as it is? Is it no wonder that marriage demands considerable attention if it is to be rewarding, exciting, and fulfilling? And, is it no wonder that so many relationships need some help along the way?

So, what can couples do about it? Are we destined to live our lives repeating the early attachment models, roles, and parental patterns that we experienced as children in all of our intimate relationships? The answer is, no. By recognizing our attachment patterns, as well as the other influences mentioned, couples can work toward changing their manner of interacting and can learn how to resolve issues that arise more effectively. It is not necessarily the attachment style itself that affects the relationship, but rather how the attachment style affects the manner in which the couple resolves issues between them or negotiates for intimacy.

When an anxiously attached wife and an avoidant male, for example, engage in a marital conflict, the anxiously attached wife may feel as though she were going to be rejected or abandoned as the avoidantly attached husband becomes more detached, self-protective, and even angry. The conflict escalates with little resolution. The issue becomes more about their attachment style than the content of the argument. If both parties were aware of their respective attachment styles, they may be able to recognize how they each may be contributing to the difficulty they are having in reaching resolution. They may be able to develop techniques for acknowledging their different styles and working around them toward reaching a resolution. For example, the wife could recognize that her husband's detached demeanor is merely his attachment style and not directed at her personally.

Similar scenarios could be developed for the various combinations of attachment style. Unfortunately, however, the limitations of space prohibit that exploration from happening here. Suffice it to say that, with effort, sometimes with the help of a psychologist or marriage counselor, these issues can be addressed such that despite the different attachment styles of the partners, the couple can develop a fulfilling and satisfying intimate relationship.

Social Issues

11

LESSONS FROM DISASTER

For 40 seconds the earth shook. We will never be the same. It disrupted our way of life and perhaps an entire way of thinking about ourselves in the world. I have heard many people say that they lived through the 1971 and 1989 earthquakes, or other dramatic events such as floods, fires, riots, and mud slides, and do not remember feeling as upset as they are feeling today. People are complaining of feeling confused, disoriented, anxious, and depressed. In addition, they are having difficulty sleeping and concentrating, and experiencing loss of or increase in appetite. *These are all normal reactions to very abnormal circumstances.*

The cumulative effect of these disasters on the human psyche is considerable. Our lives have been upended. Our sense of safety has been assaulted. We cannot even be certain that tonight we will have a roof over our heads. One moment we feel safe and secure in our beds, in our homes, in our neighborhoods, and in the next moment we don't. We no sooner adjust to one disaster than another hits us.

The human psyche can absorb only so much without

going into overload. Every energy system can reach the point of overload and the human energy system is no exception. In addition to experiencing these events, we must also absorb the deluge of stimuli from the media showing us in full color and *live* what is happening all around us. What we see is not some remote island in the South Pacific, it is not some distant country; it is our streets, our neighborhood, and our city.

Whether it is the result of riots, floods, fires, or earthquake, we are being forced to face the harshness of reality. We cannot live in denial. We are vulnerable. And when reality hits, it hits with a vengeance, leaving us exposed to all of our worst fears. We can no longer shake our heads in disbelief as we watch a news broadcast of an event that is occurring hundreds or thousands of miles away. The events are occurring all around us. We have to face the reality that even our homes cannot provide the safety that we seek. When we feel unsafe, we feel defenseless, helpless, and overwhelmed. When our customary way of life is repeatedly threatened and disrupted, we become anxious, depressed, confused, angry, disoriented, and may have difficulty sleeping and concentrating. We may seek comfort in food, drink, drugs, or anything else that eases the pain. We seek solace in something familiar.

What are we to do if there is no safety in the world? *Safety is not to be found in the world, but instead lies within each of us.* The problem is that we expect there to be safety in the world. That is, we expect safety to exist in nature, outside of ourselves. We expect something beyond ourselves to provide us with safety, rather than looking within ourselves.

An alternative way of thinking about the issue of safety is to recognize that safety is both relative and a myth. There is no concrete, absolute safety. Safety is an abstraction that we try to turn into a reality. We like the sound of the word, "safe." We are comforted by the thought that we are safe, immune from harm. And even when we believe we are safe we find that a sudden turn of events shows us that we are not. We often say with incredulity, "Imagine, we are not even safe in our own home."

The only true safety comes from within ourselves, *in our ability to confront reality and continuously re-orient ourselves to current circumstances.* Safety comes from the knowledge that we can adapt to a variety of circumstances and to the unexpected. Maintaining an attitude of preparedness, awareness, and centeredness, is our best form of safety. Safety does not come from our ability to control the world or control forces outside of ourselves. By putting our energies exclusively into trying to control our external environment, we will always be living in an illusion of safety. True safety comes from an inner sense of strength and competence to cope with life's mysteries.

Disaster or Metamorphosis?

The earth is in a constant state of flux. It is a living organism, constantly transforming itself. We often want to believe that it is inert, constant, and unchangeable. We tend to forget that it is constantly evolving. An earthquake is not a natural *disaster*; it is merely a natural occurrence. It is how mountains are formed and valleys created. We were only coincidental to that very natural process. It became a disaster because the things we built upon the back of this organic entity called earth were destroyed, and, unfortunately, so were some people. It became a disaster because we had to face ourselves as puny little people who have become so arrogant as to believe that we can control nature and are the masters of the universe. Thus, *anything* that disrupts our life is perceived as a disaster. I have heard people use the term disaster to describe anything from a fallen soufflé to an earthquake. The only common element that I can find is that in both cases we had to face a disruption in our ordinary way of doing things and to the belief that we are in control.

Both natural and social metamorphoses disrupt our sense of order. We want things to remain static, unchanged, and familiar. We strive to create that ideal set of circumstances and having achieved it at some point, we try to "freeze" that moment in time—making all other moments measure up to it. We forget that we live in a dynamic world, one that is in a constant state of change, sometimes very visible, and sometimes very subtle change. We can cope with the subtle changes because we can almost deny that they are occurring. We tend to resist change rather than embrace it. This is true both for individual change as well as social change. Not until we are forced to examine ourselves, forced to face change, do we pay attention.

Civil unrest is necessary before we recognize that we cannot continue to oppress people and live in a world of inequity. Being diagnosed with cancer or heart disease is often necessary before we recognize that we have to change our diet and our sedentary ways. A recession or depression is necessary before we recognize that we have to change our spending styles. Ozone depletion, earthquakes, floods, and fires are necessary before we change the way in which we relate to the earth and how we care for or cope with it.

Man vs. Nature

We often relate to the earth as though we were separate from it, as though it was something other than a living, breathing organic whole upon which we depend. We tend to dissociate ourselves from the earth rather than seeing ourselves as an integral to and dependent upon it for our survival. By dissociating ourselves from the earth we do not have to see ourselves as the dependent, fragile organisms that we are. We can deny our dependence. If we accepted our dependence, accepted our fragility, we would have to relate to our planet with considerably more respect. We could not pollute it, rape it, or desecrate it, because we are part of it. By creating this schism between our environment and ourselves, we can delude ourselves into thinking that we are invincible and in control. Then we become angry, shocked, and horrified when the earth demonstrates that it is indeed a living, changing entity. We see the earth as disrupting *our* lives; we place ourselves at the center and it is doing something to us. The earth is merely doing what the earth does. The earth does nothing *to us*; we are forever doing something *to it*.

We think that we can tame the planet. Thinking this way is akin to a tick thinking that it will tame the bear! We continue to believe that we can control nature rather than work in harmony with it. We use words like: dominate, conquer, control, harness, master, beat, tame, etc. All of these words suggest that we are in competition with nature and believe that we can control our environment. Perhaps we had better work in harmony with nature as Native Americans did for thousands of years. The earth keeps showing us its strength but we never seem to get the message.

An Alternative Organizing Principle

The Western, especially the American mind tends to organize the world in terms of achievement, goals, wealth, power, and domination. There is a distinctly adversarial consciousness that permeates our thinking; we think in terms of winning and losing. We divide our cities in terms of "them" and "us," "good guys and bad guys," the "good side of town vs. the bad side." This attitude puts us at war with each other and with our environment. We think in terms of "battling the elements," a "war against crime and drugs," "man over nature," and a "rule by might" brand of consciousness. An alternative organizing principle to this male-dominated, production-oriented, them vs. us approach to the world would be one that emphasizes harmony, congruence, and cooperation. Perhaps we should adopt a more cooperative, harmonious, supportive approach to our world, where we are less concerned with winning, fighting, and controlling, and more concerned with cooperating, harmonizing, and connecting with our environment and each other.

This is not a novel idea, but it is one that has only received lip service from most people in the Western world. When we compare this attitude with that of many of the indigenous peoples of this planet we see just how adversarial we have become. We do not think of how we can work in concert with our environment; we do not respect our natural habitat; we do not see ourselves as part of the animal kingdom. Rather, we see ourselves as separate and apart from both the animal world and the planet as a whole. We are in constant competition, seeking ways to be better than and have more than someone else. We often can deceive ourselves into believing that this approach works until something unexpected happens. Sometimes it is a natural upheaval as in the case of an earthquake; sometimes it's a civil upheaval as in the case of a riot; sometimes it's an economic upheaval as in the case of a recession. In each case we may have believed that we were invincible. We thought that we could maintain an attitude of separateness and this attitude would protect us.

The riots occurred on the other side of town, the fires occurred in the valley, and the recession affected only the working class or the yuppies who overspent. But we found that in each case we were all affected. We are connected. Unless we can work together and recognize that we are all part of a global society, we will not survive. This planet will go on with or without us as it has for billions of years. The question is will *we* survive, not whether the planet will survive.

A Paradigm Shift

From physics we have learned that in order to further our knowledge it is often necessary to re-conceptualize a problem and adopt a fresh perspective. One of the clearest examples of such a shift in thinking took place when Copernicus proved that the earth was not the center of our solar system, but rather was only one of several planets revolving around the sun. This new piece of information forever changed the way we think and effectively changed our self-concept. No longer could human beings believe that they were the center of the universe. We had to give up that egocentric view of the universe. However, we still seem to have a difficult time accepting the fact that we are only a microscopic part of the cosmos.

By accepting the fact that we cannot control the outcome of our lives, we must focus on the process by which we *live* our lives. Many people think that if we accept the fact that we have limited control over our universe, there is no point to doing anything. This point of view is only valid if we maintain the outcome-oriented, goal-oriented, achievement-oriented paradigm that focuses entirely on trying to control life. If, on the other hand, we adopt a process orientation, then the focus is on how we live our lives. The manner in which we live becomes the focus. From this vantage point, we become more concerned with how we live in relationship to our environment and each other, rather than how we can dominate.

Individualism or Communitarianism

Americans, especially men, historically pride themselves on their rugged individualism. We admire those rugged heroes of the old west (at least as characterized in movies and television) who appear to function on their own, dependent on no one. We see the ability to "make it on one's own" as the highest personal value. We tend to view folks who acknowledge their need for others as weaker. We deplore dependence and relegate it to childhood or old age, but this value furthers our estrangement from one another and from our environment. It pits people against people and places us at war with the environment.

However, when we have to deal with floods, earthquakes, fires, and the like, we then are glad that we live in a community. We are glad we can *depend* on our neighbors and friends. During these times we are forced to acknowledge our mutual neediness. When we watch movies portraying townspeople pulling together to cope with a common threat, we feel comforted and warmed.

Unfortunately, it seems that only when we are threatened do we value community. Only when we are threatened do we recognize that we must work together in order to survive. Under these circumstances, we are willing to accept our collective dependence and put down our barriers. When our survival is at stake, we will cooperate with one another and work as a community.

Hopefully, the recent earthquakes and other upheavals will serve to remind us that rugged individualism is not the only way, nor even the best way to survive on this planet. Perhaps such individualism should be viewed as merely a fallback position when there is no community around.

Conclusion

In this essay I have taken the position that true safety comes through confidence in one's ability to adapt to a variety of circumstances. It comes through our ability to be resourceful, to connect with our environment and with one another. We are an integral part of our physical and social environment, not separate from it. We tend to forget that the earth is a continuously evolving, living entity and cannot be taken for granted. We tend to forget that ours is a minuscule planet in the universe. We forget (deny) that we are dependent beings, dependent on each other and the planet for our survival.

If we are to survive as individuals, as a civilization, and as a specie, we must accept this dependence and invest more in connecting with our world than in trying to control it. Developing a strong sense of commitment to our community, extended families, families, and friends gives us the strength to cope with the continuously evolving, dynamic world. By relying on one another we can strengthen our ability to adapt to a changing world. We cannot maintain an attitude of separatism, isolationism, and rugged individualism mentality if we are to survive. Our greatest strength lies with individual development in the context of the community. We must reverse centuries of thinking that has outlived its appropriateness for today's world. I believe that developing a community spirit is the higher order value and one that produces the highest consciousness as a civilization, a nation, and as an individual.

12

TOUGH TIMES

These are certainly difficult and trying times for all of us. The recession has affected everyone; if we have not been impacted directly, we know someone who has. Unemployment is high, businesses are going bankrupt; even the giants of industry are posting huge losses and laying off workers. And while lower interest rates are beneficial for some, others who are living off of their savings are hurting; retailers are suffering, and the real estate market has collapsed. Not a pretty picture. This is a time when psychologists are most needed and a time when people view seeking professional help as a luxury they cannot afford. Quite a paradox. What I would like to do in this article is offer a psychological perspective on ways of coping with these "tough times" and then suggest some specific steps that we can take to reduce the feeling of powerlessness.

In difficult times, especially when there are circumstances affecting our lives over which we have no control, we need to adopt a psychological perspective. Today is no different. While we may not have control over these circumstances, we do have control over how we view these events. We can take charge of our mental attitude and exercise control in other areas of our life.

This recession has forced us to re-examine our values. It has made many folks realize just how much of their sense of purpose and well-being they have invested in material objects, financial security, and making an impression for others to admire. During the 1980s it was important for many people to be seen in all of the right places, eat in the most fashionable restaurants, wear the trendy designer labels, and live at the right street address. It has now become very *chic* to shop down, dine cheaply, and talk about just how much one has saved by buying designer knock-offs.

Between the recession, the hole in the ozone layer, the destruction of the rain forests, increased homelessness, AIDS, the savings and loan debacle, increased gang violence, the Middle East war, and the upheaval in the Soviet Union, people are becoming increasingly aware of just how small this planet is. People are becoming increasingly aware that if we don't do something—each of us—we are going to be in deeper trouble than we already are.

This increased awareness of our vulnerability has led people to reassess their values and those beliefs that offer meaning to their life. Though the immediate effects of all of this change may be very uncomfortable for all of us, I believe that the overall affect will be positive. I think that we will begin to act more responsibly in our lives and take a more active part in trying to effect social and political change. And once we do this, rather than investing solely in our personal comfort and gain, we will feel more empowered in this world.

Hopefully, people will decide to get involved and become part of the solution. Perhaps more people will even get out and vote rather than allowing a few to determine our elected officials. And once the people take action, change will occur.

Men. Historically, men and women are affected differently by economic difficulties. In our culture, men have been taught from the time they were boys that their role in life was to be a provider. Their job, they were told, was to bring home the proverbial bacon. From the time a young boy is old enough to have a conversation he is asked, "What will you be when you grow up?" And he learns that he had better come up with a good answer. Simply responding by saying "a man" was not good enough.

Men learn to develop a sense of their personal identity from what they do for a living. They fuse with their occupational identity to the point that they think of themselves as their job, whether a welder, a physician, a merchant, or artist. When men greet one another or are introduced to one another, they do so by occupation—"Meet my friend Joe, the engineer." They introduce themselves by way of their occupation as, "Hello, and what do you do?"

Thus, when a man loses his job or is not able to provide he feels less than a man. When a man cannot live up to the expectations of his wife, family, or community, he feels unworthy, embarrassed, and little. Men identify with the size of their paycheck and their ability to perform as measurements of manliness. When these are threatened, or when there is actual loss, they experience a loss of self and often develop a major depression.

During the depression of 1929, many men committed suicide after losing all their wealth. And during the recession we are now experiencing many men who are contemplating the same or are in the midst of a serious depression.

I am reminded of the story of a man who was sent to prison for 20 years. In order to preserve his sanity while incarcerated he reasoned that he would have to find something into which he could invest his time and focus. At that moment he sees a cockroach crawling along the floor and decides that he will teach the roach how to walk on its hind legs. He spends five years, day and night, teaching the roach to walk on its hind legs; he succeeded. And then he spends the next five years teaching the roach to walk on its front legs. After succeeding he spends another five years teaching the roach to talk and then the last five years how to talk with a southern drawl. Finally, he is paroled. He leaves the prison with his prized roach, the object upon which he invested his entire life and indeed his identity. And feeling freedom, he goes to a bar, orders and downs a shot of whiskey. As he is ordering his second shot he takes out the box with his prize roach, places the roach on the bar counter, and called over the bartender to show off his treasure and says, "See this here roach? . . ." "Yeah!" said the bartender bringing his big hand down upon the roach with a crunch.

This is one of the consequences of placing your entire sense of purpose, identity, and self-worth on any one set of external circumstance, especially a job. (After 20 years of work, what did our ex-convict have?) It leaves you vulnerable to events over which you have no control. Many men have felt like the ex-convict, watching their identity being unexpectedly squashed by the loss of a job, money, or ability to perform.

Women. Historically women have been taught to gain their sense of identity through "marrying well" and looking pretty. Her feeling of self-worth was achieved through her ability to attract and marry a "successful" man who is able to provide for her and the family. Women bragged about their husband's accomplishments as if they were their own, vicariously gaining a sense of self-esteem through association. Their sense of well-being and self-esteem, not to mention their economic security, became dependent upon their husbands'. And if something happened to him, many women felt devastated. Not only were they devastated by the loss of their mate but also by all that he represented.

Furthermore, women have gained self-esteem through their role as caretaker. They are the ones responsible for making their mates happy by providing a pleasant home. During difficult economic times, many women are threatened by their husband's inability to be the good provider. Their status in their own eyes may drop. In addition, they feel helpless. There is nothing they can do about making their husbands happy. And because they are feeling threatened by the circumstance, they are less able to be nurturing. After all, it is difficult to be nurturing when you are feeling threatened.

This is one of the issues that the women's movement tried to address. It attempted to help women see the folly of depending upon a man for all of their emotional and financial needs as well as their sense of self-esteem and identity. Unfortunately, many women have used the male model of success to achieve equality. They have so identified equality with being like men that they also managed to increase their risk of heart attack, ulcers, alcoholism, etc. They too have begun to develop a sense of identity through their achievements, performance, and possessions. In so identifying with men they have placed themselves more at risk and may experience similar reactions to tough times.

So we see that both men and women are affected by an economic recession. Their identity, sense of self-worth and self-esteem are intimately tied into the economic system.

Locus of Control

During the recent fires that swept through Oakland, I was watching the news and saw the devastation wreaked by the fire and the effect on the people who lost their home and possessions. I was particularly touched by an interview with two neighbors, each of whom lost everything in the fire.

One person was obviously distraught, wringing his hands, totally overwhelmed, having no idea what he was going to do next. He stated that life had little meaning. His depression and shock were obvious. The neighbor, on the other hand, had quite a different response. He stated that though it was true that he lost all of his possessions and his home, they were merely possessions. He stated that he would rebuild and move on with his life just as he always had.

The difference between the two neighbors is obvious. The first neighbor identified with his possessions; his sense of self was inextricably connected to his wealth. Whereas the second man seemed to have a sense of self separate from his possessions. His things were merely things, symbols of a life, not life itself. Clearly this man will be able to deal more effectively with his circumstances. He recognized that though he does not have control over his circumstance, he does have control over how he will deal with the circumstance. Circumstance is outside of us; a sense of self lies within us.

Those folks who are most affected by loss of possessions are those who have placed the locus of control outside of themselves. They try to control their circumstances, their environment, rather than taking charge of their own reactions and the way they view their circumstances. They believe that security comes from outside of themselves. They believe that if they can structure their world such that they are fully protected from contingencies, then they will be safe. In their attempt to structure such a world they find that they have to narrow their world, restrict possibilities, and eliminate risk.

Controlling people—those that need to control their environment, other people, and their things—tend to be more vulnerable to experiencing loss and depression. They are the folks who are most impacted by unpredictable circumstances. They tend to overreact to even minor difficulties, and have difficulty dealing with adversity and life's tragedies, especially when those tragedies touch them directly. They tend to panic during the Oakland fires, the Los Angeles floods, or economic reversals, whether real or imagined. In order to function, these folks tend to try to control every aspect of their life, thinking and re-thinking every action before deciding what course to take. It is as if by such careful consideration they could control every contingency. In reality, all that this kind of control produces is a shrinking world view, indecisiveness, anxiety, and fearful that someone or something will destroy their carefully structured world.

Howard Hughes, with all of his wealth, ended up living in a very constricted, highly structured environment. His need for control rendered him a virtual prisoner, fearful that a tiny germ would invade his space. By living in such an aseptic environment he only left himself more vulnerable rather than less.

Being in Charge

An alternative to trying to control the environment and eliminating contingency is to learn to deal with contingencies more effectively. Rather than try to control all of the variables that might affect a sailing trip, it might be better to learn how to be a better sailor. So too in life, it might be better to learn to deal with the unexpected rather than to try to insure that the unexpected won't occur.

Like Howard Hughes, we could spend considerable time and energy trying to control our home to be free of germs, dirt, etc. or we could spend our energy trying to develop a healthy body through exercise, nutritional consciousness, and learning how to deal effectively with the stresses of life through maintaining a psychologically healthy perspective.

The people who responded to the Oakland fire without total panic viewed the locus of control for their life within themselves. That is, they viewed themselves as people who could deal with contingency. Their identity was not placed in their ability to control the environment, collect possessions, and restrict their world. They gained their identity through the knowledge that they could cope with life's realities, whatever they may be. Their strength lay within themselves rather than in their possessions.

Value Restructuring

In order to effectively cope with difficult times, one must first develop a value orientation which places priority on those activities which one can master with minimum interference from outside forces. For example, one can master dealing with one's nutritional intake. One can take full charge over how one is going to feed oneself. Another simple value is that of physical exercise. With minimum interference from variables over which one has no control, one can exercise and gain a sense of mastery over the activities in which one engages.

Moving up the scale of values, we can redefine what it means to be a man or woman. We do not have to adhere to archaic and non-functional definitions of maleness and femaleness, man and woman, masculine and feminine.

Being a male could be defined as being in touch with one's feelings, learning to effectively deal with contingency, being open, warm, loving, being honest with oneself and one's world, valuing friends, family, and self. By this definition, most of us could become male with little reliance upon external factors in the environment. We do not have to define maleness as being able to bring home the bacon or accumulating lots of possessions. We do not to define ourselves by our performances. (Men seem to keep statistics on everything: how many times did you? . . . How big was? . . .)

And women could redefine femaleness to mean something other than their ability to be attractive, sexual, and have a husband who is a financial success. In earlier times women gleaned their identity through their attractiveness and the success of their mates. Thus, they were vulnerable. Looks fade and men lose their fortunes and die.

The women's movement has helped women emancipate themselves so that they do not have to rely upon men financially or intellectually. Women are capable of having the same careers that men have and performing the same jobs. However, as I pointed out earlier, by identifying with the male model of success women have also encountered the same problems facing men insofar as the negative affects on their health is concerned. In some ways contemporary women are even facing more difficulty. They are often trying to carry out roles as primary caretakers, similar to previous generations, and as independent professionals. They have placed their identity on their ability to perform equally in both arenas.

Women might define themselves through their ability to be nurturing, loving, creative, and intelligent. Work should be viewed as something that one does to earn a living and gain a sense of fulfillment. It does not define who we are. And money is merely a medium of exchange.

Personal Power

These tough times can be viewed as a prelude to significant change. And as many of us can attest, change is often fraught with chaos. In fact, some have said that chaos is merely a by-product of change. Those of you who have been in psychotherapy know that as you embark upon the path of self-discovery, there is often a period of confusion, anxiety, uncertainty, and pain. Your world seems as though you and everything in it is going topsy-turvy. But then, as the dust begins to settle, something new begins to grow out of the confusion.

Our entire planet seems to operate this way. From the upheaval caused by underwater volcanoes, islands and mountains emerge. Out of the chaos, change occurs.

We can look at this period as a signal that change is happening. And we can either resist this change and feel angry, depressed, and helpless, or we can deny this change and be ill-prepared when change is foisted upon us; or we can work with this change and embrace it as an opportunity to effect changes in our own lives.

Change is all around us. It is happening in our courts where the issue of sexual harassment and date rape are being taken seriously. It is happening in Europe and Asia, with the collapse of the Soviet Union. It is happening in an industry where we have to recognize that the United States is not the only economic power. This is the beginning of an era of cooperation among nations. The European community is banding together and soon will have a shared currency making it a formidable economic and political force. Exciting changes.

Once we accept these changes and decide that we can affect changes in our lives, we are beginning to take power into our own hands. We are deciding that we are the masters of our own destiny, rather than relying upon external forces to dictate our direction.

Personal power is the degree to which we decide for ourselves how we will lead our lives and to what values we shall subscribe. We can learn how to make wiser and better choices in our life. Each moment of each day gives us the opportunity to decide anew upon our course. We can make our ideals and our actions congruent. Often we speak one set of values but act in the opposite way, setting up a condition known as bad faith. To the extent that we live in bad faith we will feel anxious and guilty.

Personal power lies within each of us. It is not something that lies in the external world. In order to tap into this resource we must begin slowly to exercise our freedom to choose how we wish to live our life. We must decide whether we want to be healthy or sick and make choices accordingly. If we choose to be healthy, then we do everything we can to take care of our bodies and our minds to increase our resistance to disease. We must examine and re-examine our values. What role does social commitment play? What place does spirituality occupy in your life? What type of commitment have you made to your family? Friends? To your children? Are your actions congruent with your beliefs? How important is money in your life? Does it play an inordinately large part? How do you define yourself? Do you identify your sense of self with your career or job? Who would you be without it? What else do you do aside from work? How do you express your creativity? What other interests do you have? If you couldn't work how would you spend your time? How would you feel about yourself?

The Harmonious Life

Once you have completed this self-evaluation, you should have a pretty clear notion of what needs to be done. High self-esteem and a positive self-image are necessary conditions for the harmonious life. A harmonious life is experienced when the various components of one's life resonate with one another, each enhancing the other. These components include one's values and beliefs, one's work, hobbies, recreational activities, family, friends, spirituality, and community involvement. Most of these are minimally dependent upon external circumstances. To the extent that they are not in conflict with one another, e.g., expressing the belief in racial equality while supporting countries that practice genocide, is the extent which harmony can be reached. The person whose life approximates the harmonious life has enhanced his or her personal power and will be in the better position to cope with difficult times. No one area of this person's life takes on such import that without it life seems impossible to live.

13

REDEFINING SUCCESS

For as far back as most of us can remember, success has been defined in performance terms, most notably economic. As men we heard our parents say, "So and so is very successful, you should see the car he just bought." To the women these parents would say, "She married well and you should see the car he bought her." When we were in school success was measured by our grade point average. Most of our lives have been dominated by the notion that in order to be successful we had to have the trappings of success. Our success was to be measured by some objective criteria: grades, money, power (power is often money), or possessions. I propose that this definition of success has outlived its usefulness and should be changed. I further suggest that to adhere to such a narrow definition of success is harmful to our mental health and can be destructive to a society.

When we look back to the 1980s we can see just how far people will go to be "successful." Donald Trump, Michael Milken, Charles Keating, Donald Spiegel, to mention a few, all wanted to be successful. Our society thought they were geniuses. We revered these people because they amassed large fortunes. We admired them because they could manipulate vast amounts of money. We didn't concern ourselves with their values, their morals, and their attitudes. We were only concerned with their wealth. These people, and others like them, became the models of success. These were the people we wanted to emulate, and we hoped that our children would identify with them.

In previous generations we identified with various leaders, such as presidents, politicians, heads of corporations, and the like. And then came their collapse. A president was impeached, senators were found guilty of graft, the head of the FBI was corrupt and abused his power, and corporate heads were found guilty of fraud and embezzlement.

I cannot remember a time in history when so many icons of respect fell from grace. For men, this leaves a vacuum of idols. There are no models left. Even our sports heroes, in their quest for material gain or power, have been found guilty of unethical and illegal behavior. Pete Rose was guilty of violating the rules of baseball, and Mike Tyson was found guilty of rape. Where are men to turn for their models? What values should these models have? What are the appropriate criteria for a model of success?

By contrast, contemporary women have a great many models with whom to identify. Unfortunately, however, many women are using the same criteria for success that men have historically used: power and money. By emulating men, women will end up in the same place that men have ended up. We are already seeing an increase in heart disease among women, a decrease in the discrepancy in mortality between men and women, i.e., women are not living as long as they had been, and a general increase in the number of cases of what has commonly been thought of as "male illnesses." Such stress-related illnesses as ulcers, hypertension, heart disease, as well as addictions to alcohol, drugs, and cigarettes, all of which have been traditionally male problems, are becoming increasingly common in women.

Stress and Success

The human immune system is affected by stress; thus, we are more susceptible to illness under stress. The stress of trying to live up to external standards of success and achievement in an overly competitive world is one of the primary stresses of contemporary life. Learning to refocus and redefine what constitutes success would go a long way toward reducing the amount of stress we experience.

Defining oneself by external standards such as material goods, status, wealth, income, and the size of one's home leaves us vulnerable to stress, since we are always concerned with losing these attainments. And what is enough? How much of each makes for success? And if someone has more, is she/he more successful? By putting our measure of success on external variables, we are giving up control of our lives and our sense of self. We have no control over whether we will lose our job due to cutbacks, lose our wealth due to stock market crashes or recession, or lose our clients, patients, or customers. What happens in the event of disability? Is it really "success" when one has minimal family life, few friends, no hobbies, no interests other than work, minimal social life, no recreational life, limited community involvement, and no spiritual life?

An Alternative Model

Perhaps a more appropriate definition of success would include a balance of all of the above. We are all born with a certain set of genetically determined, biological givens. From that point onward we have varying degrees of control over our sense of self or what we might call our identity or self-concept. Picture a series of concentric circles moving from a small circle in the center to increasingly larger circles as you move outward, similar to a bull's-eye. The center is your genetic composition, followed in order by:

(Genetics and biology)
1. Attitudes, values, and beliefs
2. Awareness, knowledge, and insight
3. Physical care, exercise, and appearance
4. Diet and nutrition
5. Spiritual awareness
6. Hobbies and recreation
7. Family relationships
8. Friendships
9. Community involvement
10. Career and employment
11. Financial and economics

The closer to the center of the bulls-eye, e.g., 1, 2, 3, etc., the more immediate control we have and the fewer contingencies involved. We have greater control of numbers 1-6 than 7-11. As we move from the center outward, we have less control.

If your identity is based on your finances or career, for example, you have less control than those who define themselves by their attitudes and beliefs. If you define yourself by the money you make as a lawyer, for instance, and you lose clients and the public's view of lawyers diminishes, then your self-concept will take a significant drop. If, on the other hand, you define yourself by the good deeds you do or by your values, no one can take these away and your self-concept will remain constant.

As I pointed out earlier, people who define themselves by their jobs live a very precarious existence. Once they retire, by choice or otherwise, or lose their job through economic changes, these individuals often feel at a loss. They experience feelings of worthlessness, depression, anger, and a loss of self-worth.

Rather than the definition being defined by society, this alternative point of view suggests that we should define success according to the degrees to which we achieve our own balance of priorities. The more elements that go into the formula, the less vulnerable one is to failure since no one element alone comprises our self-concept. If we define success as solely based on financial achievement, for example, our self-image will go up and down at the whim of the economy.

I am reminded of the two types of balls I used to play with as a youth. One was made out of solid sponge rubber and it was virtually indestructible. Cars could run over it and dogs could chew it, and though bruised or chipped, it would still bounce. The other ball was hollow, but a very high bouncer, and hence, the ball of choice. However, if it got punctured it would quickly go flat or even split in half. The mortality rate for the hollow ball was very high. By building our self-concept based on a solid center, we might not be as glamorous or flashy as the person who builds a self-concept based on power or money, but we are likely to be more durable.

Self-concept and Success

There are two issues here: one has to do with having greater control over our self-concept, and the other relates to a new definition of success. By defining our self-concept in terms of values, self-awareness, spirituality, hobbies, etc., we have more control since these are less affected by contingency than finance and career. That is, we have greater control over the values we will adhere to than we have over economic conditions in the world. We might consider this as having an "inner-directedness" rather than an "outer-directedness." A self-concept based on inner-directedness is similar to having a solid core that can withstand adversity. On the other hand, a self-concept based on outer-directedness leaves us with a hollow core and less able to deal with adversity.

A positive self-concept is the foundation for success on the job, not the other way around. We have control over our self-concept since we can take action that directly affects how we feel about ourselves. There are certain aspects of our lives that we are more able to control than others. We can control the extent to which we live up to our values, we can strive toward accomplishing our goals, we can make a contribution to our community, we can take care of our bodies and our minds, we can develop a social and spiritual consciousness that keeps us connected to the world around us, and we can develop hobbies and interests that enrich our lives. With these attributes as the foundation of our self-concept, we are more able to function effectively on our jobs. Our jobs do not define us.

Your self-concept is how you think about yourself, your ideas about who you are. If you define yourself narrowly you will be more vulnerable to depression and anxiety. If your entire self-concept is based on being a parent, you will feel at a loss when your children grow up and leave the home. If your self-concept is based on your career, then retirement will be difficult since you will lose the basis of your identity.

It is often difficult to change your self-concept. It takes time and effort. Often we need help. Our concept of self begins to develop during childhood and is resistant to change. We learn what is expected of us first from our parents, then from friends, and in school. Society contributes to our self-concept when it defines boys as potential fathers and workers, and girls as mothers and homemakers, and when it defines success in terms of wealth, power, and accomplishment. We internalize these values and begin to define ourselves in similar ways.

In order to change our self-concept we have to take charge of our life. We have to decide what is important to us and what constitutes success. *Your* success depends on how *you* balance your priorities. Success can only be understood in terms of each person's individual formula for success. Most of us have never given it a moment's thought—we merely accepted what was handed to us. *Success begins with personal empowerment, taking charge over that which we can control and accepting that which we cannot.*

14

MEN AND MASCULINITY

What does it mean to be male in this country? Big man on campus (BMOC) ... don't be a sissy ... duke it out ... never show weakness ... be a rock ... sturdy as an oak ... a big wheel ... big boys don't cry. These have been the terms that described men. Male idols were the "strong, silent type" characterized by Joe DiMaggio, Ted Williams, John Wayne, Clint Eastwood, Sylvester Stallone, Gary Cooper, and James Arness. If a man couldn't hang tough, grin and bear it, or take it like a man, he was, by definition, less than a man. Masculinity was defined as self-reliant, competitive, achievement-oriented, independent, powerful, adventurous, and emotionally restrained. Many more sensitive men have spent a large portion of their lives feeling less than a man because they could not fit into the stereotypic definition of masculinity. The pendulum is now swinging in the other direction. Men are considering alternative models of masculinity, including incorporating the "female" parts of their personality. As such movies as *Kramer vs. Kramer, Mr. Mom,* and *Three Men and Baby* portray, more men are becoming primary caretakers for their children and performing traditionally female activities. "Macho men" are not the only models available to men.

Changing Roles

During the course of the last 30 years there has been a slow but continuous shift in the definition of what it means to be a man in the United States. In the 1950s, men were expected to work, bring home a paycheck, mow the lawn, do some maintenance around the house, and take out the trash. On the weekend there would be the family outing or BBQ. Since that time the family constellation has changed and thus, the male role has changed. By 1985, according to the Bureau of Labor Statistics, only 9.8 percent of the population was married couples with children under the age of 18 where the husband was the sole breadwinner. A wide variety of family styles have emerged including single-parent households, two-career families, and stepfamilies.

Two-career families, which may have evolved initially out of economic necessity, have become a choice for many couples. This factor alone has made it necessary for men to redefine their role. The traditional male role does not quite work when he is in the baby nursery, or when car-pooling, or while carrying out the many chores traditionally characterized as "women's work." Women want and demand an equal partner in the domestic and parenting responsibilities. Not only do they want a partner in the fullest sense of the word, they also want a friend.

Being a good provider is not enough and often not even necessary. In fact, society no longer seems to value or even recognize the traditional male way of demonstrating care, through taking care of his family, by solving their problems and being the one counted on when needed. Men are being required to take on roles that they have not been prepared for, such as nurturing children, revealing their weaknesses, and sharing their feelings. With more women entering the workplace, many men are required to share in all of domestic work in the family. And they often feel at a loss for how to accomplish these tasks. After all, women were trained from childhood to fulfill these roles. They "played house," changed dolly's diaper, and imitated mother. Men did none of these and yet they are expected to participate equally today.

A few other factors that have contributed to the changing view of masculinity are the birth control pill, the sharp influx of women into the work force, and the increased divorce rate. The result of these factors has been to permit women to earn their own income and pursue their own career without having to rely upon men for support. Control over the timing of pregnancy freed women to enjoy sex and intimacy separate from parenting. And the increased acceptance of divorce as an alternative changed the very nature of the marital commitment.

The feminist revolution contributed in no small way to the changes in men's roles. With increasing autonomy for women, men were able to explore other options than supporting and protecting women. Men no longer had to view themselves solely as providers. And women no longer had to view men as the source of their financial security. Rather than seeking careers primarily based on salary, men could consider other types of careers that were not as financially rewarding, but perhaps more personally rewarding. Since women were beginning to recognize that they could support themselves, they began to expect more from men by way of intimacy. They expected men to be more sensitive, empathic, understanding, supportive, and available. Men, being accustomed to "information talk" (communication for the purpose of sharing information) and not having been trained in what might be called "relationship talk" (communication for the purpose of forging or maintaining interpersonal connection) were at a loss as to how to communicate with women.

The Men's Movement

A plethora of self-help books dealing with a new definition of masculinity appeared on the market. The most notable of these books being Sam Keen's[7] *Fire in the Belly* and Robert Bly's[8] *Iron John.* These books spawned what has been called the "men's movement." The men's movement has made it clear that traditional definitions of men are no longer appropriate and may even be harmful to men.

The conventional definition of masculinity has led to men dying earlier than women, having more heart attacks, ulcers, and other illnesses than women. Psychologists have demonstrated that traditional male values adversely affect men by increasing physical and emotional pressures on them to fulfill roles for which they may be ill-equipped. The traditional values had created a stereotype of masculinity; if a man does not fit, he often feels inferior. Some men force themselves into the role; some just feel the burden and die early or become depressed with the responsibility. The men's movement suggests that men have another side to their personality that has not been developed. Some people refer to this side as the "feminine" side. That is, the side that is sensitive, emotional, open, warm, expressive, and vulnerable. In other words, this is the side that most men keep hidden from themselves as well as others.

The men's movement continues to challenge men to redefine themselves in terms that are more appropriate to today's world, rather than clinging to arcane definitions that have outlived their utility. The traditional definition of masculinity was based on notions of rugged individualism and physical strength. This definition developed at a time when men literally went "off to the mines" and "off to battle."

These metaphors were then used to refer to the simple act of going to work. Obviously, most of us neither go off to the mines nor off to battle. Yet we think of ourselves in just those terms and believe that it is our destiny to be the consummate provider even though our circumstances may have dramatically changed.

The men's movement argues that there are many ways in which masculinity can be defined. There is the primitive part of men that is represented by the hunter, warrior, and scavenger. And there are more highly developed aspects of masculinity that nurture and protect. There are also parts that are in need of protection and nurturance; these are the more vulnerable parts of the male identity. These latter parts of the male psyche have been under-utilized and in fact often disparaged. These are the parts that men have been told to hide, to keep in the closet. More and more men, however, are finding that it is too painful to keep these parts hidden. Likewise, it is too painful to maintain the facade of imperturbability. Increasingly, men are finding their way to the waiting rooms of mental health workers in order to deal with these identity conflicts. But this has not always been the case.

Men and Psychotherapy

Historically, men have avoided seeking and utilizing psychological services. Four major factors stand in their way: 1) they have to admit there is a problem. The "sturdy oak" concept of maleness implies that men should conceal weaknesses; 2) they have difficulty asking for help. Men believe that they should be able to solve all of their own life problems; 3) men have difficulty processing emotional states, stemming from early training which states that boys should tune out painful feelings (e.g., the macho attitude of "it's only a flesh wound" and "big boys don't cry"). As a result, men are often unaware of what they feel; 4) they fear intimacy. Men prefer to shake hands rather than hug. They fear that physical contact equates to sexuality. When men enter psychotherapy with a female therapist, they tend to eroticize the relationship; with male therapists fears of homosexuality emerge.

Ideally, men should be able to enter psychotherapy for any number of reasons and should be able to benefit from a wide variety of therapy modalities that could be entered at any point along their overall journey. However, traditional male socialization has made this very difficult because most men, to some extent, have been trained to resist psychotherapy as representing everything they fear and despise: loss of control, dependency, vulnerability, and femininity. Such clients require special handling.

Psychologist Dr. F. Pittman described an "invisible male chorus that haunts men's lives." This male chorus—made up of all man's comrades, rivals, buddies, bosses, male ancestors, cultural heroes, and his father—pushes a man to "sacrifice more and more of his humanity for the sake of his masculinity."

Although men often function in the public sphere, surrounded by work associates, and often report a large number of "buddies" or casual friends, most contemporary men live lives of marked emotional isolation. Men tend to have friendships characterized by "activity sharing" (e.g., hunting, fishing, bowling, cards) whereas women are likely to have friendships characterized by interpersonal intimacy and discussion of feelings—side-by-side friendships rather than face-to-face.

Because they lead these emotionally isolated lives, many men may find therapy groups to offer immense potential for interpersonal connection and recognition of common struggles. In an all-male therapy group, participants commonly discover the universality of men's issues, such as the challenges of the worker and good provider role, and doubts about one's ability to meet the expectations of male family leadership. Insecurities about sexuality and emotional distance from children are often topics of discussion. When group members find that most other men share these concerns, they usually feel a powerful sense of relief.

Because men limit emotional expressiveness and dependency with other men, they tend to become emotionally overdependent on women. Psychologists have noted that married men are much less self-disclosing with male friends than single men, do little to keep male friends intact, and depend on their wives for friendship and dependency needs. It is therefore not surprising that one of the formidable challenges for divorcing men is the need to replace the multiple emotional contributions of the lost spouse. Because men have allowed themselves to become so significantly dependent on women for social facilitation, nurturing, and validation, the all-male therapy group can offer an especially valuable corrective emotional experience, as men learn to trust and value intimate male friendships.

When men enter psychotherapy, they are often quite anxious. They frequently come into treatment either under duress or pressure from a significant other or as a last alternative. Therapy, for most men, is the antithesis of masculinity. Visiting a psychologist violates the very essence of the traditional definition of manliness. It means admitting that a problem exists that cannot be fixed by oneself. Men have hard enough time asking for directions while driving or reading the instructions for putting chair together! Asking for help with one's emotional life is another order of magnitude. Admitting to being in pain or that their life is not working the way they want or as expected is at best, difficult. Often, they would rather turn to alcohol than ask for help.

Once men do enter treatment, being trained to be

emotionally constrained, and to avoid intimacy (especially with a man), they are often focused on obtaining immediate, measurable results. This demand for measurable progress is one way in which the male's resistance to therapy surfaces. This concern with results also serves to maintain the problem that brought them into therapy in the first place, since often a man's problems are a result of his need to maintain control while ignoring his emotional needs. They are cautious about the therapeutic process, wanting to stay in control and fearing the intimate relationship with the therapist where they might lose power. When they do reveal themselves, they feel both relieved and weak, feeling obliged to apologize for their feelings. They fear becoming attached to and dependent upon their therapist, especially if the therapist is a man. They fear acknowledging fear and weakness. They may even come to enjoy the intimacy and connection with their therapist, but they are also frightened by these feelings. At this point they often want to flee treatment.

Men have been so acculturated as to believe that all intimate relationships with men are to be avoided. Yet it has become apparent that most men suffer from what might be called "father hunger." This father hunger relates to the need for contact with men which has been unsatisfied, forcing men to rely almost exclusively on women for satisfying their dependency needs. Because of the traditional role ascribed to men, most of them did not spend much time with their fathers. They often look back nostalgically at the time spent with their fathers fishing, playing ball, or sometimes doing homework. These times, however, were often few and far between.

Fathers were somewhat enigmatic men with whom they could do things; they often were not men from whom they could receive nurturing. However, the need persists. We can see the magnitude of this need in this country with men's obsession with predominantly male events—sports, poker nights, boys' night out, smokers, etc. Men long for contact with other men, but can only tolerate it in small doses under controlled and competitive circumstances where intimacy is indirectly achieved and vulnerability is minimized. The therapeutic context, on the other hand, encourages men to become vulnerable, to self-disclose, and to reveal their fears, anxieties, and insecurities. And in this context they often discover how important the male-male bond is to them, and how much they miss and/or long for the intimacy that occurred among the "guys" of their youth.

During the past decade, I have noticed a dramatic shift in the gender composition of my practice. For the first twenty years my patient population was overwhelmingly comprised of women. Today, the majority of my practice consists of men.

Problems In Living

15

COPING WITH DEPRESSION

Depression is one of the two of the most common complaints expressed by people coming to a psychologist's office. Anxiety is the other. Frequently they are experienced together. We often use the term "depression" when we feel "blue," sad, or down in the dumps. Most times these feelings are "normal" reactions to life's difficulties. They will pass, usually in a short time, once the situation with which they are connected passes or is resolved. We refer to these reactions as situational when the feelings are appropriate for the circumstances. It is appropriate to feel sad when you lose your job or when your best friend moves to another city or state. It is normal to occasionally feel down in the dumps when things go wrong or when life seems a bit overwhelming.

Some people, however, have a chronically depressed outlook on life. They are more prone to experience depression when faced with some misfortune. These people expect the worst out of life; for them, the glass is always empty. They tend to blame themselves for everything that goes wrong, even events over which they have no control.

Depressed folks exaggerate failures and minimize successes. Their world is very constricted, perceived choices are limited, and they always expect the worst out of life. Depressed people are pessimists for whom life is a constant struggle. Even the simplest tasks are monumental and the smallest decision seems overwhelming.

Depression is characterized by: (1) feelings of helplessness, worthlessness, and hopelessness; (2) poor concentration, confusion, indecisiveness, and forgetfulness; (3) decreased ability to enjoy life (dysphoria); (4) sleeping too much (hypernosmia), sleeplessness (insomnia), constant fatigue or agitation); (5) increased or loss of appetite; (6) unusually slow or rapid speech and physical movements; (7) narrow range of affect; 8) withdrawal from social contact.

Types of Depression

"The Blues" or the "Blahs" is that feeling when we experience when our normal, everyday activities seem to lack purpose. We may feel as though we lost our sparkle. The "blues" often comes upon us suddenly in reaction to some event or series of events such as a series of disappointments, or even as the result of being bored. Just as suddenly, the blues may disappear when something new enters our life or when the circumstance that precipitated the experience changes.

Situational Depression is a prolonged period of the "blues" usually in reaction to some life event such as a loss or disappointment. Losses come in many varieties. Sometimes they are obvious, while at other times they are subtler. Obvious losses are: loss of a loved one through separation, divorce, or death, loss of a job, loss of a friendship, loss of limb or body part through accident or illness, loss of health. Less obvious losses are: loss of one's youth associated with life transitions, children growing up and moving out of the home, a particular lifestyle or career path, retirement from a career, loss of childbearing capability, loss of long-held dreams.

There are many losses that human beings experience. Most individuals readily accept these losses, while others experience them more profoundly. The latter individuals may experience depression. In a situational depression, the depression disappears once the triggering event fades. Some of the symptoms of situational depression are:

- Sense of helplessness and gloom
- Grief
- Feeling that life is empty or meaningless
- Loss of appetite
- Weight loss (or increase)
- Anxiety
- Worry
- Irritability
- Tendency to retreat from interacting with others.

Major Depression is a more severe form of depression than situational depression. People who experience a major depression become incapacitated. They are not able to function in their customary roles in life. They often feel that life is not worth living. They feel so overwhelmed with life and are so filled with grief or remorse that they are not able to carry out their daily functions of life. These individuals experience:

- Overwhelming grief
- Loss of self-esteem
- A sense of desperation
- Loss of interest in activities that they normally engage in
- Withdrawal from people
- Loss of energy
- Difficulty getting out of bed
- Self-reproach and inappropriate guilt

- Suicidal thoughts
- Lack of response to environmental changes
- Change in physical demeanor, i.e., change in speech pattern, gait, and posture, which makes one unable to enjoy life or function in their work or within their family.

A major depression may be triggered by a situational depression or may slowly develop without any precipitating trigger. Some people gradually begin to doubt themselves, feel that they have not accomplished their life's goals, feel like total failures in their life, and see themselves at fault for all of the difficulties that their family experiences. They take on inappropriate amounts of responsibility and experience overwhelming guilt when they are not able to accomplish the impossible.

Organic Depression There are essentially three types of organically based depressions:

Manic-depressive illness (bipolar disorder) is evidenced by extreme mood swings. The individual alternates between periods of manic behavior where they feel all-powerful with incredible amounts of energy and periods of extreme depression where they have no energy at all. These episodes are often cyclic and the feelings are so intense that they take over the person's life. Medication is necessary for treatment of these disorders.

Organic brain damage sometimes associated with dementia, is often observed in elderly people. The combination of brain deterioration, loss of intellectual functioning, loneliness, and isolation converge to leave the person experiencing a profound depression.

Depression can be associated with the habitual use of illicit drugs and alcohol and as a side effect of some medications.

Causes of Depression

There is no single cause of depression. Many factors may contribute.

- *Situational factors* relating to stressful life events
- *Helplessness* stemming from a lack of control over one's life
- *Social and economic class factors* such as homelessness, unemployment, chronic inability to provide adequate care for one's children, and social oppression
- *Repressed anger*—when we turn our anger inward for fear of losing love or fearing rejection, or tend to deny these feelings
- A *response to loss*—job loss, retirement, empty nest, and even completion of life goals
- *Low self-confidence and self-esteem*—seeing yourself as a failure or a loser
- *Passivity*—the belief that you are not in control of your own destiny and the tendency to let life happen to you rather than taking an active role
- *Sex roles*—females, because they are raised to think and behave more passively, are more prone to depression than men. More married women experience depression than single women. Stereotypic roles in either sex can foster depression.
- *Biological factors*—some people seem to be born predisposed to experiencing depression. Circumstances may stimulate the predisposition to become active. Hypothyroidism often results in symptoms of depression, as does other bio-chemical processes.
- *Nutritional factors*—some vitamin insufficiencies, as well as too much sugar in one's diet, is known to result in symptoms of depression. Hypoglycemia may yield depressive symptoms.

- *Physical illness*—depression often accompanies such illnesses as thyroid disorders, diabetes, multiple sclerosis, hepatitis, anemia, and infectious diseases.

Grief and Bereavement

It is important to distinguish between normal grief and bereavement experienced at the death of a loved one from situational depression. While grief and bereavement may lead to depression, it is not necessarily the case. Most people experience a profound sense of loss when a loved one dies. Research has indicated that most people experience stages of grief: separation and loss, anger, forgiveness and acceptance, letting go, growth and change, and new beginnings. The bereavement and mourning period make take anywhere from weeks to years without the person slipping into a depression. During the mourning period people are able to carry out daily functions though they may do so without much enthusiasm. Reminders of their loss will bring moments of sadness and tears. When the bereavement results in the symptoms we have discussed, however, we are dealing with depression and professional help is often necessary.

Treatment for Depression

Research has demonstrated that in most cases a combination of methods is most effective in dealing with depression. Certain types of depression, such as loss and bereavement, require special treatments. Brain chemistry can result in depression and may require medication. In some instances it is difficult to determine which came first, the chemical imbalance or the depression. Because of the mind-body connection, it can work either way. That is, severe depressions may create a chemical imbalance in the brain that can exacerbate the depression, and chemical imbalances may predispose us to reacting with a depression.

Psychotherapy

Psychotherapy has been found to be effective in treating depression, both situational depression and major depression. It has also proved to be valuable to prevent depression in cases of bereavement or significant life changes, such as illness, divorce, and loss of job and/or economic status. While most psychotherapy has been found to be beneficial when compared to no psychotherapy, cognitive-behavioral approaches have been found to be especially effective with major depressions.

Psychotherapy is helpful in aiding an individual understand why the depression occurred and what aspects of their life, past and present, may have contributed to setting the stage for depression. Did the precipitating event trigger a long-repressed conflict that occurred in childhood? Has the individual been suffering from low self-esteem for many years and the event was more than she/he could handle? Is there unexpressed anger that has been accumulating for many years that results in depression?

Cognitive behavior therapy (CBT) has been effective in helping individuals recognize and change the faulty beliefs that contribute to depression. Learning how to change these beliefs and the actions taken on the basis of the beliefs alleviate the depression and the symptoms. Developing new belief systems and challenging old systems with attendant new behavior patterns gives us more power and control over our lives.

In some cases, depending on the severity and duration of the depression, a combination of treatments is necessary for resolving the depression. Current research indicates that while psychotherapy alone can be sufficient for dealing with most depressions, a combination of anti-depressant medication and psychotherapy may be required in cases of more severe depression. Anti-depressive medication alone is frequently not sufficient for lasting results, though temporary and limited relief can often be found.

There is evidence to suggest that in the case of major depressions, without psychotherapeutic intervention, the individual is more prone to have additional bouts of depression over time. With intervention, however, there is less likely to be a recurrence of a major depressive episode.

Anti-Depressant Medication

In some cases of depression, anti-depressant medication is prescribed, in addition to psychotherapy. Research has suggested that some depressions affect brain chemistry. In some instances, brain chemistry may actually precipitate the depression. Most often it is difficult to definitively state which came first. Empirically, however, we have found that anti-depressant medications tend to alleviate some of the symptoms of depression in some people. Research also suggests that anti-depressants alone frequently have short-term ameliorative effects but these effects tend to wear off over time. However, anti-depressants in conjunction with psychotherapy have more lasting effects. In cases of major depression anti-depressant medication is always suggested at least in the beginning of treatment; the medication makes the patient more accessible to psychotherapy.

Exercise

Physical exercise is highly recommended in general for maintenance of a healthy mind and body. It is especially indicated for warding off or attenuating depression. During aerobic exercise endorphins are released in the brain. These endorphins are natural anti-depressants. In addition, exercise increases the amount of oxygen received by the brain that also helps to alleviate depression. The general nature of physical exertion counters the feeling of helplessness associated with depression.

Diet

Diet can affect our mood. Some vitamin deficiencies can leave us feeling depressed. Sugar often gives us a lift when we are feeling down, but the euphoria is followed by a let-down feeling. This is often referred to as "sugar blues." Some research suggests that too much sugar and fat in our diets leaves us prone to feeling depressed, as does overeating. People often use food as a means for dealing with depression as well as anxiety and boredom. Some practitioners suggest that beneath all eating disorders there is a depression that needs to be treated. Hence, watching one's diet for any changes, watching one's weight for significant fluctuations may indicate an underlying depression in need of attention. Maintaining a low-fat, low-sugar, and low-salt diet along with high fiber, fruits, and vegetables is one way of alleviating depression rather than masking it.

Meditation

Meditation has also been found useful in treating depression. Most people think that meditation is mystical and difficult to learn. Or they think that it is some form of new age approach to healing. The truth is that meditation has been around for centuries and many of us meditate without calling it meditation. Many people engage in prayer as meditation. For others, taking a few minutes a day, sitting quietly, allowing our thoughts to meander without trying to capture them, without focusing on anything but our breathing, is probably the simplest form of meditation. Whether you engage in formal meditation or self-hypnosis or progressive relaxation, any form of meditation will be helpful in combating depression.

Conclusion

Depression is common among Americans. Statistics suggest that approximately six million people each year are treated for depression. Untold others experience depression but are not treated at all. As with other medical and psychological difficulties, early detection and treatment of depression is important for most effective treatment. It has been found that if a depression goes untreated there is a greater likelihood of recurrent episodes. Most treatment programs include combinations of the following: exercise, diet, medication, meditation, and psychotherapy.

16

UNDERSTANDING SHAME AND GUILT

Shame and guilt are two very powerful human emotions that affect our lives to varying degrees. In moderation, they are both normal human emotions. However, they both can become so overwhelming as to interfere with healthy functioning. Despite their similarities, guilt and shame are different emotions and serve different purposes in our lives.

SHAME

In the healthy person, *shame* is that emotion that lets us know when we have crossed a social boundary of expected behavior or committed a social *faux pox*. Similar to embarrassment, it operates as a signal, letting us know that we have acted in such a way as to expose ourselves, often inappropriately, or acted with impropriety. We often blush; we feel exposed and vulnerable. Embarrassment may occur when a man finds that his fly is open as he stands at a dinner table. Normal shame may occur when he passes gas at the dinner table. Embarrassment is similar to normal shame but the feeling is not as profound and is more transitory. When we feel shame, we experience our personhood on the line. It is not merely the act, for the act may be insignificant as in the case of the open fly. We experience shame as something being wrong with us as a person.

Shame lets us know that we are, after all, human; we make mistakes. Shame reminds us that we are finite beings and have limits. Darwin, when asked how the human animal differs from other animals, replied, "Humans are the only animals that blush." Blushing is a manifestation of our human limits. It serves to keep us humble, reminding us that we are not perfect, that we are mortal.

Shame is that feeling that we experience with regard to who we are as a person, as contrasted to something we have done. Shame refers to feelings about one's self as a human being as in, "I am ashamed of myself." We may feel guilty about something we have done, but feel ashamed of who we are. We can be ashamed and guilty at the same time. For example, we can feel guilty for a behavior and ashamed for not having the moral fiber or will power to behave differently.

Shame is experienced at our very core of being. Neurotic shame is the experience of feeling unacceptable as a person for something that was above and beyond our control. For example, some people feel shame for being born out of wedlock, or for being the child of an alcoholic, or for not being as courageous as we might like to be. In neurotic shame one feels badly about one's sense of self for the circumstances in which one finds oneself. Neurotic shame persists over time, as compared to the transitory shame one might feel in any given circumstance, and is destructive to human growth.

The Development of Shame

Through the bond between parent and child, the child learns to trust. Through *positive* mirroring in the eyes of the parent, the child develops a sense of self-worth. The child learns what is expected. But because the child cannot differentiate between self and behavior, all disapproval is experienced as very personal. It is not simply disapproval of behavior, but disapproval of self, and is experienced as shame. This process helps the child learn limits and boundaries, and begins the process of differentiating self from others. How caretakers mirror the child's behavior will determine whether the child develops normal shame or toxic shame.

Neurotic or toxic shame is the internalized sense of shame that leads us to feel that we are worthless as a human being. It is a feeling of self-loathing, a sense of contempt directed toward the self. With toxic shame we feel that we are flawed, that we are defective as a person. This experience goes beyond the recognition that we are limited, finite beings. It views these limitations as fundamental defects for which one feels shame. A person filled with toxic shame feels isolated and empty, not worthy of being part of a community. People with toxic shame may, therefore, withdraw from others, isolate themselves, and become depressed.

Neurotic shame can be internalized and become part of one's identity. As such, a person then identifies with others who are filled with shame and so this self-image is reinforced. Some people filled with toxic shame may associate with other shame-filled people that reinforces their negative self-image but gives them some sense of connection with others. In their attempt to cope with the excruciatingly painful effects, they may try to cover these feelings in ways that look like opposites. They may become perfectionists or slobs, substance abusers or self-righteous.

Often when talking with these people, I have found that the only objective thing that they can point to for which they feel shame is the very behavior that they are engaged in to deal with their sense of shame. In other words, their sense of shame stems from an internalized belief system about themselves, rather than from anything they actually did. Toxic shame is experienced as a disease of the soul—a fundamental flaw of personhood.

Among the many steps needed to dissolve toxic shame, two are most important: recognition and disclosure. Shame must be recognized before it can be resolved. Once recognized, it needs to be made public; that is it must be shared, taken out of the closet. And then the underlying belief system must be examined. In psychotherapy, it is this belief system that must be modified in order to resolve the sense of shame.

GUILT

Guilt is at the core of conscience. Guilt is the experience we have when we behave in ways contrary to our values or morals. Guilt is the emotion that lets us know when we have strayed from a set of internalized rules. Without guilt, anarchy might result. There are three general categories of guilt: normal guilt, existential or ontological guilt, and neurotic guilt.

Normal guilt is experienced when we act in ways that we know are socially or morally proscribed. We feel guilty when we do something that we know is wrong. When we violate a social or moral taboo guilt lets us know that we have stepped over that invisible line. Normal guilt is akin to our conscience. In psychoanalytic terms, it is the superego, reminding us that we have transgressed social, moral, or legal boundaries.

Guilt operates as an overseer, protecting the self from potential punishment. We can experience guilt merely by thinking of crossing a boundary. And when we do cross the boundary and experience guilt for our actions, confession, punishment, and forgiveness affords us relief. The pain of guilt is often greater than the pain of punishment. It is the internalization of values that precipitates the guilt and allows for civilized society to operate without the omnipresent threat of a physical overseer. When the child internalizes parental values, the continuous physical presence of the parent is no longer necessary to control behavior. When these values are not internalized, and there is no guilt, only the imminent threat of punishment prevents proscribed behavior.

Existential guilt is a form of guilt we seldom hear about, but often experience. It is the guilt built into the human system; it is the guilt associated with knowing that we are not being all that we can be at any given moment, when we know we are not living up to our potential as a human being. Existential guilt (or ontological guilt—guilt associated with being), as existential anxiety, is an integral part of being human. It refers to the limiting of our choices, often knowingly choosing a course of action that limits our potential for growth, for being the person we know we can be.

Existential guilt can be experienced in relation to oneself, one's fellow human being, or to the environment. When we detach ourselves from others, separate ourselves from our fellow man, we experience guilt. Likewise, when we detach ourselves from the world around us, we experience existential guilt since we are an inextricable part of our environment.

Often we find ourselves feeling an undercurrent of guilt or anxiety that we cannot affix to some event or circumstance. It is easier when we can concretize these feelings, when we can attribute them to something outside of ourselves. However, existential guilt cannot be disposed of in this fashion, for it relates to the core of our being. Attempts at externalizing only serve to camouflage or distract us from these feelings, sometimes successfully—at least for a while. Then they return.

Neurotic or irrational guilt refers to either excessive guilt over minor transgressions or guilt for acts never committed. Neurotic guilt also refers to guilt associated with inappropriate beliefs, such as the belief that one is the cause of another person's heart attack or the guilt a child may feel for "causing" his parents to divorce.

People experience guilt for their thoughts as well as their actions. For some, thoughts are tantamount to actions. If you think it, you did it. If it were true that we are as responsible for our thoughts as we are for our actions, then we should all be in jail! Sometimes, we might have a thought of wishing harm to someone and, coincidentally, that person experiences some misfortune. Guilt-prone individuals take on the responsibility for the misfortune as if they actually caused it through their thoughts. Yet these very same people do not take credit for the fortune that people may receive subsequent a positive thought! Believing that thoughts are same as action and can cause events to happen is referred to as "magical thinking," and is normal in children, but not in adults.

Children are especially prone to take on responsibility for events over which they have no control. Children often make faulty connections between their own behavior and harmful things that happen to them or others. Since children are by nature egocentric, omnipotent in their thinking, and prone toward magical thinking, they often experience themselves as the cause of events outside themselves. Parents may reinforce this thinking process thus, leaving children filled with remorse and inclined toward blaming themselves for anything traumatic that might happen to family members.

Children have a difficult time attributing malevolent intent to their parents, and, wanting to love and be loved by their parents and to trust their parents, they would rather blame themselves when things go wrong. They rely upon their parents to interpret the world. Thus, children often will believe their parents when they blame the child for some event or situation. Children will easily believe that they are at fault and begin to see themselves as basically bad while preserving the image of the parent as good. Children also blame themselves for their parent's misfortunes and unhappiness. They take on the responsibility of making the parent happy. Failing in this mission, they label themselves as bad, incompetent, or unworthy. As adults, these individuals may find themselves working hard at being successful as if through their efforts they could make an unhappy parent happy and thereby, exonerate themselves.

Neurotic guilt takes many forms that share certain painful characteristics. Some forms of irrational guilt are: survivor guilt (the guilt experienced by survivors of a disaster who question why they were spared or believe that they could or should have done something to prevent the disaster, whether possible or not); separation guilt (experienced by grown children who leave their parents to begin a life of their own often in another geographical area or to marry, etc.); omnipotence guilt (stemming from the erroneous belief that one could have saved a loved one from illness or death if only they would have . . .); disloyalty guilt (the belief that if one stands up for oneself or someone else in disagreement with a parent or significant other that they are disloyal). These are but a few of the overlapping forms that guilt may take.

Guilt may exist on various levels of consciousness ranging from fully conscious to unconscious. Often guilt is denied and defended against, making it all the more difficult to resolve. Some psychologists believe that unconscious guilt is a root cause of psychopathology. As with the experience of shame, guilt can be excruciatingly painful. It can affect our sense of well-being, invade our self-concept, and constrict us emotionally. In an attempt to deal with these feelings, the individual may repress the events that precipitated the feelings, as well as the feelings themselves. In order to keep these feelings at bay, considerable psychic energy must be expended, often at the expense of emotions.

People experiencing repressed guilt are frequently seen as emotionally restricted, rigid, compulsive, and overly moral. Should they step out of line, they experience overwhelming anxiety. A great deal of the anxiety these people experience is related to the dreaded guilt re-emerging. The guilt is so painful that they will do anything in their power to avoid experiencing any form of guilt. Even the mere threat of guilt is enough to generate a sense of panic.

Sometimes, in an attempt to make restitution or receive punishment for some real or imagined act for which one feels guilty, the individual may either submit to the injured party's wishes rather than take a stand against them. Or the person may take on some form of analogous form of punishment upon oneself, living a life similar to the person about whom they feel guilty. Thus, a man feeling guilty for some thought or act toward a parent may submit to that parent's wish for him to be a "good boy" or may live a life similar to that person. In the process, he sacrifices his identity, individuality, and sense of self.

Resolving Guilt

Existential guilt is part our make-up as human beings and must be recognized, accepted, and dealt with differently than either normal or neurotic guilt. It requires that we accept the human condition and see ourselves as beings in the process of becoming. We are connected with each other as well as with the world around us. We are constantly evolving as human beings; if we stop moving toward self-actualization, fail to take part in the world, we will experience existential guilt.

The principles for dealing with normal and neurotic guilt are similar. However, resolving the latter is far more difficult and may require professional assistance; unconscious guilt, of course, is even more difficult and requires professional help.

Forgiveness is an essential aspect for the resolution of guilt. Sometimes that forgiveness comes from others, and sometimes it comes from us. In order to obtain forgiveness from others, we must make amends, which means we must contact those against whom we have transgressed. When this is not possible, we must learn to forgive ourselves. To be effective, the latter cannot be done in lieu of direct contact. The act of making amends is healing.

Where there is neurotic guilt it is necessary to fully examine the grounds for guilt. In neurotic guilt there is always an underlying belief system that is faulty. This belief system must be challenged. Once the faulty beliefs have been recognized and worked through, the process of amends and forgiveness can follow leading to healing. Some people hold on to their beliefs as a form of self-punishment. Until they are finished punishing themselves for real or imagined transgressions, no amount of reasoning will prevail unless the underlying beliefs have been challenged and rectified. In these instances professional help is recommended.

17

SEXUALITY AND SEX THERAPY

Despite the fact that we live in the post-Victorian, post-human potential movement, post-free love movement, we are still uncomfortable with our own sexuality. One would think that with all of the talk about sex, all of the books written about sex, and all of the movies depicting sexuality, we would finally have reached a point in our evolution where we would be as comfortable talking about and experimenting with sex as we are talking about food, and sharing sexual information as readily as we share recipes. But this is not the case.

We are uncomfortable talking to our friends about sex; we are uncomfortable asking for help with our sexuality, and we certainly would not take lessons in how to increase our enjoyment of sex. We will take cooking classes to learn how to prepare a gourmet meal. We will take dancing lessons to better be able to trip the lights fantastically. We will take golf lessons, tennis lessons, and any number of other lessons to increase our expertise and enhance our abilities. However, when it comes to sex we assume that we should be able to function optimally without help. Furthermore, if we should want to increase our sexual pleasure or should we feel uncomfortable with some aspect of our sexual life, we feel embarrassed in seeking counsel.

Generally we carry the belief that we should know everything there is to know about sex as if sexual behavior was encoded in our DNA. Most of us carry attitudes about sexuality that we learned when we were adolescents. We seldom take the time to update that information and so as adults we operate on the basis of adolescent notions of sexuality. Ignorance is one of the most effective deterrents to effective sexual functioning.

Human Sexuality

There are no rules for the human sexual response. We can respond to the same sex or the opposite sex. We can have a sexual response when we are alone or with someone. We respond to living beings and inanimate objects. Human sexuality includes all of the senses—smell, touch, sound, sight, and taste. Sexuality involves imagination, fantasy, and imagery.

Boys tend to learn about their sexuality through locker-room talk, erotic magazines and movies, and trial and error. Girls gain their sexual knowledge through conversations with other girls and women, love stories and movies, and experience. For men the sexual act is a combination of pleasure, sexual release, and power. For women, sexuality is intimacy, affection, and pleasure. Just think about the terms men and women use when referring to sex. Male terms tend to be aggressive, even hostile, while female terms are gentle, loving, and even spiritual. Women make love, men get laid.

These attitudes and values affect the manner in which the genders approach sexuality and, in large measure, contribute to their appreciation of the sex act. Furthermore, these values affect how men and women perceive themselves and how they view each other. Generally, men establish their identity through performance. From childhood through adulthood, they measure themselves by such things as how far they can spit, how fast they can run, how far they can throw a football, grade point average, penis size, salary size, staying power in bed, and the number of women they can "conquer." One way or another, performance matters. Women measure themselves by how attractive they are to men, the power held by the men that are attracted to them, and by how they are treated by these men. If men treat them kindly then they are good, if men treat them poorly they perceive themselves as bad.

Men and women bring these attitudes into the bedroom, playing out their roles as performer and seductress. During love making, the male is concerned with whether he will perform well enough or whether he will fail. Rather than focusing on his loved one, he is concerned whether she will be pleased with his performance. She, on the other hand, is concerned with whether he will think she is attractive enough. Is her buttock too big or are her breasts too small?

The Dance of Sex

Lovemaking is similar to ballroom dancing. Each person may or may not be a good dancer. One person may be a great dancer and the other may not be terrific. However, it is how they dance together that matters. Some people can dance well alone, but not with a partner. To be beautiful and satisfying, ballroom dancing demands cooperation, communication, and consideration. One partner must not go on his or her own without communicating to the partner; and the partners must cooperate.

No couple expects to dance well together, no matter how well either one may dance alone, without practicing together. It does not matter how easy it might be to dance with other partners, one's current partner is the one that matters if you wish to become a good ballroom dance team.

All of this is true for lovemaking as well. Yet we often believe that good lovemaking should "come naturally," without education. We covet beliefs that somehow people should know how to make love together and should not have to talk about it or practice with the intent of improving our style so that it is mutually satisfying. Clearly, if your dance partner continuously stepped on your toes and was unwilling to discuss the matter, it would not take long before you either stop dancing or find a different partner. Yet the majority of couples do not communicate about their lovemaking and are not open to exploring their sexuality with one another. Even the most experienced lovers often practice poor lovemaking strategies. People, especially men, become defensive when their partner wants to discuss their sex life as if they were about to be criticized.

Communication between dance partners and lovers is essential for having a satisfying experience. The partners must frequently communicate verbally and non-verbally with one another in order to learn to anticipate each other's moves. With sufficient practice, the dance of love seems effortless. Lovemaking should be fun, playful, affectionate, intimate, and fulfilling. When something goes awry, either because of faulty communication, inappropriate attitudes, or antiquated beliefs, a sexual dysfunction may emerge.

Causes of Sexual Dysfunction

Most sexual dysfunction occurs because of faulty beliefs and attitudes about sexuality, poor habits, ignorance, and early experiences. There are some sexual dysfunctions that are precipitated by physiological, biological, or chemical factors. However, all physiological dysfunctions have a psychological component. When men are unable to obtain or maintain an erection, whether from physiological or psychological causes, they feel inferior, less manly. When a woman is unable to reach orgasm, she feels less feminine. Therefore, *in all cases of sexual dysfunction it is necessary to attend to the psychological aspects of the difficulty* and what it means to the individual.

Physiological factors. Some of the more common non-psychological precipitants of sexual dysfunction include hormonal imbalance, medications, neurological impairment, physiological disorders, and even vitamin deficiency. Certain illnesses and medications can have side effects that affect sexual functioning including impotence and increased or decreased libido.

Many people prefer to think of only a medical approach to sexual dysfunction since it is more acceptable to one's self-image to believe that there is an organic basis for the dysfunction. Even in those instances when there is a recognizable medical condition affecting sexual functioning, the psychological component cannot be overlooked. We all have varying psychological reactions to physical illness or impairment. This psychological reaction can exacerbate the physical problem. This is especially true for infertility problems. Most people who have difficulty conceiving a child choose to investigate the medical aspects to the exclusion of the psychological aspects. Yet we all know of many cases where a couple after years of frequenting the fertility clinics to no avail, finally decide to adopt a child only to conceive a few months afterward. Clearly this would suggest that psychological factors were at play.

Psychological factors. Most sexual dysfunctions have a psychosocial etiology. Dr. Helen Singer Kaplan states, "In a general sense we see the immediate causes of the sexual dysfunctions as arising from an anti-erotic environment created by the couple which is destructive to the sexuality of one or both. An ambiance of openness and trust allows the partners to abandon themselves fully to the erotic experience." She lists four specific sources of anxiety and defenses against full sexual enjoyment: 1) Avoidance of or failure to engage in sexual behavior which is exciting and stimulating to both partners. 2) Fear of failure, exacerbated by pressure to perform, and overconcern about pleasing one's partner, rooted in fears of rejection. 3) A tendency to erect defenses against erotic pleasure. 4) Failure to communicate openly and without guilt and defensiveness about feelings, wishes, and responses.

Common Sexual Dysfunctions

The following are the most common forms of sexual dysfunction. They are all treatable, with a high probability of success.

Male Dysfunctions

Inhibited Sexual Desire Inhibited sexual desire or response refers to the lack of desire for erotic sexual contact. In almost all cases when there is a lack of sexual desire, the underlying causes are psychological in nature. Avoidance of sexual contact because of fears of rejection, failure, criticism, feelings of embarrassment or awkwardness, body image concerns, performance anxiety, anger towards a partner or women in general, or lack of attraction towards a partner, all play a part in reducing or eliminating the sexual response. Most men are too uncomfortable to talk to their partner or anyone else about these issues, preferring to simply avoid sex or attribute their lack of sexual appetite to stress, worries, etc. Some of these men have a very active fantasy life and prefer the solitude of masturbation to the intimacy of sexual relations.

Premature Ejaculation Premature ejaculation is the most common dysfunction and it is the easiest to treat. Masters and Johnson define premature ejaculation as the inability to delay ejaculation long enough for the woman to orgasm fifty percent of the time. (If the woman is not able to have an orgasm for reasons other than the rapid ejaculation of her partner, this definition does not apply.) Other therapists define premature ejaculation as the inability to delay ejaculation for thirty seconds to a minute after the penis enters the vagina.

For the most part, premature ejaculation occurs as a function of a learned response. Early sexual experiences were hurried in nature. Even masturbatory activity had to be hurried for fear of being caught. From youth onward men have trained themselves to be more concerned with the end result and their own pleasure rather than with the sexual process and their partner. The object of sex for most of these men was and often continues to be, ejaculating as quickly as possible. This rapid ejaculating pattern can easily become a way of life after even only a few episodes. It then begins to create a pattern of anxiety in the male each time he engages in coitus thus, increasing the probability of it occurring. Fearful of displeasing their partner and feeling inadequate as a function of it, men would rather avoid sex rather than experience the humiliation and discomfort.

Retarded Ejaculation or Ejaculatory Incompetence Ejaculatory incompetence is the opposite of premature ejaculation and refers to the inability to ejaculate inside the vagina. Men with this difficulty may be able to maintain an erection for 30 minutes to an hour, but because of psychological concerns about ejaculating inside a woman, are not able to achieve orgasm. One of the reasons this dysfunction goes undetected is because the male's partner is satisfied and indeed often is able to achieve several orgasms. Most of these men can readily achieve orgasm through masturbation or in some cases through fellatio. Many factors contribute to this condition, some of which are because of religious restrictions, fear of impregnating, and lack of physical interest or active dislike for the female partner. In addition, such psychological factors as ambivalence toward one's partner, suppressed anger, fear of abandonment, or obsessional preoccupation also plays a significant role in developing retarded ejaculation.

Erectile Dysfunction: Primary and Secondary Impotence Primary impotence refers to a man who has *never* been able to maintain an erection for purposes of intercourse either with a female or a male, vaginally or rectally. In secondary impotence a man cannot maintain or perhaps even get an erection, but has succeeded at having either vaginal or rectal intercourse at least one time in his life. The occasional failure to get an erection is not to be confused with secondary impotence. Familial, societal, and intra-psychic factors contribute to primary impotence. Some of the more common influences are: (1) performance anxiety, (2) a seductive relationship with a mother, (3) religious beliefs in sex as a sin, (4) traumatic initial failure, (5) anger toward women, and (6) fear of impregnating a woman.

Female Dysfunctions

General Dysfunction. These dysfunctions, according to Kaplan, "are characterized by an inhibition in the general arousal aspect of the sexual response. On a psychological level there is a lack of erotic feelings" manifested by lack of lubrication, her vagina does not expand, and "there is no formation of an orgasmic platform. She may also be anorgasmic. In other words, these women manifest a universal sexual inhibition which varies in intensity."

Orgasmic Dysfunction. The most common sexual complaint of women involves the specific inhibition of orgasm.

Orgasmic dysfunction refers solely to the impairment of the orgastic component of the female sexual response and not arousal in general. Non-orgasmic women can become sexually aroused and in fact enjoy most other aspects of sexual arousal. Inhibition and guilt about masturbation, discomfort with one's body, and difficulty giving up control, contribute to orgastic dysfunction. With a combination of education and practice, most women can be taught to achieve orgasm.

Vaginismus. This relatively rare sexual disorder is characterized by a conditioned spasm of the vaginal entrance. The vagina involuntarily closes down tight whenever entry is attempted, precluding sexual intercourse. Otherwise, vaginismic women are often sexually responsive and orgastic with clitoral stimulation. Similar attitudes to those found in impotent males are often found in these women. Religious taboos, physical assault, repressed or controlled anger, and a history of painful intercourse all contribute to this dysfunction.

Sexual Anesthesia. Some women complain that they have no feelings on sexual stimulation, although they can enjoy the closeness and comfort of physical contact. Clitoral stimulation does not evoke erotic feelings though they do feel a sensation of being touched. Dr. Kaplan believes that sexual anesthesia is not a true sexual dysfunction, but rather represents a neurotic disturbance and should be treated through psychotherapy rather than sex therapy.

As with sexual dysfunctions in men, the female dysfunctions also have to be understood from a social, familial, and psychological perspective. Attitudes, values, childhood experiences, adult trauma, all contribute to the sexual response in women. The attitudes and values of her partners as well as their sexual technique play a major role in the sexual response as well. An inept or misogynistic lover can significantly affect the female response. Since a woman often does not want to "damage the male ego," she will try to accommodate her responsiveness to him, often sacrificing her satisfaction in the process. She then builds up a secondary inhibition to sexual arousal in order to avoid the frustration accompanying an unsatisfying sexual experience. This inhibition or accommodation then becomes a habituated conditioned response.

Sex and Aging

There is no reason for elderly persons to discontinue sexual activity merely because of the aging process. Human beings can enjoy an active sexual life well on into their 80s or beyond. Many senior citizens hold on to invalid beliefs about their sexuality believing that sex should be reduced or eliminated during the latter years of one's life. Enjoyment of sexual relations is largely a function of the breadth of activities in one's repertoire and the degree to which one is open to learn and explore. Again we can use our dancing analogy. It is true that as we age we may no longer be able to jitterbug or engage in a fast mambo. However, we can develop a beautiful waltz and fox trot. New forms of sexual activity can be added to the sexual experience. One of the problems faced by many elderly folks is that they believe in the adage that, "you can't teach an old dog new tricks." Nothing could be further from the truth. There are many things that we can no longer do or do as well or in the same way as we could when we were younger. However, we are perfectly capable of discovering alternative ways of performing certain activities. Necessity gives us the opportunity to discover new approaches to old activities.

As we age we can become *better* lovers, depending on our attitude. Being a good lover does not mean doing sexual acrobatics or being able to orgasm a half dozen times. Being a good lover means that we are sensitive to our partner's needs; we are responsive to their wants. Being a good lover means that we communicate and listen with an open heart and mind. It is unfortunate that we don't learn these things when we are young. As we age we are "forced" to have to learn how to be good lovers because we cannot get by with the same old performance orientation. Aging gives us the opportunity to explore alternative lovemaking styles and techniques that we may have avoided when we were younger.

Sex Therapy

Sex therapy provides information and counseling on all aspects of human sexuality, including enhancing sexual pleasure, improving sexual technique, and learning about contraception and venereal diseases. Sex therapy is used in the treatment of all of the dysfunctions discussed earlier. In many cases treatment is relatively short, requiring specific techniques, homework, and practice. In some cases, the underlying issues are more complicated requiring an exploration into historical and psychological factors, both conscious and unconscious, that are contributing to the dysfunction. However, there is a very high probability of success even in those cases if people are motivated, cooperative, and willing to learn. Unfortunately, most people would rather live with a sexual dysfunction and a less than satisfying sexual life than seek help. The embarrassment they feel in discussing their sex life with a professional is too great. And there are others who have adjusted to their sex life and despite the fact that their spouse might be unhappy, they refuse to seek help. When these people hear that their spouse is unhappy about their sex life they experience it as a criticism, become defensive, and often become either hurt or angry, rather than open themselves up to exploration with a sex therapist.

Stress often produces temporary sexual dysfunction that

can become permanent. Unfortunately, people often consider sexuality such a private matter that they are reluctant to discuss it with others. Even those who have had sexual difficulties as a consequence of disease or surgery, have difficulty seeking sex therapy to facilitate adjustment to the dysfunction. Many men prefer to needlessly avoid sex altogether rather than seek professional help. Their pride gets in the way of sexual satisfaction.

One of the most significant contributing factors in sexual dysfunction is your attitude toward the dysfunction. If you view it as diminishing your self-worth and reflecting negatively on your overall value as a human being, sex therapy will take a little longer since we first have to overcome these initial feelings. Another contributing factor is your motivation and that of your spouse or partner. Your partner's cooperation, participation, and support can accelerate the process and in many cases is essential for effective treatment. Remember, when one member of the dance team is impaired, the team is impaired. Sex therapy, like sex itself, is a cooperative venture.

18

COPING WITH STRESS

Stress is an integral part of our urban lifestyle. It is the body's *adaptive response* to abnormal circumstances. In psychology, the term stress refers both to certain heightened mental and body states and to the causes of such states. A person in a physically or mentally demanding or dangerous situation is said to be under stress. Internal medical and mental disorders can also produce stress responses. Chronic repetition of certain emotions such as anger or despair, changes in work or home situations, or reactions to surgery, are just a few of the other ways in which stress can occur. And, more than one factor causing stress can be present at one time.

Stress is a normal part of life. Some producers of stress such as physical exercise, various emotional states, and creative activity are usually healthy. However, prolonged and unwanted stress can have undesirable effects on mental and physical health, although reactions to such pressure can vary greatly among individuals. We know a number of stress-related disorders, even though we do not fully understand the interactions of body and mind in the development of such disorders. Mental states, such as severe melancholic depression, are closely linked with stress-inducing anxiety; the complex syndrome known as post-traumatic stress disorder is produced by traumatic situations such as war and natural disaster. Physiological effects linked with stress include ulcers, high blood pressure, and heart disease. Stress can also adversely affect the immune system, causing the body to be less resistant to a wide range of other health problems.

The effects of stress can be complex, but they all involve a certain group of basic body responses. These responses arose in the course of evolution, as organisms met situations of physical danger. When the human body perceives danger (whether real or imaginary), the pituitary gland releases a hormone called adrenocorticotropic hormone. This in turn triggers the adrenal glands to release epinephrine and various other hormones that speed up the heart rate, raise blood pressure, and increase muscle tension. These effects are all part of the "fight or flight" response of the body to a threatening environment. We observe these same effects in certain social or occupational situations, or when under emotional stress, however inappropriate they may be in such circumstances. Usually such responses are of short duration. If their effects persist beyond a reasonable length of time they can also lead in complex ways to the above-mentioned mental and physical problems.

Recognizing Stress

Many people are not aware of when they are under stress. Some are under so much stress so often that they assume that the way they are feeling is normal. This is especially true for those individuals who are not very tuned in to their emotional responses. For these people it is often necessary to rely upon the physical manifestations of stress. Some of the signs (observable manifestations of a disease) and symptoms (experienced or subjective manifestations) of stress are insomnia, digestive problems, irritability, headache, upset stomach, and fatigue. Old habits, such as nail biting and hair twirling, may reappear or increase in intensity. You may feel more criticized by others, become more pessimistic, cynical, or resentful than usual. You may feel unappreciated, misunderstood, and feel like a victim. Things that you normally look forward to may seem like a burden. Sometimes the changes you experience may be so gradual that they go unnoticed until your health or relationships change.

Dealing with Stress

There are various stressors in our life that trigger an adaptive response. These stressors vary from person to person, though there are some that appear to be virtually universal: death, marriage, relocation, change in or loss of a job, and having children.

The first step in learning to manage stress is to recognize the triggers or stressors in your life, those things that are particularly stressful to us individually. Each individual may have different reactions to the same stressor depending on how one interprets the event. For some individuals relish change; others fear it. A great deal of stress has to do with the degree to which we need to be in control of events in our life. *Thus, people who have less of a need to be in control of their environment tend to experience less stress.*

One of the ways in which we adapt to change is to attempt to gain more control of the stressors. Thus, identifying the stressors would be an important first step. Another step is to be more accepting of our reactions to events. Many of us are critical of ourselves, expecting our reactions to events to fit some pre-conceived standard.

Interpersonal Stress

Interpersonal relationships are often stressful. Trying to have different personalities interact within the context of a system is very demanding. There are three systems that are the most complex and hence, are potentially a significant source of stress.

Family. Families are a complex network of interactions. Each family is a system and hence, each interaction and each personality affects the entire system. If one person is ill in your family it is clear how that illness disrupts the everyday flow of the system. Likewise, it affects the system when one member of the family is angry or depressed. An alcoholic in the family disrupts the system and often leads to the system trying to adapt to the family member. Sometimes that adaptation creates difficulties as well. The family, like the human body, tries to compensate for an organ that is not functioning up to par. Our entire body may be thrown out of alignment by an injury to an arm or a leg, for example. Similarly, the family, in an attempt to compensate for one of its members, may be thrown out of alignment and become dysfunctional. When this occurs it is time to seek professional help. Psychologists and family therapists can help the family focus on the communication styles that throw the family out of alignment.

Marital. The institution of marriage in itself is stressful. Two people, each with different histories, different personalities, different needs, and different ways of doing things are trying to live under the same roof and get along with each other on a daily basis. That's a pretty tall order even under the best of circumstances. One of the main difficulties that couples face revolves around expectations. Each person in the marriage brings a set of explicit expectations, a set of implicit expectations, and a set of unrealistic expectations. These expectations, when in conflict with the other person's expectations, can create a great deal of conflict; and this conflict is stressful. During the course of marriage each partner may go through a series of transitions, such as the death of a parent, the loss of a job, or physical illness. The couple may go through transitions, such as relocation, the birth of a child, or the change of a job. All of these changes have an impact on the marriage and produce stress on the relationship.

Occupational. Work is a significant source of stress for many people. Conflicts on the job, dissatisfaction with one's supervisor or with the job itself, insufficient financial compensation, fear of losing one's job, fear of changing a job for greater advancement, feeling stifled in a quest for power, or not feeling appreciated or acknowledged, all produce significant stress. Each of these can produce significant amounts of stress. The degree of stress will vary depending on the personality of the individual and the amount invested in each issue.

How we think. Stress increases as a function of how we think about events. Some folks tend to catastrophize events, making mountains out of molehills, or exaggerating the consequences. They tend to react to small things that happen with larger than warranted feelings, exaggerating the event to match their feelings, rather than adjusting their feelings to the event. *People with low stress reactions tend to make molehills out of mountains.*

The following questions can help gain a perspective on situations to reduce the impact and hence, the stress.

What is the worst that can happen?

What is the likelihood of the worst happening?

Have I done everything that I reasonably can do to alter the outcome?

Will my life change substantially and will I even remember it years from now?

How would I counsel a friend in a similar situation?

Methods for Dealing with Stress

There are several common activities that are useful in reducing or coping with transitory, situational stress. These techniques, when applied regularly, can significantly reduce or soften the brunt of the stress reaction to temporary events.

Relaxation Techniques

There are many different forms of relaxation techniques including autohypnosis, progressive muscle relaxation, and some forms of yoga, to mention a few. One that I have found helpful combines several aspects of these approaches.

- Start by seating yourself in a comfortable position in a quiet area. Loosen your clothing so that you do not feel constricted in any way.
- Close your eyes and squeeze them shut as tight as you can. Progressively move from one muscle group to another, teeth and jaw, neck, shoulders, arms, fists, chest, back, thighs, buttocks, calves, and feet.
- Tighten each in turn until your entire body is tight.
- Then relax one group at time, feeling the contrast between the tight experience and the relaxed experience. Notice the tingling or whatever sensation you have. Just notice it, don't do anything about it.
- And as you relax each area, focus on your breathing. Breathe slowly and rhythmically until your entire body relaxes.
- Finally, imagine yourself in a location that you find especially relaxing, safe, and comfortable. For some people, it might be a secluded beach, for others a mountain lake. Each of us has our own place.
- Once you have the image in mind, make it as clear as you can, almost as though you are there. Let your thoughts

go, don't try to capture them or block them; just let them go by like so many butterflies fluttering.

- Stay in your "place" for five or ten minutes and then slowly remind yourself to come back to present time or home.
- Gently open your eyes and gradually reorient yourself. This approach takes about 15 to 20 minutes. You should feel refreshed when you are through.

Breathing

Deep breathing has long been known to have relaxing properties. All forms of yoga, athletic exercises, and meditation have a breathing component. Oxygen itself tends to revitalize; it both energizes and relaxes as we cleanse our system. Breathing exercises are simple. Sitting quietly, breathe in as deeply as you can through your nose and exhale through your mouth expelling all of the air. Repeat this three times. Then, focusing your attention on your breathing, breathe in slowly through your nose and exhale through your mouth. Breathe rhythmically. Repeat this ten times. You will notice the difference.

Physical exercise

All form of exercise, aerobic exercise in particular, has relaxation qualities. Getting oxygen into your bloodstream, releasing stored toxins in your body through sweat, and increasing the production of endorphins into your bloodstream will have a calming effect on your entire system. That is one of the reasons so many people are participating in these forms of exercise across the nation.

Conclusion

Stress is the body's adaptive response to unusual circumstances and can come from internal and external sources. Prolonged, intense stress can and often does have deleterious effects on mind and body. It can affect the immune system, making us vulnerable to disease. It has been linked to high blood pressure, ulcers, and heart disease. It can affect our judgment, our perceptions, our interpersonal relationships, and our job performance. Different personality types will have different reactions to situations and thus, have different levels of stress. Some people tend to exaggerate events thus, heightening their stress response, while others tend to minimize events and have an attenuated stress response. Some people are more prone to experience stress than others. For example, people who have difficulty accepting change or being out of control have higher levels of stress than those who are adaptive and accepting of the contingencies of life. Psychotherapy is often helpful in dealing with chronic stress reactions and post-traumatic stress disorders. Meditation, yoga, relaxation techniques, exercise, and hobbies can ameliorate temporary stress reactions and can even be helpful in preventing stress reactions if practiced regularly.

19

SHYNESS AND SOCIAL PHOBIA

Many people have had the experience of feeling awkward in social situations, nervous about giving a speech, and finding it difficult to call someone up on the telephone to ask out on a date. Many folks have dreaded being called upon in a class situation, sat in the back of the auditorium during a lecture, and hugged the wall at a dance or party. They may have had the experience that their mouths were filled with cotton and their armpits and hands were drenched with sweat. In new situations they may feel a bit awkward and self-conscious. They have even hoped that an event such as a company picnic would be canceled so that they would be off the hook and not have to attend. They tend to be quiet when in unfamiliar surroundings and prefer to stay with people that they know. Tending to be somewhat self-conscious and uncomfortable with strangers, they feel more comfortable one-on-one or in small familiar groups than they do in large gatherings, and they prefer to entertain in their own home rather than in someone else's.

These people describe themselves as being shy. Such shyness may have been a characteristic of personality since childhood or it may have developed later in life. Typical social shyness, which affects almost everyone at least occasionally, can cause trepidation and uncertainty, particularly in new situations. Even people who are normally very aggressive tend to become meek and timid under special circumstances, such as when meeting others held in high esteem or when having to "perform" under pressure. While most shy folks are able to function fairly well in daily life, there are others for whom shyness is quite extreme.

Social phobias. Their shyness is debilitating and interferes with daily functioning. These individuals are forced to shrink their world so as to avoid many situations that they experience as overwhelming. For them even the thought of the event is enough to send them into panic. For some of these folks it may be very specific such as the fear of speaking in front of a group, while for others it may be more pervasive such as the fear of meeting new people, going to a party, or having a conversation. Extreme timidity, social inhibition, and intense fear of social situations characterize social phobias. We often characterize these individuals as "painfully shy." When shyness becomes so extreme as to affect the quality of one's life, we speak of it as *social phobia.*

Social phobia revolves around the fear of being judged; the opinion of others becomes so all-important, so consuming, that the social phobic feels he or she is being constantly judged, especially when in the presence of strangers or those not well known. Consequently, if he or she is alone or in familiar situations, everything is generally fine. Social phobics feel scrutinized and judged by others— and the judgment projected is negative, a reflection of their own low self-esteem.

This may involve specific performance situations (e.g.,

having to give a speech), general social contact, or both. These folks are overwhelmingly concerned with how others perceive them, how they are going to be judged, and whether they will do or say something that will embarrass themselves. They fear doing something foolish, or appearing less intelligent than others. The most common social fears include (in descending order of prevalence):

1. Formal and informal speaking
2. Eating and drinking in public
3. Writing in public
4. Taking tests
5. Other observational situations (e.g., golf, bowling, tennis)

In addition to pervasive negative self-perceptions and of their abilities, social phobics experience somatic arousal, particularly heart palpitations, trembling, sweating, and blushing. These latter symptoms frequently acquire secondary fear-producing qualities so their possible appearance becomes a source of apprehension and when they do occur they exacerbate the emotional response.

There is substantial use of alcohol among social phobics, as well as the use of other anxiety reducing drugs, to control the anxiety. Additionally, there are increased suicidal thoughts. Most social phobics cannot form and maintain satisfying interpersonal relationships and have a chronic restricted range of social activities. They have increased difficulties with work, incomplete educational attainment, and lack of career advancement. There is a tendency toward avoidance and the presence of rigid and perfectionist tendencies often combine with high general anxiety and fear.

Specific and Generalized Social Phobics. Psychologists have divided social phobics into two types: the *specific* type and the *generalized* type. The *specific* type is characterized by anxiety and fear associated with a very limited range of social activities. An example is a speech phobia or a very specific performance situation such as an athletic competition. The *specific* type constitutes about 30 percent of all social phobias with about 70 percent being of the *generalized* type. This type has a more pervasive pattern of social fear, more severe anxiety, depression, avoidance and fearfulness, and greater self-consciousness. The *generalized* type seems to have an earlier onset, more neurotic and introverted features, and a stronger family history of anxiety than the specific subtype.

Demographics. Recent studies indicate that about 13 percent of the population in the United States is affected by social phobia. Surveys in other countries indicate similar results. Social phobia occurs equally in men and women, Caucasian and African-American. This makes social phobia the most common form of anxiety disorder in the general population. In addition to social phobias, there are untold numbers of individuals who experience varying degrees of shyness. While shyness is not defined as a psychiatric disorder as is social phobia, it is nonetheless uncomfortable and even painful to those who experience it. Social phobias and shyness are very common and yet they often go unrecognized and untreated. This group of individuals has been described as the "silent sufferers."

Developmental Considerations. Research suggests that developmental factors may play a role in the development of social phobias. Some infants and children demonstrate early social inhibition and fear of novelty that may predispose them to social phobia. However, there is strong evidence to suggest that familial factors, parenting styles, and early traumatic conditioning experiences—especially in the specific type of social phobia—influence later development. The *generalized* social phobia appears to have a more insidious onset process, according to researchers.

Shyness begins, naturally enough, in childhood. All children tend to be shy for the first two or three years of their lives. You can see them clutching at the legs of their mothers and fathers, peeking out carefully to see if the stranger giving them attention is safe. How the parent responds to the child's social fear will, in large part, determine how the grown child responds to social situations. If a parent, fearful for his or her child (especially when newspapers are full of stories about child molestation and kidnapping), unintentionally passes along that fear, the child may learn to be afraid; the reinforced shyness then develops into an abnormal fear of unfamiliar people, places, and situations, and eventually, it generalizes into a constant, gnawing anxiety which makes it impossible for the sufferer to function properly in the world.

Shyness may also result in children who suffer an early loss of one or both parents. As a method of avoiding too much closeness or intimacy for fear of losing another loved one, they withdraw into themselves, hoping to erect an impenetrable shield as insulation from hurt. At the same time, the child with one remaining parent may cling pathetically to that parent, terrified of some unknown catastrophe occurring and making him or her an "orphan"; likewise, the remaining parent may tend to overprotect the child, feeling that the emotional attachment is necessary support. Both situations tend to encourage and exacerbate shyness.

Children with physical disabilities or severe childhood illnesses often develop into shy or fearful adults because they have been taught to be hyper-afraid of hurting themselves or catching additional diseases. To these children, all strangers are viewed as threatening.

Chronic shyness in adults may also stem from two other causes: frequent relocation of the family, which continually thrusts the child into unfamiliar situations and doesn't allow time for the child to establish close relationships with others of the same age; and very critical, demanding and perfectionist parents, whose children feel that they can never live up to the parents' expectations of them.

As children grow into adults, the manifestations of shyness evolve into more complex and subtle expressions. From clinging onto a parent's leg and begging not to be left alone at a school party, the older child may concoct an imaginary playmate with whom "safety" can be easily found. A few years later, the adolescent's imagination may construct elaborate fantasies as a method by which he or she regains some control over the world. And finally, adults who may develop grandiose styles in order to compensate for their underlying shyness and social inhibition complete the evolution.

In order to function as normally as possible, these people tend to confine their experiences so as not to have to deal with the full extent of their inhibitions. They may withdraw into their specific area of expertise, whether it is academia, auto mechanics, art, etc. In their own little universes, they are able to function entirely without anxiety, or minimal anxiety. It is only when forced to make contact outside of these spheres that their symptoms arise.

Almost all adolescents feel awkward; it comes with the territory. So many changes are occurring—physically, psychologically, socially—that the adolescent must constantly work to integrate them all. As a teenager, he or she is exceedingly aware of and sensitive to criticism, peer pressure, and performance. Everything is experienced in a BIG WAY; everything that goes wrong is a catastrophe, while everything that goes right is "the best ever." Middle ground does not exist and neither does perspective. Look at the words teenagers use to describe impressions: devastated, crushed, blasted, blown away, annihilated, etc. Even mildly disappointing events are blown up bigger than life.

Adolescent experiences can leave scars that last for years, or a lifetime. So in later years, the young adult unwilling to admit immaturity must remember the event with equally overwhelming emotions in order to justify the experience of those feelings. Often then, what remains in adulthood as the basis for a rationale which says that he or she need not respond maturely, is a larger-than-life reality—one that doesn't respond to reason or facts—one that "comforts" the sufferer with a belief system intended to validate the sufferer's lack of self-esteem.

Psychological aspects of shyness. At their core, shy people dread being evaluated; they anticipate that their performance will not be adequate. Among children, test taking is one common form of anxiety associated with shyness. Adults fear that no one will like them, that they are not worthy of attention and affection, that they have nothing to offer. And if, by chance, they are given an opportunity to express themselves, they fear that they will be "found out," exposed as shams.

Of course, such anxieties, whether they're as simple as test taking or as insidious as self-deprecation, become self-fulfilling. The anticipatory anxiety interferes with normal functioning, obscuring all abilities and positive traits. What remains after the fear of failure is only the failure itself—a failed grade or a failed attempt at relationship. "I can't succeed" becomes "I didn't succeed" begets "I can't succeed"; while "You couldn't like me, could you?" becomes "I knew it—she/he didn't like me" begets "I know you won' like me, but . . ." The worst-case scenario raises the shy person's fears and inhibitions, increasing the likelihood of that exact scenario occurring.

In like fashion, some shy people seek to prevent further psychic damage by refusing to try for the fear of failure— the fear of fear. They call upon a core of memories in which their efforts weren't rewarded or appreciated, and they remember the laughter, real or not, of their detractors. Of course, they never intended to succeed, sabotaging their conscious intentions with the subconscious fear of humiliation, embarrassment, or rejection. "I'd rather not try," they reason, "than get hurt." Again, the fear of fear.

The shy person's grossly exaggerated fears include the belief that an inept performance in a social situation will strike a fatal blow to his or her aspirations. "I will be absolutely ruined if I'm rejected," is the thought, but placing that expectation on the situation—making it life or death—creates a burden that is impossible to carry. Any attempt to shoulder that burden ensures certain failure.

The fundamental difference between shy people and more outgoing people seems to be encapsulated in their definitions of rejection. Outgoing people, comfortable in most social situations and unafraid to try to meet new people, define rejection much more narrowly than do shy people, who apply the term anytime someone doesn't jump into bed with them after saying "hello."

Treatment. Generally speaking, social phobias are highly responsive to psychotherapeutic intervention. Specific social phobias, however, are more easily treated than the generalized social phobias. In the case of the specific type, there is a specific activity, situation, or event that can be the focus of treatment, whereas in generalized type the individual's anxiety level affects a wider array of situations. As mentioned earlier, the generalized subtype has an earlier onset and is characterized by additional personality factors affecting functioning. Because of its more insidious course of development, it is often more severe on all areas of functioning.

Behavioral treatment. Most behavior strategies include some form of exposure-based treatment combined with relaxation techniques. Exposure-based treatment involves controlled exposing of the individual to the circumstances, usually through imagery, that generates the anxiety. The images are then paired with the relaxation. Once the person can conjure an image associated with high anxiety and effectively utilize the relaxation technique to reduce or remove the anxiety, she/he is then exposed to real-life situations in the same fashion.

So, for example, when dealing with the fear of public speaking, we may first start with images of beginning with preparation for the speech, going to the venue, standing in front of the audience, and finally delivering the speech. Once this can be accomplished in images, we may follow it up with the real thing.

Often these behavioral approaches utilize both individual and group sessions as part of the treatment program. The addition of the group component reinforces a bond with others who experience similar feelings to oneself.

Cognitive treatment. Cognitive approaches to social phobias involve examination of the belief system that underlies the phobia. Irrational beliefs and unrealistic assumptions account for much of the anxiety experienced by social phobics. Social phobics tend to catastrophize the outcome of situations based on their fantasies or upon limited experience. Often the irrational beliefs developed in childhood or adolescence have never been challenged. Because these beliefs are difficult to relinquish, cognitive treatment is most effective when combined with the behavioral approaches described above. Thus, we can address both the underlying belief system and the behaviors.

Social skills training. This treatment modality has been devised specifically for treating the generalized social phobias. It combines exposure with an explicitly developed social skills training program that is administered over about a 4-month period. It also combines individual exposure sessions with group social skills training sessions.

Most people who suffer from social phobias also

experience other concomitant psychological difficulties such as depression, substance abuse (food, alcohol, or drugs), perfectionism, and compulsive behaviors. Therefore, when they come into treatment the practitioner not only has to focus on the social phobia, but also on treating these other conditions. Similar to physical disorders, the individual has learned compensatory measures for coping with their phobia. These compensatory measures often become difficulties in themselves.

20

FORGIVENESS IS A CHOICE

We most often associate the topic of forgiveness with religion. It is a concept that clergy talk about, not psychologists. Our religious training tells us that we should forgive; after all, "to err is human, to forgive divine." Forgiveness has profound implications for mental health. We confront the issue when we have been betrayed, either by a friend, a business associate or, most profoundly, by a spouse who has cheated on us. We also have to deal with issues of forgiveness when we have experienced emotional or physical abuse, current or past traumatic events, and humiliation. Intuitively we know that if we could forgive we would feel less bitter, less resentful, and less burdened; we know that it would be good for us to forgive. It is easier said than done.

In this article I will discuss the meaning of the term forgiveness, its psychological implications in terms of personal growth, and an approach toward learning to forgive. Perhaps through a deeper understanding of what it means to forgive, why it is important for human development, and how we can learn to forgive, it will become easier for us to do so.

What is forgiveness?

When most of us think of forgiveness, we think in terms of making amends with someone who has offended us or whom we have offended. One party or the other holds the power to release the other from the guilt associated with the occurrence. We also think of apology. We ask to be forgiven for some transgression and seek to be absolved. We want to feel reconnected. Being asked for forgiveness puts us in the position of strength; seeking forgiveness leaves us feeling weak or humble.

When we forgive, we are saying to the person who has offended us that we will hold no grudge and, that while we do not condone the behavior of the offender, we will not hold it against him or her and may be willing to move on with the relationship. When we receive forgiveness, we feel uplifted and sometimes even grateful toward the one who grants us forgiveness. Forgiveness renews our spirit and helps us move forward.

By contrast, when we do not forgive, we feel resentful, angry, and even bitter. We are hurt and seek revenge or retribution. We want the person who has offended us to suffer as we are suffering; we want them to feel pain for their transgression. We may feel a sense of righteousness; after all, we were wronged. This righteousness, however, may be short-lived. The resentment we feel may build, leaving us feeling emotionally constricted and even debilitated. The thought that the offending party may not be experiencing guilt is even more offensive to us and causes us even greater resentment.

For the most part, we have associated forgiveness with receiving an apology from another person. We believe that without contrition on the part of the offender, there can be no forgiveness. Take a look at the reactions of the survivors of the Oklahoma bombing. Timothy McVeigh showed no remorse for his action. Without such remorse the survivors find it difficult to forgive. McVeigh holds the power to keep these people suffering as they harbor their resentment, anger, and bitterness. They want retribution; they want him dead. Only then will they feel a sense of relief and closure.

What if we could make forgiveness a one-way street? What if we could forgive without depending upon the offender to express guilt? What if we did not need to be asked for forgiveness, but could grant it nonetheless? What if we could say to an offender, "whether you wish it or not, I forgive you." What would such unilateral forgiveness do for us?

Let's examine the case of a spouse who has betrayed his wife by having an affair with another woman. When this happens, the aggrieved party experiences a myriad of emotions. She feels deeply wounded by her husband's actions. He violated a basic trust. Their marriage contract stated that he would forsake all others. He violated the contract as well as the trust. She feels diminished. Her husband chose to be intimate with another woman; he preferred to be with her rather than with his wife. The wife feels less than the chosen woman. Her pride is wounded and her self-esteem is damaged. His actions reflect poorly on her as a woman. She was not able to keep him from seeking the attention of someone else. She experiences herself as the victim of a heinous act perpetrated against her. She wants to hurt him as he hurt her. She wants revenge. She wants him to suffer as she has suffered. How can she ever forgive him?

Yet, we see that some spouses are able to do just that. They are able to get beyond their personal hurt and see the larger issues that may underlie the transgression of their spouse. Some are able to go so far as to continue the relationship and use the experience to rebuild the relationship. In some instances the marriage becomes stronger as the couple faces the various factors that led to the affair.

On the other hand, some spouses can forgive the transgression but are not willing to maintain the relationship. In effect they say, "I can forgive you but I am not willing to stay with you. The risk of your doing it again is too great and I am not willing to chance it." Or they say that, "that while I can forgive you, our relationship will never be the same, so I choose to continue without you."

Forgiveness does not mean that we condone the behavior of the transgressor. It does not mean that what you did to me is all right. Nor does it mean that we will forget what happened.

Forgiveness requires that we let go the anger and hurt that we are carrying. If we want to move forward with our life after being betrayed or hurt by someone else, we have to be willing to let go of the resentment, bitterness, hurt, and anger. Forgiveness becomes a choice.

Forgiveness is a choice

Most of us do not think of forgiveness as a choice. When we feel harmed, wounded, betrayed, or damaged we want relief and often we want revenge. Just as revenge is a choice, so is forgiveness. Our initial emotional response does not have to determine our behavior. We have a choice in how we will respond to any circumstance or situation. We can choose to act angrily, we can choose to act sullen; we can choose to withdraw or we can choose to move forward. We can choose to experience ourselves as a victim of an act of betrayal. Or we can choose to see ourselves as a survivor of a betrayal. We can choose to act with vengeance or to act with forgiveness. The call is ours and ours alone.

The problem arises, however, that in our culture, to forgive without having received an apology leaves us feeling foolish; we end up thinking that the perpetrator is getting away with something. This thought is intolerable. For many people, forgiveness is related to weakness rather than to strength. Hence, we excuse ourselves for not being more forgiving rather than aspiring to a higher standard. We accept holding the grudge, holding the anger, holding the resentment, as if it were more noble than forgiving.

What does holding on to resentment, hurt, and anger toward someone who has transgressed against us do to us? Where does it leave us? What happens over time? Harboring anger, resentment and hurt often leads to depression, insomnia, emotional constriction, distrust, physical complaints (e.g., ulcers, insomnia, headaches, muscle pain, lethargy, etc.), brooding, dysphoria, to mention a few of the consequences. Holding on to resentments and anger takes psychological energy away from more creative pursuits. Over time, it can emotionally deplete us. Yet we often continue to suffer because we believe that if we forgive the offender, he or she is getting away with something and is not being punished. We believe that every crime deserves a punishment. More often, however, we pay a greater price for holding on to the resentment than to the person who committed the offense will ever pay. We continue to suffer while the other person goes on with his or her life. We lock ourselves in the time period that the betrayal occurred, e.g., the spouse who continues to relive the day he learned that his wife has had an affair.

When someone harms us, we feel vulnerable. We recognize that we are exposed to the vagaries of life and the whims of circumstances. We are confronted with our mortality. Thus, feeling so vulnerable, we seek to re-establish a sense of power and control. With retribution, vengeance, or some form of reprisal, we can establish ourselves as powerful, if only for a moment. We can temporarily suspend the truth of our own vulnerability. In order to truly forgive we must come to terms with our own vulnerability and our mortality. We must come to terms with the existential truth that we live in a contingent world, where things happen, often for no apparent reason. And we often are hurt by these events. Nothing we can do can change the events; nothing we can do can leave us less vulnerable. When we sentence to death the Timothy McVeighs of the world, we have the illusion that somehow we have made ourselves less vulnerable, at least to him. However, our vulnerability continues to exist. Another bomber, another sniper, another terrorist, and another betrayer lurks just around the corner. When we kill McVeigh we believe that we have increased our safety. Such an experience of safety, however, is both temporary and illusionary.

By letting go of the anger, hurt, and resentment, we free ourselves to move beyond our pain. We learn that we can survive a betrayal; we learn that we can heal. However, there can be no healing if we do not forgive. We only make the wounds deeper and create emotional scarring. In short, there is no payoff for not forgiving.

Some people hold on to their anger and resentment lest they forget the event, especially if it were perpetrated against a loved one. Let's take the example of someone whose spouse was murdered. The surviving spouse may be loath to forgive the killer for fear that they would forget the deceased spouse or even be disloyal to the memory of the deceased. They hold on to the hatred as a self-inflicted punishment for surviving.

Forgiving does not mean one forgets. It does not mean condoning an action. It only means letting go of the past and deciding that one wants to transcend the tragedy and celebrate living by moving ahead rather than remaining in the past. If I forgive someone who has betrayed me, murdered my spouse, or raped my daughter, it is because I have made the decision to honor a higher sense of self that refuses to remain stuck in a circumstance over which I have no control. The event happened. I cannot change that. I cannot undo it. I can only decide how I choose to behave and whether to move forward with my life. My future actions will determine how I honor the memory of those harmed, not how long I can hold to the anger, resentment, and bitterness of the past.

How do we forgive?

Forgiveness is both a value and a process. We aspire to be a forgiving person. To honor this value we must learn to forgive. Is it something we can train ourselves to do? It is easy to forgive someone if they step on our toe or even dent our car. It is relatively easy to forgive an accident. How does one forgive an act of malfeasance? A violation of a contract? A betrayal in a relationship? How does one forgive an act of intentional harm? How does one forgive a rapist, a murderer, a serial killer, an Oklahoma bomber, an Adolph Hitler?

If we find a method for learning how to forgive, it must be applicable for a variety of circumstances along the dimension of inflicted harm, whether by accident or by design. I do not purport to have discovered an absolute, ironclad system for learning how to forgive. I do believe, however, that we can train ourselves to forgive and to become a forgiving person. I believe that forgiveness can be taught and practiced. I further believe that forgiveness ought to be a central value in our lives, along with such values as honesty, integrity, loyalty, kindness, generosity, civility, to mention but a few. And just as we must practice these other values and honor them in our daily lives, we should practice forgiveness.

We would begin by practicing forgiving folks who may have transgressed against us in minor ways and work up to forgiving more difficult acts of hurt and betrayal. Forgiveness is a process of letting go of resentments and emotional hurts inflicted by others. It is about making a decision not to dwell on the past, incorporating forgiveness as a part of our value system, and honoring that value by acting in ways that moves us toward that higher self to which we aspire. The following are some steps that may assist in this process:

- Make a conscious decision that harboring resentment over past hurt only does you harm. You must be able to understand that there is no value to maintaining a resentful, angry position. In other words, it does not serve you.

- Frame forgiveness as strength, rather than a weakness. Once you understand that forgiveness facilitates growth and represents a commitment to embrace life, it will be easier for you to let go of resentment and anger.

- Develop a vision or image of yourself as a forgiving person rather than an angry, resentful person. You cannot be both forgiving and resentful at the same time. These two attributes are mutually exclusive. To the extent that you hold on to resentment, you become less forgiving, and vice versa. Commit to the ideal of forgiveness. Imagine yourself being the person you want to be. Picture various scenarios and imagine how this forgiving person would deal with them.

For dealing with a specific hurt inflicted by someone, Dr. Everett Worthington, Jr. suggests, *"recall the hurt as objectively as possible. Don't rail against the person who hurt you, waste time wishing for an apology that will never be offered, or dwell on your victimization. Instead, admit that a wrong was done to you and set your sights on its repair."*

Dr. Worthington suggests that you *"commit to forgive. When you forgive, you can eventually doubt that you have forgiven. When people remember a previous injury or offense, they often interpret it as evidence that they must not have forgiven. If you make your forgiveness tangible, you are less likely to doubt it later. Tell a friend, partner, or counselor that you have forgiven the person who hurt you. Write a 'certificate of forgiveness,' stating that you have, as of today, forgiven."*

Remember, forgiveness does not mean forgetting. It means letting go of the pain, anger, and resentment associated with the event or memory.

21

ANXIETY AND PANIC DISORDERS[10]

Your heart starts to pound, your palms sweat, your breathing is erratic, you feel dizzy or light headed, and you think you're having a heart attack. The chances are it is not a heart attack, but a panic attack. Everyday tens of thousands of people experience panic attacks. For some, the fear of having an attack is so great that they curtail their daily activity, sometimes refusing to drive or even leave their home for fear of having an attack.

Anxiety is a normal part of life. We anticipate an event with trepidation; we worry about the outcome. Most of the time we forge through our anxiety and feel relieved when the event is over or when the outcome turns out better than we had expected. These anxious moments are short-lived and we learn to accept them knowing that we will get through it. However, when anxiety becomes frequent and excessive it may indicate the presence of a clinically diagnosable anxiety disorder.

There are several types of anxiety disorders covering a

wide range of symptoms. Those experiencing any of the following symptoms may have an anxiety disorder:

• Panic or anxiety attacks
• Persistent senseless disturbing thoughts, excessive worrying
• Phobias or fears of common objects or situations
• Restlessness, feeling tense, keyed-up
• Sleep problems
• Unexplained heart palpitations, stomach problems
• Feelings of unreality
• Concentration difficulties

TYPES OF ANXIETY DISORDERS

Panic Disorder: characterized by panic attacks, sudden feelings of terror that strike repeatedly and without warning. Physical symptoms include chest pain, heart palpitations, shortness of breath, dizziness, or abdominal stress.

Obsessive-Compulsive Disorder (OCD): Repeated, intrusive, and unwanted thoughts that cause anxiety, often accompanied by ritualized behavior to relieve this anxiety. These thoughts and behaviors can be so severe as to prohibit normal, daily functioning. They come on suddenly, often in response to a triggering event, sometimes for no apparent reason. The person feels compelled to carry out the ritualized behavior, often in automatic fashion. Interruption leads to further anxiety necessitating starting all over again. Treatment for this disorder usually requires a combination of medication and behavior modification.

Phobias: Extreme and disabling fear of something that poses little or no danger and leads to avoidance of objects or situations.

Specific Phobia: fear of specific objects or situations such as flying, heights, and animals.

Social Phobia: fear of being the focus of attention or scrutiny or of doing something that will be intensely humiliating.

Post-Traumatic Stress Disorder: Persistent, frightening thoughts that occur after undergoing a frightening and traumatic event.

Generalized Anxiety Disorder: Chronic or exaggerated worry and tension; almost always anticipating disaster even though nothing seems to provoke it. Worrying is often accompanied by physical symptoms like trembling, muscle tension, headache, and nausea.

Since we focused on shyness and social phobia in the last *Psychotherapy Update*, in this issue we will examine panic attacks and generalized anxiety disorders.

PANIC DISORDER

"It started ten years ago. I was sitting in a seminar in a hotel and this thing came out of the clear blue. I felt like I was dying."

"For me, a panic attack is almost a violent experience. I feel like I'm going insane. It makes me feel like I'm losing control in a very extreme way. My heart pounds really hard, things seem unreal, and there's this very strong feeling of impending doom."

"In between attacks there is this dread and anxiety that it's going to happen again. It can be very debilitating, trying to escape those feelings of panic."

People with panic disorder have feelings of terror that strike suddenly and repeatedly with no warning. They can't predict when an attack will occur, and many develop intense anxiety between episodes, worrying when and where the next one will strike. In between times there is a persistent, lingering worry that another attack could come any minute. You may genuinely believe you're having a heart attack or stroke, losing your mind, or on the verge of death. Attacks can occur any time, even during non-dream sleep. While most attacks average a couple of minutes, occasionally they can go on for up to 10 minutes. In rare cases, they may last an hour or more.

Panic Attack Symptoms

* Pounding heart
* Chest pains
* Lightheadedness or dizziness
* Nausea or stomach problems
* Flushes or chills
* Shortness of breath or a feeling of smothering or choking
* Tingling or numbness
* Shaking or trembling
* Feelings of unreality
* Terror
* A feeling of being out of control or going crazy
* Fear of dying
* Sweating

Panic disorder strikes at least 1.6 percent of the population and is twice as common in women as in men. It can appear at any age—in children or in the elderly—but most often it begins in young adults. Not everyone who experiences panic attacks will develop panic disorder; many people have one attack but never have another.

For those who do have panic disorder, though, it's important to seek treatment. Untreated, the disorder can become very disabling. Panic disorder is often accompanied by other conditions such as depression or alcoholism, and may spawn phobias, which can develop in places or situations where panic attacks have occurred. For example, if a panic attack strikes while you're riding an elevator, you may develop a fear of elevators and perhaps start avoiding them.

Some people's lives become greatly restricted—they

avoid normal, everyday activities such as grocery shopping, driving, or in some cases even leaving the house. Or, they may be able to confront a feared situation only if accompanied by a spouse or other trusted person. Basically, they avoid any situation they fear would make them feel helpless if a panic attack occurs. When people's lives become so restricted by the disorder, as happens in about one-third of all people with panic disorder, the condition is called *agoraphobia*. A tendency toward panic disorder and agoraphobia runs in families. Nevertheless, early treatment of panic disorder can often stop the progression to agoraphobia.

GENERALIZED ANXIETY DISORDER

"I always thought I was just a worrier. I'd feel keyed up and unable to relax. At times it would come and go, and at times it would be constant. It could go on for days. I'd worry about what I was going to fix for a dinner party, or what would be a great present for somebody. I just couldn't let something go."

"I'd have terrible sleeping problems. There were times I'd wake up wired in the morning or in the middle of the night. I had trouble concentrating, even reading the newspaper or a novel. Sometimes I'd feel a little lightheaded. My heart would race or pound. And that would make me worry more."

Generalized anxiety disorder (GAD) is much more than the normal anxiety people experience day to day. It's chronic and exaggerated worry and tension, even though nothing seems to provoke it. Having this disorder means always anticipating disaster, often worrying excessively about health, money, family, or work. Sometimes, though, the source of the worry is hard to pinpoint. Simply the thought of getting through the day provokes anxiety. People with GAD can't seem to shake their concerns, even though they usually realize that their anxiety is more intense than the situation warrants. People with GAD also seem unable to relax. They often have trouble falling or staying asleep. Their worries are accompanied by physical symptoms, especially trembling, twitching, muscle tension, headaches, irritability, sweating, or hot flashes. They may feel lightheaded or out of breath. They may feel nauseated or have to go to the bathroom frequently. Or they might feel as though they have a lump in the throat. Many individuals with GAD startle more easily than other people. They tend to feel tired, have trouble concentrating, and sometimes suffer depression, too.

Depression often accompanies anxiety disorders and, when it does, it needs to be treated as well. The feelings of sadness, apathy, or hopelessness, changes in appetite or sleep, and difficulty concentrating, that often characterize depression, can be effectively treated with anti-depressant medications, or, depending on their severity, by psychotherapy. Some people respond best to a combination of medication and psychotherapy. Treatment can help the majority of people with depression. Usually the impairment associated with GAD is mild and people with the disorder don't feel too restricted in social settings or on the job. Unlike many other anxiety disorders, people with GAD don't characteristically avoid certain situations as a result of their disorder. However, if severe, GAD can be very debilitating, making it difficult to carry out even the most ordinary daily activities. GAD comes on gradually and most often hits people in childhood or adolescence, but can begin in adulthood, too. It's more common in women than in men and often occurs in relatives of affected persons.

It's diagnosed when someone spends at least 6 months worrying excessively about a number of everyday problems. Generally, the symptoms of GAD seem to diminish with age.

TREATMENT

Studies have shown that proper treatment—a type of psychotherapy called cognitive-behavioral therapy, medications, or possibly a combination of the two—helps 70 to 90 percent of people with panic disorder. Significant improvement is usually seen within 6 to 8 weeks.

Cognitive-behavioral approaches teach patients how to view the panic situations differently and demonstrate ways to reduce anxiety, using breathing exercises or techniques to refocus attention, for example. Diaphragmatic breathing, which involves slow, deep breaths, is one such exercise. This is necessary because people who are anxious often hyperventilate—taking rapid, shallow breaths—that can trigger rapid heartbeat, lightheadedness, and other symptoms.

A form of cognitive-behavioral therapy called exposure therapy, can often help alleviate the phobias that may result from panic disorder. In exposure therapy, people are very slowly exposed to the fearful situation until they become desensitized to it. Such psychological forms of treatment, like cognitive-behavioral therapy, can help to prevent panic attacks or reduce their frequency and severity.

Cognitive-behavioral therapy teaches patients to react differently to the situations and bodily sensations that trigger panic attacks and other anxiety symptoms. However, patients also learn to understand how their thinking patterns contribute to their symptoms and how to change their thoughts so that symptoms are less likely to occur. This awareness of thinking patterns is combined with exposure and other behavioral techniques to help people confront their feared situations.

For example, someone who becomes lightheaded during a panic attack and fears he is going to die can be helped with the following approach used in cognitive-behavioral therapy. The therapist asks him to spin in a circle until he becomes dizzy. When he becomes alarmed and starts thinking, "I'm going to die," he learns to replace that thought with a more appropriate one, such as, "It's just a little dizziness—I can handle it."

Some people find the greatest relief from panic disorder symptoms when they take certain prescription medications. Two types of medications that have been shown to be safe and effective in the treatment of panic disorder are anti-depressants (e.g., Zoloft, Prozac) and benzodiazepines (e.g., Xanax, Klonopin).

A relative recent medication found useful in treating GAD is buspirone (BuSpar), especially when taken in conjunction with psychotherapy.

Taking Charge

22

PSYCHOLOGY AND YOUR HEALTH:

THE MIND-BODY CONNECTION

Scientists are becoming increasingly aware that mind and body are inseparable. The earlier belief that mind and body are two separate systems has not stood up to the test of scientific scrutiny. The mind influences the physical body and the physical body influences the mind. How we think and feel influences our bodily functions. When we are depressed or anxious, measurable physiological changes take place. When we are physically ill, it affects how we think about ourselves. The mind can affect our wellness and the course of an illness. Our emotions, our attitudes, and our beliefs can influence the healing process as well as our immune system, both positively and negatively. Bill Moyers' book[11] and PBS television series, based on studies from a variety of sources around the world, demonstrated the intimate connection between mind and body. Likewise, Norman Cousins' book, *Anatomy of an Illness*[12], points out how we can influence the course of an illness through our attitude and through laughter. Hypnotherapists have demonstrated the power of the mind to increase or speed up heart rate, to anesthetize parts of our body sufficiently to have surgery performed, to reduce bleeding, and decrease the experience of pain.

Health psychology concerns itself with understanding the interaction between mind and body. It focuses on the various ways in which psychological processes can influence illness, healing, and the prevention of disease and illness. Many scientists are stating that every physical illness has a psychological component; the mind can influence the course of the illness. We are all aware that some people have intense reactions to minor illnesses while others can have minimal reactions to even a major illness. We tend to view our illnesses and ourselves in unique ways. We internalize illness as part of our sense of self. We identify with our bodies and see ourselves as less than whole when something happens to us. Illness can often be a metaphor for how we see ourselves. People with cancer often feel powerless over a raging enemy and merely succumb, while others put up a valiant fight against the invasion. The manner in which they cope with illness often represents how they live their daily lives. By becoming aware of how our minds can influence our body, we can have considerably more control over our physical health.

There are various methods available that can affect our physical well-being. These methods include:

Individual psychotherapy is familiar to most folks. It can be described as the process by which a trained mental health professional collaborates with a patient/client in a series of psychological interviews designed to help the patient gain greater awareness of his/her inner world; this awareness facilitates personal growth with subsequent changes in attitude and behavior.

When dealing with physical illness, psychotherapy

focuses on the psychological factors that may be affecting the course of the illness or trauma and recovery as well as the psychological affects of the illness. Our attitude about the illness, and infirmity in general, can influence the course of the illness. Some people feel victimized and helpless when they become ill, while others view it as an opportunity to be pampered. For some there is a conscious or unconscious secondary gain derived in being ill and as such, the illness lingers longer than medically indicated. For others, it is something to get through quickly, often too quickly, not permitting sufficient time for complete healing. Individual therapy, even for only a few sessions, can significantly contribute toward a more complete recovery.

Individual psychotherapy can help significantly attenuate the intensity of the experience of being ill and even reduce the length of time for the illness to run its course. Psychotherapy has been found helpful in reducing the incidence of gastrointestinal disturbances such as ulcers, colitis, and irritable bowel syndrome. It has also been demonstrated to be useful in helping individuals reduce the stress associated with cardiac arrhythmia, tachycardia, and adjustment to cardiac surgery.

Group psychotherapy is the second most commonly known, albeit poorly understood, form of psychological treatment. In group therapy six to eight people plus a group therapist meet for ninety-minute to two-hour sessions for a period of time, either time limited or on-going. The members of the group usually have at least one common concern that brings them into the group. That concern could be an illness, tragedy, trauma, life transition, or addiction. The effect of group therapy is very powerful. In the safe confines of the group, people share their feelings and thoughts about their concerns. As members share and empathize with one another, and as group cohesion develops, a synergy evolves. The group begins to heal itself. People learn new ways of relating to themselves, to each other, to their work and to their concerns. Learning from one another lessens the feeling of being alone and promotes greater self-understanding and a sense of connection to a larger whole. That connection has been demonstrated to be healing.

There is evidence that cancer patients in group therapy can experience symptomatic remission; one study demonstrated that when comparing two groups of cancer patients diagnosed as terminally ill, one group receiving group therapy and the other not, the former lived from three to five years longer than the latter. Similarly, it has been suggested that cardiac patients receiving group therapy tend to have a quicker recovery rate than others. The same seems to hold true for other illnesses. It has also been demonstrated that adjustment to the effects of catastrophic accidents is facilitated by group therapy. Addiction groups, incest groups, victims of violent crimes or natural disasters, and other self-help groups have repeatedly demonstrated the healing power of the group.

Family psychotherapy involves bringing the entire family unit together. Illness or trauma that affects one person affects the entire family system. Each person plays a vital role in the healing process. When it is functioning at its best, the family unit provides a nurturing, healing environment for each of us. People who are cared for at home rather than in hospitals often recover sooner, and in cases of terminal illness, often live longer. When the family unit is disrupted by death, illness, or tragedy, the entire system is disrupted. Family therapy helps people deal with their own reactions to the crisis and helps to restore the healing power of the system.

Families adjusting to the chronic illness of a family member are helped to work through their feelings of helplessness, despair, anger, and anxiety. By working these feelings through, and restructuring thinking, the family can serve as a potent healing force for each member and the patient as well. Family therapy can facilitate understanding and support for each member affected by the circumstance.

Marriage counseling is naturally thought of when a marriage is in trouble. People think of going to marriage counseling when the marriage is faltering and communication is lacking. However, marriage counseling is also another psychological intervention that has been found beneficial in healing the disruption that a catastrophe, loss, or illness can cause to the marital unit. Often the physically ill person feels guilty for the upset she/he is causing to the spouse. The spouse feels helpless to do anything for the ill person, while at the same time may be worried about his or her own well-being. Sometimes this normal reaction leaves one spouse feeling guilty. Whenever one person in a marriage experiences a physical or emotional upset, it has repercussions on the other. Sometimes these repercussions are difficult to understand and integrate. Skillful marriage counseling can help the couple integrate the new circumstances into their lives and facilitate re-establishing of the healing union.

Biofeedback is a modality that helps individuals monitor their physiological reactions to stress. By receiving biofeedback training we can learn to modify our emotional reactions to stressful situations that in turn will affect our physiological response. For example, when we are under stress, the temperature of our skin rises. By hooking up a device that measures skin temperature and attaching it to a buzzer, people can be trained to either raise their skin temperature and increase the sound of the buzzer, or lower their skin temperature and reduce the sound of the buzzer. In the same way we can be trained to increase or decrease the electrical response on the surface of our skin (i.e., the galvanic skin response or GSR). By learning to monitor and control our physiological responses we can dramatically reduce the stress reactions that are associated with these responses. Thus, people have learned to reduce their blood pressure, decrease the acid flow in the stomach, and control migraine headaches. Clearly any catastrophic illness or physical disability increases our stress level. With increased control over our response to stress, we can increase the efficiency of our immune system and perhaps accelerate the healing process.

Meditation training, hypnosis, and visualizations are other techniques that psychologists use to help people cope with the stress of physical illness, physical and emotional trauma, and stress-related illnesses. Through these techniques, the individual autonomic nervous system's response to stress can be altered. They are very effective in controlling stress reactions and can be used to help cope with chronic pain. They work by helping individuals focus their energy on the healing potential within the body and the power of the mind to affect physiological processes.

Meditation teaches us how to focus our attention away from our pain and frees us to harness the power of the mind to slow down our autonomic nervous system. It teaches us how to put our mind in neutral, away from the pressures and worries that concern us. It has been found that twenty minutes spent twice a day in a meditative state can dramatically reduce our heart rate and our blood pressure.

Visualization is a technique that psychologists use to help individuals focus on the healing powers within us. It is usually combined with a technique called progressive relaxation wherein an individual learns to relax each part of her or his body to reach a profound state of relaxation. While in that state the psychologist helps the individual develop an image of the diseased organ or area of pain. Then utilizing other images, the patient is guided to find healing powers within to combat the illness, disease, or pain.

Hypnosis is an extension of the progressive relaxation technique mentioned above. The psychologist induces a trance with the client's cooperation wherein a deeper state of relaxation is achieved. Once in the relaxed state, the psychologist will help the client tap into the hidden powers of the mind to uncover areas that are affecting the healing process. Through this form of heightened awareness the individual can learn how to raise pain thresholds, lower blood pressure, reduce heart rate, and achieve an overall sense of strength in one's ability to recover from illness. Psychological aspects of the patient's illness can also be uncovered and resolved through hypnosis. One study has found that even one 20-minute hypnotic session prior to surgery, on average, decreased hospital stay by five days.

Psychologists are increasing our understanding of the power of the mind to heal as well as to cause physical and emotional pain. Through research we are expanding our knowledge of the interaction of mind and body. Psychologists have been able to help people recovering from illness participate more actively in their treatment. Rather than remaining a passive recipient of the ministration of physicians, patients can become active partners in their healing. Psychological interventions can reduce the length of hospital stays, increase compliance with medical interventions, reduce re-admission to hospitals, reduce utilization of medical services, and speed recovery from surgery.

Summary

Though some people think of going to a psychologist for emotional, psychological issues and problems coping with life, visiting a psychologist can also be helpful in dealing with physical illness as well. The mind and body are interconnected. Our psychological state of mind can influence our immune system and our recovery from illness. It can also create physical problems. Excess worry creates an increase in acidity in our stomachs causing such illnesses as ulcers. Excess agitation and anger affects our blood pressure. Likewise, illness affects our psychological state. When illness or accident strikes it also affects our family system. This paper discussed various interventions used by psychologists to help us take a more active part in our own healing process; these interventions include: individual and group psychotherapy, family and marital counseling, meditation, hypnosis, and visualizations. Each plays a part in helping us increase our sense of physical and mental well-being.

23

HOW DO WE CHANGE

Q: How many psychologists does it take to change a light bulb?
A: One, but the light bulb must want to change.

Whether light bulbs or people, for change to occur we must want to change. The first step toward behavioral or personality change is intent. No one can make us change. We must make that decision alone. The thought that comes to us that says, "This is not the way I want to live the rest of my life. There must be a better way," is the beginning of the journey to change. As many of us have found when we intend to exercise or lose weight, intent alone is insufficient. We can be quite sincere in our intent to change and still no change occurs.

There is another ingredient that is necessary for change: commitment. Commitment refers to the action part of the process of change. Commitment is what you actually do. Thus, while intent may get us started in thinking about change, commitment is what produces results. Commitment is what gets us out of bed and down to the gym. Commitment is what keeps us from eating the quart of ice cream that beckons us from inside the freezer.

Who amongst us hasn't experienced the desire to change and even began the process intending to change and made the commitment to change only to find that while the intent remains, the commitment seems to fade? We started out going to the gym five times a week and we watched how many excuses seem to come up so that by the end of some finite period we are not exercising at all. What happens?

Resistance to Change

While on the one hand human beings have a basic drive to grow, to develop, and to change, there is also another drive to remain quiescent. While we may seek change, we also resist change. We can see this phenomenon in children. While on the one hand the toddler seems to seek out novelty through its insatiable curiosity, on the other hand the very same toddler may have a fit if you change the position of one its toys or fail to read a story exactly as you read it before. This apparent contradiction is within all of us. We struggle between forces of change and forces of sameness. We will both to self-stimulate and seek homeostasis.

What makes for some people constantly seeking change while others seem to prefer routine and sameness? Why is it that some people seem to be driven to grow while others seem imprisoned by their routines? In short, why do some people resist change or growth?

People come into therapy expressing a desire to change. They say, "I wouldn't be here if didn't want to change." Yet, they seem to resist whatever interventions the psychotherapist offers. The therapist's advice, urging, active involvement, and brilliant interpretations are to no avail. The patient is far better at resisting than the therapist is at effecting change. Remember, "the light bulb must want to change." Here, the commitment to change is not as great as the intent to change.

As the psychoanalyst, Dr. Allen Wheelis[13] has so aptly pointed out:

> *"Some patients don't want to change, and when a therapist takes up the task of changing such a one he assumes a contest in which the patient always wins. The magic of insight, of unconscious dynamics, proves no magic at all; the most marvelous interpretation falls useless—like a gold spoon in the hands of a petulant child who does not want to eat his spinach."*

A great many variables intervene between the intent and the commitment. Going back to our toddler, many folks when they were toddlers were discouraged from change and exploration. They were told, directly or indirectly, that change, growth, and risk-taking were to be feared or avoided. They were rewarded for routine, for doing things the same as their parents. Fear of change frequently is passed down from parent to child. The negative consequences of change were reinforced, while the joys of change were dismissed. Sameness and security became more important than growth, change, and discovery.

It is the material that intervenes between intent and commitment that constitutes the bulk of the psychotherapeutic process. Many people who seek help are impatient. They want change to simply happen. They want the therapist to behave similarly to their parents and simply tell them what to do; after all, why should they approach the therapy process any differently than the rest of their life? The joys of self-discovery elude them. Thus, even if the therapist were to tell them what to do, they would resist. Hidden in the recesses of their mind is the agenda that says,

"I'll let you help me providing that I do not have to change."
They really want their current system to work. They would
like nothing more than to have the therapist figure out how,
with minimal effort, to make their system work. I have had
more than one patient ask me, "Doc, can you just give me a
pill?"

These people cannot comprehend the value of discovery.
Embracing change is a foreign concept. Maintaining
sameness is their style. They were not encouraged to explore,
to discover, to experiment. Novelty was eschewed, and
security exalted.

The biblical allegory of the Exodus is an apt metaphor
for the process of psychotherapy. The Israelites, seeking food
in a time of famine, migrated to Egypt. As they increased in
number, the Pharaoh became concerned that the Israelites
would side with Egypt's enemies. He therefore enslaved the
Israelites. They remained enslaved until Moses came to lead
them from Egypt. Despite their slavery, the hardships they
were forced to endure, and despite their wish to be free,
the majority of the Israelites chose to remain enslaved. They
feared their own redemption for it meant they would have
to endure the difficulty of crossing the desert and the vast
unknown. They would have to give up the security of the
life they had where, though enslaved, was familiar. At least
they knew they would eat and they knew what was expected
of them. The years of enslavement squelched their spirit,
their drive, and their desire for discovery. Of course they
wanted to be free, but they wanted it to just happen without
any effort or commitment on their part. They wanted it to
occur by magic. Moses was available to lead them out of
bondage, but they would have to choose to act. They would
have to endure crossing the desert and doing without food
and trusting the unknown process. Only a relative few were
willing to make the commitment.

Similar to the Israelites, many people are enslaved by

their neuroses, phobias, habits, fixed beliefs, and behavior patterns. Each of these developed early in life as a means for survival. They helped to cope with a world that was difficult and threatening. By capitulating to environmental demands and the demands of their parents, the young child survived. But in time the behavioral style becomes a way of life. Adults become enslaved by the fears of the child. As much as they want freedom from the bondage of their own enslavement, they are afraid. They visit a psychotherapist in the hopes of being set free. However, when the psychotherapist suggests that she/he can only lead, and that the major part of the work will be the patient's, many patients drop out of therapy. They are so frightened that they choose bondage over freedom.

Dr. Wheelis puts it this way:

> "Many patients go to a psychiatrist as if to a surgeon, and many psychiatrists regard themselves as psychic surgeons. When such a patient comes to such a therapist a relationship of considerable length many result, but little else. For the job can be done, if at all, only by the patient. To assign this task to anyone else, however insightful or charismatic, is to disavow the source of change. In the process of personality change the role of the psychiatrist is catalytic."

Some folks enter psychotherapy because they recognize that change is necessary, but they are not quite ready to change. For these individuals, psychotherapy is more of a holding pattern. The safety of the therapist's office, as well as the therapist, serves to help these people maintain their equilibrium that they are ready to change. For these people the therapist serves as a container for affects, ideas, beliefs, or projections that the patient is not ready to confront or change. Sometimes this process can go on for years. To the outside world watching, no change would seem to occur. But for the patient, the psychotherapy serves a very important, sometimes vital, function; namely, it helps them maintain daily functioning. The therapy session serves as a decompression chamber that stabilizes the individual so that she/he can carry on with reduced inner stress. For many people, the therapeutic hour is a safe harbor where the patient can gain a respite from the chaos of his/her everyday world. Frequently, this holding pattern sets the stage for change to occur at some later date.

The Role of Action

Without action there can be no change. Insight, understanding unconscious motivations, and discovering the connections to our past, all play an important and even necessary part in the process of change. However, none of them are sufficient. For change to occur we must do something differently.

A man visits a surgeon after having spent years in a wheelchair unable to walk. The surgeon, determining what the problem is, suggests surgery. After extensive surgery and a period of recovery, the patient finds that he still cannot walk. He complains to the surgeon. The surgeon asks the patient if he had gotten out of his wheelchair. The patient responds that it is uncomfortable and even painful. It was apparent to the surgeon that the patient had grown accustomed to his non-walking state and that he had expected that the surgery alone was going to be sufficient to walk. It was as though the patient believed that after spending a lifetime in a wheelchair, after six hours of surgery he would then be able to walk immediately. After the surgery, the patient had the choice of walking as an option. He could now exercise that option and go through painful, frustrating actions that would lead to change. The same holds true for people in psychotherapy. Psychotherapy opens up the possibility for change. The agent of change is the patient, and the vehicle is action. The patient must behave differently for permanent change to occur. Baby steps may be necessary at first. It will be uncomfortable, awkward, and even painful. But it will happen.

As Wheelis points out: "Personality change follows change in behavior. Since we are what we do, if we want to change what we are we must begin by changing what we do, [we] must undertake a new mode of action. Since the import of such action is change, it will run afoul of existing entrenched forces that will protest and resist. The new mode will be experienced as difficult, unpleasant, forced, unnatural, anxiety provoking. It may be under taken lightly but can be sustained only by a considerable effort of will. Change will occur only if such action is maintained over along period of time."

The Process of Change

Once there has been the commitment to change, the psychotherapeutic process can be likened to two people sitting down and pulling together a giant jigsaw puzzle without the aid of a box top to show the final picture. And many of the pieces of the puzzle may be missing. The patient brings in as many of the pieces as are available. The therapist and the patient engage in a process of seeking the pieces, putting them out for examination, and gradually fitting them together. During the course of this cooperative venture, issues may come up between patient and therapist. These issues often represent characteristic modes of the patient's behavior. The patient may perceive the therapist as some person from his past onto which she/he projects feelings and attitudes. The therapist responds differently than the patient expected and thus, acts as a catalyst for change.

All of this must be worked through as the collaborators continue to piece the puzzle of the patient's life together. With this increasing clarity the patient is able to make new and better choices upon which to act. Acting differently bated on the new information and understanding produces change. As the patient acts differently, new feelings and belief systems emerge. Gradually, the patient develops a new, more rewarding world view.

24

LIVING CONSCIOUSLY

During the past 30 years that I have been in practice as a clinical psychologist, I have often worked with individuals who have considerable difficulty maintaining a sense of balance in their lives. They are compulsively driven to attain more and more goods, toys, money, or titles to assure themselves of their identity and worth as human beings. These individuals are chronically anxious lest they lose their possessions or positions. They have defined themselves in terms of their work. Many of them are tormented by feelings of inadequacy. As much as they want to change, and as clearly as they are able to see that the way they are organizing their lives is not bringing them the joy that they had hoped for, they feel incapable of reversing the process.

Some of them recognize that as children they had a sense of freedom and a fuller appreciation of life. As they grew up, often beginning in grade school, they learned that life was not to be enjoyed and appreciated, but rather was to be taken seriously. Life was work. They learned that their value in this world, and indeed their very identity, was going to be based on what they did for a living and how much money or power they had. Parents and other adults around them, in their often well-meaning concern for the future of these people, overemphasized the need to find purpose and meaning in life through work. In their zeal to produce responsible adults they imparted the message that what one did as an occupation was all-important to the detriment of what one did for one's own personal fulfillment.

As I have worked with these people to help them create balance in their lives, and a greater sense of personal harmony, many of them have asked for some principle that would guide them. They wanted some sort of reminder on which they could focus, especially when they felt caught up in the press of everyday activities. Similar to the alcoholic suffering from a hangover, they remember only in retrospect what they should have done in a given situation. By then, it is too late. They have asked for a reminder that might help before the fact, rather than afterwards.

As I thought about this issue, it occurred to me that these individuals were not distinguishing between what they did for a *living* and what they did for their *life*. What they did for a *living* has taken over their life to the point that they virtually had no life. I began exploring the distinction between these two words with these folks and found that for most of them there was no distinction. Their *life* was dominated by their work. They spent more time and energy physically and mentally involved in their work than all the rest of their time and energy combined. I began to think about these terms as two different worlds, the world of *for-a-living* and the world of *life*. The mission for these people was to develop more of a world of *life* and less of a *for-a-living* world. The world of *life* includes family, friends, hobbies, recreation, community involvement, spirituality, and self-awareness. There is no financial reward and less power or status in the world of *life*. *Life* is a process of appreciation in its own right.

The more I pondered this issue, and the more the thoughts I was having and expressing with my patients, the more it sounded familiar to me. Then I realized that thousands of years ago the biblical sages must have been dealing with similar issues. They were concerned with having people realize that they were not on this planet for the purpose of merely working to achieve some end and to procure more material possessions nor to merely follow our instincts and emotions as animals do. Rather, the human beings had *consciousness*. This *consciousness* differentiates us from lower animals and some might consider it to be divinely inspired. Others have said that it is through this *consciousness* that God speaks to humans and/or operates through them. Whatever the belief, it is through *consciousness* that humans have the capacity to reflect on their behavior, are able to have a higher order guiding principle, and can develop a code of ethics, values, and beliefs to guide their behavior.

Frequently, we do not utilize this *consciousness* and thereby reduce ourselves to lower levels of development relying upon habit, emotions, instincts, needs, and drives to determine our actions. The ancient religious leaders recognized this tendency in people. They saw, even in ancient times, that people would spend their lives trying to amass fortunes, gold, land, goods, etc., often at the expense of their own integrity as well as that of others. They went off to wars for the sole purpose of power, glory, and money. They killed in the name of that belief system. And these wise men also recognized that people were easily enslaved, either by others or by themselves. They were enslaved by the promise of riches or because they failed to use their *consciousness* to determine a more appropriate path.

It seems to me that these ancients were dealing with a society that tended to get caught up in the materialistic world, whether it was the world of ancient Egypt, where they chose to remain slaves rather than crossing the hot desert, or were more interested in being Hellenistic, with all of the material things, than in fighting for religious freedom. And here I am faced with a number of people who are involved in their personal struggle between freedom and slavery, between *consciousness* and habit, between what one does for *life* and what one does for a *living*.

The Old Testament states that the Israelites were commanded to place the words, "Hear, Oh Israel, God is One," on doorposts, doorways, and gates and to tie them on their arm and on their forehead each day as a constant reminder that there is but one God. If we equate God with *consciousness*, then this idea suggests that human beings are in need of a constant reminder to utilize their *consciousness*, lest they fall back on their animal instincts and become enslaved by either their own ignorance or by the ignorance of others. Perhaps this is why there is such a high value placed on education by many civilizations. Education demands *consciousness*.

Many cultures have embedded within them rituals, symbols, and traditions designed to bring adherents to a higher level of consciousness. When performing the rituals or gazing at the symbols, one is supposed to direct one's thoughts away from the mundane and toward enlightenment or a more spiritual focus. It occurred to me, for example, that the *mezuzah* (the ornament that Jews hang on their doorways which contains those biblical words) and the *tefilin* (the leather boxes containing the biblical words that traditional Jews place on their arms and foreheads each morning) could be viewed as visible, symbolic reminders of the need for human beings to be *conscious*. These devices can be understood as daily, frequent reminders of the continuous struggle to maintain one's humanity on a daily basis. Lighting candles or morning meditations are common with other cultures and serve to remove the participant from the daily thoughts of earning a living and to bring him/her to a higher *consciousness.*

To the individuals whom I described earlier who have asked me for reminders to help keep their lives in balance, I have suggested that they might think about ways in which they can alter their days so that each day would begin with an appreciation of *life.* I suggest that they might meditate, find a special place where they can stand or sit, and reflect on the meaning of *life* and the distinction between what they do for *life* and what they do for a *living.*

I further suggest that they develop some physical symbolic reminders that they can see and even carry with them. For some it might be a special figurine, a special bracelet, or a unique amulet. These can be carried or placed strategically in their environment. For those who are religious, I suggest that they reinterpret their religious or cultural symbols in the above light. Thus, rather than being merely a religious artifact that has spiritual, traditional, or ornamental value, these symbols can have contemporary value in their own lives. For the Jew, the mezuzah, the Chai, and the tefilin could be symbols of *consciousness*; a reminder that *life* is more important than what one does for a *living.* For the Christian it could be a crucifix, a statue of the Virgin Mary or other saint, or a St. Christopher's medal. Almost any object can serve as a reminder of our essential humanity, our *consciousness,* providing that we impart that meaning to it.

In this light, even the very act of eating can serve to keep us in touch with our humanity. Special dietary laws of many cultures can be viewed as another way for us to remind ourselves that we are *conscious* human beings. It does not matter whether it is the Hindu practice of avoiding beef, the Muslim practice of avoiding pork, the Christian practice of Lent, or the Jewish practice of keeping a kosher diet. We can distinguish ourselves from animals by choosing what we eat, when we eat, and how much we eat. We do not have to be driven by our hunger, but rather we can choose. We can choose not to eat bacon or fats or sugars or salt, or any number of other foods that we know we would be better off not eating. In this act of choosing, we are exercising our uniqueness and can recognize that we eat for *life*. The simple act of eating can become an affirmation of our commitment to *life* rather than to what we do for a *living*. Missing meals in the service of what we do for a *living* would be counter to this commitment to *life*. Consciously fasting, if done for spiritual or health reasons, by contrast, might be considered an act of higher consciousness.

One can view mealtime as an opportunity to commune with one's inner self, one's higher power, or any other form of higher *consciousness* that might serve to remind us of our uniqueness. Each of us can decide on a particular form of dietary style that will serve as a tangible reminder of our commitment to the world of *life* as different from the world of what we do for a *living*. Most animals eat standing; humans can eat seated, as a reminder that they have the choice. Even this act can be seen as an act of higher *consciousness*.

From this perspective, it is possible to find many symbols into our lives to remind us to remain conscious, to be fully human, to maintain connected to our own inner strength. It further suggests that there are many simple acts that we execute daily that could bring us in touch with a higher self, if we were to be *conscious* when we performed them. There are many acts in which we could engage that would elevate us to a higher level of consciousness, and that would make this world a little better place, make us feel a little better about ourselves.

25

TWEAKING YOUR LIFE

When we consider changing some habit, some behavior, or even the direction of our life, we often come up with some grand plan for doing so. We think big. It's the American way. If we want to lose weight, we establish a goal of, for example, 20 lbs. We decide to go to the gym four or five days each week for an hour each day. Of course, for most people this plan lasts for about a week, if that much. When we want to cut back in our spending, we decide to give up buying clothes for the next year. When it comes to our spiritual life, we say we will begin going to our place of worship every week. In each instance our resolve lasts for a very short time, leaving us feeling guilty, down on ourselves, and disappointed. We accuse ourselves of being failures, lazy, lacking in discipline, and generally as losers. Our self-esteem drops and we feel worse about ourselves than before we made the resolution. We add one more self-recrimination to the long list of past unfulfilled promises to ourselves.

Each time we fail, we feel just a little bit worse about ourselves. Our disappointment in ourselves grows to the point where we may either give up trying to change, or we begin to accept ourselves as born losers–failures. We begin to look at ourselves as incompetent. We become depressed and feel hopeless. In order to avoid falling into despair, we may simply give up. We say, "This is the way things are, I am doomed to living my life this way, so I might as well just accept it." What we don't realize is that it may not be that change is not possible, but rather it is our approach to change that may not be working.

INSTANT GRATIFICATION

Most Americans have a penchant for instant gratification. We want immediate results. We also have a tendency to think, "More is better." I have gone to the gym to work out and watched very out of shape men go over to the weight machine for the first time and try to bench press their body weight! Finding they cannot lift this amount of weight, they give up and go off to some other machine. I have heard people say that they are going to lose 50 pounds in three weeks. These folks are setting themselves up to fail.

Many health clubs and diet plans count on the tendency of people to bite off more than they can chew in order to stay in business. They offer big discounts to people to sign up for a year or more in advance knowing that the vast majority will go for a few weeks and then quit. If those who signed up attended every day, there would be no room to accommodate everyone. The same is true for diet centers. They count on people's desire for immediate results. Yet we all know, in the intelligent part of our brains, that weight loss, body building, and as in learning any other activities, takes patience, persistence, and time, in order to achieve lasting results. But our desire for immediate gratification takes over and we set ourselves up for instant failure.

TWEAKING

This is where the concept of "tweaking" comes into play. Literally, "tweaking" means to gently pinch or jerk something or someone. Colloquially speaking, we use the term to refer to slightly improving or changing a situation. We say, "We tweaked our offer a bit and were able to make the deal," or "we tweaked the volume on the audio just a bit for better acoustics." The same concept of "tweaking" can be applied to aspects of our lives. We can tweak our lives in small ways. Over time these tweaks add up to significant shifts and changes. In each instance, we can make a slight alteration in what we were doing in order to get a better result. They don't have to be big changes, but minor adjustments. This concept tweaking, or making minor adjustments to situations or areas of our life, can have a significant impact on the overall direction of our life. A series of tweaks can, over time, have the same overall effect as one significant change, without the pain of a large sudden shift.

Consider trying to straighten one's teeth. We go to the orthodontist to have braces put onto our teeth. The orthodontist doesn't try to straighten our teeth all at once because the pain would be too great and damage might be done to our teeth and gums. If the pain is too great we will want to quit the process before the job is done. However, through a series of tweaks–gradually tightening the braces— over a period of many months or years, we see our teeth straighten and remain straight even after the braces are removed. The same is true when we want to straighten a tree that has been growing crooked. We tweak it gradually over time, each week tightening the brace that pulls the tree into position. If we were to do it suddenly, the tree might break. A series of tweaks does the job of straightening the tree, almost imperceptibly over time.

We can apply a similar principle for straightening our life. Change normally does not occur suddenly, overnight. It occurs by degrees, often without our awareness. When it does occur suddenly, it usually is precipitated by circumstance or necessity. We may be forced to change when confronted with trauma, precipitous occurrences such as sudden economic reversal, earthquake, and so forth. For the most part, however, lasting change occurs gradually over time.

Let's examine four areas of our life: relationships, occupation, physical and mental health, and spirituality, to see how the concept of tweaking might apply.

RELATIONSHIPS

Relationships, especially in a marriage, often get stale. Couples fall into habitual styles of relating. Sometimes relationships become dysfunctional, while at other times the relationship may simply lose its sparkle. In both cases, the couple may think that there is no way of revitalizing the relationship without a massive overhaul. If they think in terms of a complete overhaul, they may get overwhelmed and simply either accept the status quo, or think that they ought to divorce. In my opinion, many relationships can be salvaged or spruced up if each party makes a commitment to seek ways that each party can tweak the relationship. Below I will list a number of ways couples have found to tweak their relationship. It is not necessary that all of these suggestions be followed. Rather, you could do one of them for a month or two, and then when the mood strikes you could add a second, then a third, and so on. Each of these tweaks, when added together over time, adds up to significant movement. As with losing weight, it happens one pound at a time.

Tweaks for your relationship:

- Set aside one hour per week at a specific time and place for an uninterrupted conversation with your mate to discuss anything that is on your mind. Each party takes a half hour just to talk, with no interruptions by the other party. The listening party is there just to listen for a half hour. Then the roles are reversed.
- Set aside one night a week for a "date night," an evening consisting of at least two hours alternately planned by each partner each week. The date night could be something as simple as going out to a coffeehouse for espresso or a local pub for a glass of wine. Or an evening picnic, such as Chinese food or a hoagie sandwich at the beach or local park. Just getting out of the house during the week can be refreshing.
- Take an "in-town" mini-vacation by spending the night in a local hotel or motel. Leave from there to go to work the next morning. Or spend the weekend at a local hotel. It does not have to be a major, planned event to be fun or relaxing.
- Go with your partner for a massage at a local spa or health club. Or even bring one to your house. The cost is not that great compared to the payoff.
- Set aside time in the evening for a relaxing ritual, such as preparing tea and cookies before retiring.
- Take a bath or shower together at least once a week.
- Do something risqué that you might have done when you were dating. Think of the fun you will have talking about it and remembering it afterwards.

YOUR OCCUPATION

At first blush it may seem that only those who are self-employed would have the freedom to tweak their job. To be sure, it is easier to tweak when it is your own business, but this does not mean that it is impossible to tweak when you are working for someone else. You just have to be more creative. The chances are that you have never given it much thought. You have never thought of the ways you can make your work more pleasurable. Let's take a look at some of the ways you might tweak your work experience, beginning with the commute to work.

Tweaks for work:

- Listen to a book on tape while driving to the office. Or learn a language on tape. You often complain that you don't have the time to read a novel or those motivational tapes you hear about. Well, the morning and evening commute would be an ideal time to do so. Rather than complaining about the traffic, you will look forward to finding out what happens next in that novel you are listening to.
- Take a ten-minute break in the morning and again in the afternoon to leave the building and take a walk around the block.
- At least once a week have your lunch in a park rather than either in the office or in a restaurant.
- Have your wife or husband, friend, or child meet you for lunch once a month or more.
- Bring your child to the office once a month.
- Put pictures of your family and other personal items on your desk or around your office.
- Take a personal mental health half-day (or full day if you can) off several times a year. Don't wait until you become ill. And take yourself to a movie or hit some golf balls during that time off.
- Practice deep breathing exercises or meditation often during the day.

- Develop a relaxing ritual that you can look forward to each day while at your place of employment, e.g., a tea break.

YOUR PHYSICAL AND MENTAL HEALTH

It is in this area that we set ourselves up for the biggest failures. One would think that we would do whatever we could to build our self-esteem and to enhance our self-image. Yet, by virtue of our desire for immediate results, we achieve just the opposite. We resolve to be a totally new and improved version of ourselves, fail, and end up feeling worse about ourselves than when we started.

The trick once again is in tweaking. Rather than promising to be a totally new you, think tweak. Think about one area you could spruce up just a bit. Below are only a few suggestions; they should not be done all at once. Choose just one of them, or any other of your choice, and do it consistently until it become as much a part of your life as brushing your teeth. Then add another one, and another, and so forth. Take your time. Gradually, by virtue of here a tweak, there a tweak, you will end up with that new and improved version of you. But it will not come upon you suddenly. Rather, it will happen gradually, almost imperceptibly.

Tweaking your physical and mental health:

- When it comes to the commitment to increase your reading, rather than committing to read the entirety of *War and Peace*, think about reading one article a day from a magazine of your choice.
- Rather than saying that you are going to learn how to meditate, take 10 minutes a day just to sit quietly and focus on your breathing. Increase at no more than five

minutes every two weeks until you are able to do it 20 minutes a day.

- Instead of promising to power walk for 45 minutes a day, commit to walking around the block either in the morning before getting dressed for work or in the evening, either before or after dinner. Make it at least a ten-minute walk. When that becomes comfortable, add five minutes. Add only five minutes, and not more often than one addition a week, until, over a several month period you are at 30 minutes a day. It could take you months to get there.
- Give yourself a treat by having a professional massage once a month. Start with a half hour session. If you like it, increase it to an hour over time.
- Spend ten minutes each morning stretching before you take your shower.
- Take a warm bath by candlelight before retiring, while listening to your favorite soothing music and enjoying a cup of tea. If you find it pleasant and relaxing, increase the frequency.

Imagine how you might feel about your life next year at this time if several of these ideas were a regular part of it. For example, how would it feel to know that you were reading an article (chapter of a book) every week, walking for 30 minutes a day, having a monthly massage, and enjoying a warm bath by candlelight several times a week? Then imagine how it would feel if you were also tweaking your approach to work as discussed earlier.

SPIRITUALITY

I think it was Charles Darwin who said that what differentiates humans from animals is that only human beings can blush. Human beings can reflect upon their own behavior. They can experience a sense of something beyond themselves and can feel connected to one another. They have a higher consciousness. Human beings are conscious of right and wrong, good and bad; they are conscious of their own finitude. As such, we can say that human beings have a spiritual awareness as part of their existential make up.

Most of us enjoy a beautiful sunrise or sunset, appreciate a mountain view, feel calmed by the ocean, and feel peaceful when stargazing on a clear night. At these moments, we feel connected with the universe, a part of something larger than ourselves. We feel moved by the good works of others, and feel a sense of awe at the birth of a child. We feel blessed when someone we love recovers from an illness.

We often vow that we will stop to smell the flowers more often. We promise to attend our place of worship more frequently. We tell ourselves that we will make a contribution of time and energy to make this world a better place. Though we are sincere in these desires, somehow we seldom find the time to follow through. We want to feel connected to others and to our world, yet the time eludes us.

Again, we believe that in order to be connected to our spiritual self, we have to make a significant change. We believe that we have to have a big impact. Overwhelmed, we gradually slip into our routine, everyday life, feeling just a bit disappointed in ourselves for not being the person we would like to be.

As with the other aspects of our life discussed thus far, we can tweak our lives spiritually as well. The following suggestions might serve to stimulate your own thinking about creative ways to bring spirituality into your life.

Spiritual tweaking:

- Each day when you awaken, before getting out of bed, spend a moment reflecting on the miracle of just being alive.
- Before starting your day, think about your blessings and

how you might make a difference in someone else's life.
- Once a week put a coin in an expired parking meter to prevent someone from getting a ticket.
- Several times a week, pay someone a compliment.
- Make it a practice to say "thank you" to someone for taking the time to criticize you.
- Create a picture in your mind of the self you would like to be. Each day pause in the middle of the day to reflect on that higher self.
- Tell someone you care about that he/she is important to you.
- Periodically contact a friend whom you have often thought about but have not taken the time to call.
- Once a month spend an hour volunteering at a local community agency or shelter.

CONCLUSION

We all have the power to improve the quality of our life by making slight adjustments–tweaks–to the way we do things. These tweaks add up over time, with the same net effect as major adjustments without the pain of sudden, drastic change. The traditional wisdom of, "no pain, no gain" does not apply when it comes to making significant life changes. People often think that they have to wait until the children grow up, or that they have to divorce, in order to lead the life they would like. They then become overwhelmed with the enormity of the task. My contention is that we should think small. You do not have to wait; you can start tweaking today. Remember, don't put off until tomorrow what you can tweak today.

26

INTEGRITY AND YOUR MENTAL HEALTH

You make a promise to do something for someone. You forget. You believe you are an honest person. You tell a lie. You commit to participate in an exercise program or diet. You do not even begin. You talk the talk, but you do not walk the walk. Are you a person of integrity? You would like to believe that you are, but you find your life peppered with examples of hypocrisy. Your words and your actions do not line up.

What is integrity? What does it mean to live life with integrity? What are the psychological effects of not doing so? *A Comprehensive Dictionary of Psychological and Psychoanalytical Terms* define integrity as, "the quality of being whole or undivided; moral consistency; honesty and truthfulness." As you can readily see, living one's life with integrity by this definition is not always easy. Forces that would lead us off the path of integrity, making living with moral consistency, honesty, and truthfulness difficult, continuously bombard us. Most of us have a sense of what it would mean to live our life with integrity. We have a picture of our "ideal self" in our minds. Yet, we frequently find ourselves falling short of that ideal. We make a decision that will give immediate, albeit temporary, satisfaction, but one that does not leave us feeling good about ourselves. In order to live with integrity, our actions have to comport with our higher order beliefs. We must *consistently* act in a manner that reflects our integrity. Our challenge is to maintain our integrity in a society that does not necessarily reflect these values. It is a lot easier to live with integrity when the larger society reflects, supports, and encourages these values. Unfortunately, our society does not always do so. We often are viewed as suckers or chumps when we make a choice to take the higher ground since it is so much easier and often more profitable to do otherwise. We often glorify the con man or the hustler. We admire people who can get away with something. It is not easy to live a life of integrity in a world that emphasizes bottom lines, material possessions, end results, winning at any cost, and bigger is better. It is difficult to consistently live with integrity, but what is the price we pay if we do not?

False Self

People visit a psychologist seeking relief from anxiety, panic, and depression. Frequently, they are seeking to change ineffective behaviors or habits. Generally, they want to live more productive, fulfilling lives. Intuitively, they know that they are not feeling whole. There are parts of themselves that they do not like and would like to disown. Many psychologists describe individuals who are so estranged from themselves and their world that they develop a "false self" in order to cope with the world. They see the human drama as a quest for the real self, believing that the road to psychological health is the degree that we live an authentic life. They see the human struggle as a search for meaning in an absurd world. Collectively, these practitioners suggest that much of what we call psychopathology is the result of inauthentic behaviors, coping mechanisms that result from the "false self," or attempts to make meaning in the world.

The existential philosopher and playwright Jean Paul Sartre used the concept of bad faith to refer to the degree to which human beings fail to develop their potential as human beings. He suggested that we all live in bad faith since we are not able to develop all of our potentialities at all times. However, to the extent that we struggle to live an integrated, authentic life, we can approach good faith. The more complex the society, the more difficult it is to live an integrated, authentic life.

When we seek expedient solutions to complicated problems, we stop struggling and seek short-term fixes rather than long-term solutions. The end becomes more important than the means. We often come up with all sorts of excuses for why it is acceptable for us to do what we are doing despite the consequences. We know that we are not living up to our highest potential. We know that we are falling short of our ideal self. However, we excuse ourselves by saying that living an authentic life is not practical. We claim that we all have to live less than honorably if we want to survive or be successful in this world. We fail to see that our short-term, so-called practical solutions to the complexities of modern life only bring more grief, pain, and distress upon themselves in the long run.

We want psychologists to help us find a way to live without integrity but without the painful consequences. Some of us may seek relief through anti-depressant or anti-anxiety medications, hoping these drugs will help us deal with the pain of living an inauthentic life. No medication can heal or cure a malaise created by living without integrity. Bad faith or inauthentic living is not a chemical imbalance.

It is my belief that many of the symptoms of psychological

stress with which people struggle and for which they seek psychotherapy are exacerbated, if not caused by, living lives without integrity. Though people enter psychotherapy wanting to feel whole, fulfilled, and content with their lives, they also do not want to struggle with such issues as integrity. They fail to see the connection between how they live their lives and the emotional consequences they experience. I contend that it is not possible to feel a sense of personal wholeness and feeling of internal integration while living in ways that undermines one's integrity.

Mental health professionals too often attribute emotional pain *solely* to poor parenting, chemical imbalance, unconscious unresolved trauma, repressed memories, and so on. While it is true that these all significantly contribute to emotional distress, the manner in which we live our lives contributes greatly to how we feel about ourselves. Integrity has received scant attention by many mental health professionals who ordinarily leave such issues to religious leaders.

We are familiar with the feeling of guilt we experience when we act in ways that run counter to our self-image. Depending on the magnitude of the transgression, we may lose sleep, condemn ourselves, lose concentration, or become depressed. Most of us can understand these reactions when the transgression is significant. But what happens when there are a series of smaller transgressions spread out over time? What happens when we live everyday doing things that we know are not in our own best interests or violates our internal set of values? I believe that the negative effects of living out of integrity build within us gradually, eroding our sense of self. We try to ignore the feeling. We tell ourselves, "Everybody does it." We may make excuses, we may rationalize, but the effects go on. Like a little bit of rust on our car, these transgressions spread and gradually erode our spirit.

Parenting Today and Yesterday

We look around us and we see children killing their parents, parents killing their children, spouses killing one another, we see our leaders being accused of moral turpitude, our movies make paid assassins appear like regular guys, and we expect that this will not affect our values.

When I was a boy growing up in the '40s and '50s, I knew the difference between good guys and bad guys. Presidents were good. Soldiers, police, and professional athletes–they were all good. War movies always depicted our soldiers fighting the good fight. It represented a triumph of good over evil. Values were clear and most people upheld a similar standard. There were few shades of gray.

The values I learned in my home were reinforced by my neighborhood, my community, my school, my friends, movies, and (later) television. Today it is difficult to tell the good guys from the bad and social values do not conform to parental values. When I was a child, parents could feel comfortable knowing that the school, the neighborhood, and the society at large would reinforce their values. Today's parents do not have that luxury. Two-career families often relegate much of the value training to others.

With less involvement on the part of parents and mixed support from the community, it is difficult for today's parents to help a child develop a sense of integrity. It becomes even more important that parents live a life of integrity so that the child constantly sees their parent modeling what it means to live with integrity. Parents can no longer afford to say, "Do as I say, not as I do." It is important that their words and deeds conform.

The impact of the media's words and images is far greater than the words of mere parents. A thirty-second ad on television can influence millions. These ads do not necessarily represent the values parents would have their children internalize. Television shows, movies, and record albums frequently give messages that are quite contrary to those that a parent would want to have inculcated in their children. Parents frequently do not have the time to influence their children. And what little time they have cannot balance out the effects of the media and society in children. Too often parents do not teach their children the value of integrity. Frequently, parents themselves do not understand the meaning of integrity.

Adults are not immune to the media. Even those who developed a strong sense of ethics and were taught the value of integrity find it difficult to maintain their focus. The media bombard us with information about those who we believed were people of integrity. We see elected officials espousing morality and the importance of being honest while they, themselves, are found to be less than honorable. Sport figures, celebrities, clergy, business tycoons, you name it, all have been found guilty in the court of public opinion of not living up to their word. Movies glorify and make paid assassins, adulterers, and devious political officials into lovable people. How can we hold on to a set of values when the world around us is saying that a touch of larceny is really acceptable? Over time our values will shift. We find ourselves doing things that as a child we were taught were not acceptable. We gradually shift from living a life where integrity mattered to one where we can make excuses for lying, cheating, failing to live up to our word, and not honoring contracts or agreements. We think nothing of using bankruptcy as a way to avoid paying creditors. We think it is clever to cheat on our taxes, betray our spouses, or steal from our employers. We think little of the impact of such behavior on others or on ourselves.

Maintaining Integrity

Even under the best of circumstance it isn't easy to live one's life with integrity. We always have to face difficult dilemmas. These are the challenges in life that help us grow. If it were easy, there would be minimal growth. It is easy to refund incorrect change to the cashier when the amount is small and you are not hungry. But what about when you are hungry and the amount of incorrect change is large? The issue is the same in both instances, but the challenge is greater in the latter.

We have become so numbed to the effects of minor breaches of integrity that it takes years before we recognize the symptoms. We may often feel more of a struggle to make a decision based on integrity than to do otherwise. The minor decisions we make every day may have more of an effect on our self-image than the big decisions demanding a moral choice.

Many of us do not even think about the times we have failed to deliver on a promise, or have cheated on our taxes, or lied to someone, or taken advantage of someone's error. But these add up over time, leaving us feeling depressed, agitated, anxious, and disgruntled, to name a few of the psychological affects of damage to our sense of self. Often we try to deal with the sense of internal dissatisfaction through various forms of self-medication: alcohol, drugs, work, sex, etc. None of these are effective for very long.

Perform an honest appraisal of yourself. Ask yourself how close you have come to reaching your ideal self. Are you being the model to your children that you would want to be? Would you like others to treat you the way you treat them? Would you want your children to grow up to be like you? Do you embellish upon your accomplishments in order to appear better to others? Do you make excuses for yourself when you fail to deliver on a promise? Do you sometimes make a promise that you know you cannot keep? Do you break your commitments just because it is not convenient for you or without thinking about the effects on others? These are but a few of the smaller ways in which we undermine our own integrity. To the degree that we can align our words and our actions to increase our self-esteem we will at least not contribute to the emotional distress in our lives.

A patient of mine gave me the following poem suggesting that integrity is being able to look yourself in the eye and liking what you see.

"The Man in the Glass"
(Author unknown)

When you get what you want in your struggle for self,
And the world makes you king for a day,
Just go to a mirror and look at yourself,
And see what that man has to say.

For it isn't your father or mother or mate,
Upon whose judgment you must pass;
The fellow whose verdict that counts most in your life
Is the one staring back from the glass.

Some people may think you're a straight-shootin' fellow,
And call you a wonderful guy.
But the man in the glass says you're only a bum,
If you can't look him straight in the eye.

He's the fellow to please, never mind all the rest,
For he's with you clear up to the end,

*And you've passed your most dangerous, difficult
test,
If the man in the glass is your friend.*

*You may fool the whole world down the pathway of
years,
And get pats on the back as you pass,
But your final reward will be heartache and tears,
If you've cheated the man in the glass.*

27

THE STORY WE TELL

When most of us think about clinical psychology we think about Sigmund Freud and the unconscious. The unconscious has played a prominent role in theater, books, movies, and even in general conversation. We are intrigued by the mysteries of the mind, the unknown recesses where our demons lodge, and the awesome power it seems to have over our behavior and our thinking. This unknown force that seems to influence every aspect of our life has intrigued human beings for hundreds of years, long before Sigmund Freud and his followers began to explore and map this area of the mind. According to many, the unconscious dominates our personality and our behavior. We have little control over it; it controls us.

Most of us do not like to think of ourselves as being dominated by a force over which we have little control, except when it suits us. For example, when we behave in ways that gets us into trouble with the law, we appeal to unconscious forces that made us act in a certain way. We view abnormal behavior as largely controlled by unconscious forces. Psychoanalysts delve into the unconscious in order to find antecedents for neurotic or psychopathologic behavior. They believe that when unconscious material can be made conscious, one can then integrate this material into one's consciousness, and behavior will change. This idea has some appeal. However, many of us know people who have spent many years in psychoanalysis exploring their unconscious are quite at home discussing their Oedipal complexes, Electra complexes, penis envy, and other psychoanalytic concepts. However, their behavior does not change! They may feel differently, but they act the same.

It is for this reason that many psychologists have turned their attention toward another aspect of the human mind, consciousness. While not as mysterious or romantic, the conscious mind plays a significant role in understanding how we develop and change. In fact, many psychologists believe that it is the conscious mind that is most important and, when developed, can affect the greatest impact on behavior and personality change. The conscious mind has the capacity for understanding, integrating, conceptualizing, creating, focusing, reasoning, and determining action. The problem is that many people do not seem to exercise their consciousness. Training the conscious mind takes work. Hence, they act out of habit. Even psychoanalysts and psychoanalytically trained psychologists have recognized that delving into the unconscious is often not sufficient to change human behavior. They are turning their attention to studying the role of the conscious mind in healing and behavioral change.

Victim vs. Survivor

There is enough data available in the universe of data to support whatever belief system we choose. If we choose to believe in aliens from another planet, there is data available to support it. If we choose to think that we are losers and failures, there is data in our history to support that belief. If we choose to believe that we will not succeed, that we are ugly, or that there is no point in getting up in the morning, we can find evidence to support the position. By the same token, we can find data to support the contention that we are successful, beautiful, intelligent, and athletic; we can find the evidence to back it up, if we choose to look for it.

We can look at our lives and see ourselves as victims of circumstance, destined to stay exactly as we are, or we can see ourselves as survivors capable of great achievements if only we apply changes to ourselves. The data is available for both points of view. Our behavior will change depending on the story we tell about ourselves. If we tell the story of being a victim, we will see ourselves as helpless and at the mercy of forces outside of ourselves. If we tell the story of how we survived a tragedy or trauma, we will see ourselves as heroes capable of forging our own destiny. The choice of what story we tell is ours.

In a literal sense we are both the victim and survivor. We were victims of a perpetrator or act of violence and we managed to survive. The issue is how are we going to identify ourselves? A reporter asks the question and we respond, "I was a victim of abuse," or "I am a survivor of abuse." We have no choice as to the abuse itself; we do not have to question the abuse. We do have choice over how we define ourselves. The victim sees him or herself as a helpless pawn, acted upon by forces outside him or herself over which she/he has no control. The survivor experiences him/herself as a powerful force capable of withstanding assault, abuse, or tragedy and coming out of the experience whole and confident. Both individuals went through the tragic event; however, they come out differently by virtue of how each chooses to define themselves. This self-description will affect how they experience themselves in other aspects of their life. The victim will see him/herself as having little influence in the world around himself/herself. The victim will walk through life afraid, uncertain, wary, with a pervasive feeling of helplessness and a sense of powerlessness to effect any change in their circumstance.

The survivor, by contrast, will experience himself/herself as a powerful force capable of coping with life and all it has to offer. Having experienced a tragedy and seeing that she/he survived, she/he is more likely to face life as a challenge, with the confidence that no matter what, she/he will survive. The survivor knows firsthand that life has contingencies; knows that tragedy can strike unexpectedly. But the survivor has also learned that she/he has the skills necessary to effectively deal with these contingencies. This gives him/her the confidence to undertake challenges without fear.

The stories we tell

Just as we can find data to support whatever belief system to which we chose to adhere, we can also create a story of who we are based on these data. We can weave a story based on all of the negative data that occurred in our lives to demonstrate that our parents were evil people under whose rule we suffered. Or we can tell a story of well-meaning parents who were struggling with their own problems and choices, and, out of benign neglect or ignorance, did not respond to our specific needs. While the net effect on us may be the same, i.e., we may feel neglected, the psychological impact of believing that the damage was caused by design or ignorance can affect our outlook on life. Just as it makes a psychological difference when someone steps on our foot intentionally or by accident, we feel differently toward the perpetrator in each case and it affects our perception of the perpetrator and the world at large. In the first case we may develop a world view that states that people are hostile and out to damage us, while in the latter case we may develop a world view that recognizes that accidents happen.

Some people firmly adhere to a negative story that defines their life and affects their perception of the world. This perception, in turn, affects their judgment and their behavior as well as their self-perception. If we can develop a different, more positive world view based on the available data, we can change our behavior, our beliefs, and our outlook.

Marty's Story

Let's take an example on how this might work with Marty, a painfully shy young man who is so inhibited that he finds approaching people all but impossible. His shyness affects all areas of his life. He has difficulty making friends, approaching women, and despite his intellectual abilities he cannot rise within his profession because of his difficulty conversing with his supervisors, customers, and colleagues. Marty describes his parents as self-centered individuals whose primary focus in life was to do the socially correct thing. They emphasized the importance of education and performance, with little concern for the psychological development of their children. Family conversation was virtually non-existent except when there was an obvious problem that impacted directly on their lives. Marty defined himself as a loser and a misfit who could never please his parents. He perceived his parents as totally competent and successful, believing that they favored his more outgoing, aggressive older brother who was always held out to him as an example of what Marty should be like. Marty was filled with self-contempt, resentment toward his brother, self-pity, and anger toward his parents for their self-absorption.

After exploring his life in greater detail, it came to light that his parents, children of immigrant parents, married quite early in life and had children almost immediately. They were expected to fulfill the role as parents long before they themselves had fully matured. They both worked in order to give their children a better life than they had as children. It was very important for them that their children were successful by contemporary standards. They wanted to demonstrate to the world that was against their early marriage that they could be effective parents. They doted on their first-born child, expecting him to represent their success.

When Marty was born, his parents passed the responsibility for his social development onto their oldest child. They paid less attention to their newborn child, expecting him to develop in the footsteps of his older brother. They wanted the older brother to lead the younger brother, thus, creating a hierarchy between the brothers, with the older expected to mentor the younger. The older brother experienced his authority as both license to criticize his younger brother and as a burden of having to look after him. Marty developed a narrative of his life as one of being a neglected child at the mercy of the tyrannical older brother whose expectations he could never meet. Since his parents seemed to laud the virtues of the older brother who could do no wrong, Marty felt that he was simply a failure who could do no right. He hated his brother and himself.

During the course of our work together Marty began to develop an alternative perception of his brother and his parents. He began to see his parents as immature people who abrogated responsibility for parenting leaving a child, his brother, in charge. He began to see his brother's life as one in which he was burdened by the responsibility of a younger brother. Rather than being angry with his parents for imposing such a responsibility on him, he took out his anger on Marty. Marty began to see himself as a survivor of the abuses of his brother who was deprived of his own childhood by incompetent parents. He began to see his parents as simple folks who received no guidance in what it meant to be parents.

At this writing Marty is in the process of rewriting the story of his life. The facts remain the same, but as he redefines his life story, his world view is undergoing a radical change wherein he is seeing himself as a person who virtually raised himself, capable of withstanding the abuses of a resentful brother who himself had little guidance and was robbed of his own childhood. He sees them both as the progeny of two insecure, immature parents, who themselves had little guidance in their roles as parents. Rather than blaming his parents and his brother for his shyness, Marty is beginning to understand that his shyness was the result of his youthful attempt to make sense of his life. He had woven together the data of his life in such a way that it became an organizing principle that defined his life. It was the only way he knew how, to make sense of his world.

After re-examining the data of his life, he began to see that he has a choice as to how he wishes to define himself and how he will organize his world view. He can either choose to continue to hold to the story that he developed as a child that to make sense of his world at that time, one that portrays him as a victim of neglectful parents and a tyrannical brother, or he can choose to define himself as having been born of ignorant parents who, because of their own immaturity, abrogated parental responsibility by laying too much responsibility on an older child for raising a younger sibling. He therefore, was forced to raise himself and overcome familial circumstances.

Sam's Story

Sam had always viewed his father as a tyrant. He saw him as a larger than life figure who was fearless, critical, and tough.

By comparison, he experienced himself as weak, small, and incompetent. His father was a super-salesman and constantly bragged about his own accomplishments while at the same time he would belittle Sam and dismiss his achievements. Sam, himself, was very bright and by other's standards, very successful. He was an attorney and spoke several languages. Yet his father would demean him and emphasize his shortcomings. The net result was that Sam always felt poorly about himself, especially when around his father. He harbored considerable anger toward his father, thus, he stayed far away from him.

As Sam worked in therapy, he began to understand his father through the eyes of an adult. He recalled that his father had always wanted to be an attorney, but did not think himself intelligent enough. He tried to hide this insecurity from his son through an intellectual bravado and by being an outspoken critic of others. He proclaimed that circumstances were such that he could not afford law school so he settled for being a salesman. However, Sam knew that this was not true. As Sam re-examined the data of his life, he began to recognize that his father was an insecure, dissatisfied man who may have been jealous of his son and fearful of his intellect. Not wanting to be seen as weak, he intimidated Sam. When we combine the natural perception of a child of a father as a superman, with overbearing intimidation tactics, the result was overwhelming to Sam. It was difficult for Sam to see his father as jealous of him or generally insecure. Yet, the data was available to support the hypothesis.

By rewriting his life story to include these additional data, Sam began to see himself as well as his father, in a different light. Rather than being a small, incompetent person, he saw himself as successful and accomplished. He also saw his father as more human. This allowed him to approach his father with less fear and resentment, opening the possibility of a better relationship.

Choosing a different story

All of us have the opportunity to choose how we integrate the data of our life. Like Marty and Sam, we create a narrative of our life based on the information available to us at the time and our limited cognitive ability to create meaning out of chaos. Most of the time, the story that we created in childhood or youth becomes fixed in our minds. This story becomes the guiding influence or principle by which we define ourselves and by which we live our lives. Unfortunately, we seldom create a story that leaves us feeling good about ourselves. Rather, we often create a story that leaves us feeling like a victim of forces over which we have little or no control. The story we create disempowers us, rather than empowers us. We seldom re-examine the story we have created in the light of new information, new cognitive abilities, and new experiences. We may embellish it or modify it, but we seldom change it. To do so requires a belief that there might be other ways to organize the date and that additional data exists. Most people who do are not aware that there might be other possibilities.

Challenge yourself. Think of the story by which you identify yourself. How do you present the narrative of your life to others? Are you a hero in your story? Are you a victim? Has the story changed over the years or are you still telling the same story that you told when you were an adolescent? Does your story empower you or does it leave you feeling poorly about yourself and your future? Does it doom you to continuing to live a life that is unfulfilling or does it give you the courage to change your life and face new challenges undaunted?

If your story leaves you feeling hopeless or helpless, I

suggest you re-examine the data upon which you have based the story. But this time, examine all of the data. Are there data that you have left out of your narrative that contradicts the story you have been telling? How could you incorporate that data into your story or better yet, how could you rewrite the story based on the additional data? How old is the data upon which you have based your life? Is it based on childhood experiences to the exclusion of all the adult data you have accumulated? Is it based on the child's perception and interpretation of the data? How about looking at the data through adult eyes?

In the John Irving novel *The World According to Garp*, a young man tells the story of being fearful of swimming in the ocean because of the sea-monster called the "*under-toad*." In his mind as a child, the word under-tow conjured images of a monster of the deep. Where is the *under-toad* in your life and what is the story you've been telling? Perhaps it is time to change that story.

28

COACHING AND PSYCHOTHERAPY

More and more people are hearing the terms personal coach or life coach. There have been newspaper articles and professional articles written on the subject. Several people have asked me, "What is a life or personal coach and how is personal coaching different from psychotherapy?" Until recently, personal coaching has been confined to corporations where it is known as executive coaching or executive consulting. Today, personal coaching has found its way into the public domain. This issue of the *Psychotherapy Update* will discuss personal or life coaching as a new trend that will become more available over the next decade to assist people in achieving a more fulfilling, rewarding, and balanced life. Perhaps personal coaching is just what you've been waiting for to help you enrich your already satisfying life.

Coaching has been around for a long time. It is usually associated with sports, e.g., tennis coach, golf coach, track coach, football coach, or baseball coach, to name a few. You want to get better at something, whom do you call? A coach.

You want to become more physically fit, you call a personal trainer. Just as there are athletic coaches, voice coaches, and acting coaches, there are personal coaches. Personal coaches, sometimes referred to as life coaches, are usually professionally trained mental health practitioners, who, in most instances, have been successful in their professional and personal life. In addition to their professional training, they have developed special skills in helping individuals develop their potential and fulfill their goals.

Within the past years the practice of personal coaching has mushroomed. In 1994 it was estimated that there were approximately 1,000 personal or life coaches nationwide. Today, it is estimated that there are close to 5,000. As people seek to achieve greater fulfillment from their work, their marriages, and their life in general, the need for personal coaches will continue to increase. Previously, many people sought psychotherapy for personal growth not just for treatment of emotional problems or mental illness. Others wanted some other form of assistance without the association to mental illness carried by psychotherapy. Now people can turn to personal coaches, whose focus is on growth and development of all areas of one's life, rather than on internal stress and emotional conflict.

Coaching and Mentoring

Mentoring has been around for as long as there have been relationships. Mentor was the name of the royal advisor to Odysseus in Homer's *Odyssey*. A mentor is a trusted person to whom we turn for counsel, advice, and support who may act as a guide or consultant suggesting a path or course of action.

Many of us may have been fortunate to have in our lives an important person to whom we would turn for advice and counsel. This person may have been a revered uncle, a respected teacher, a member of the clergy, or our scoutmaster. We often refer to these individuals as mentors. We look to them for assistance in helping us fulfill a part of ourselves. We want to develop a better self, whether that self is in relation to our school, work, business, or profession; or we want to develop more effective skills in organizing our life. These mentors may assist us in fulfilling our dreams and aspirations, and may become role models as well.

Coaching and mentoring have a great deal in common. A personal coach is similar to a professional mentor. The coach's role is more clearly defined. The coach has no other relationship to the client than that of a coach. Therefore, there is no hidden agenda or conflict of interest. Often we seek a coach to help us achieve balance in our lives. Personal coaches believe that when all aspects of one's life are in harmony, a synergy is formed that can propel an individual forward to achieve greatness.

When we turn to a personal coach, we want to become better at whatever it is that we are focused on. We want to actualize our potential. We know that we have the potential, we know that our business can grow, or that our life can be better balanced, but we have difficulty in developing a plan of action that will help us reach our vision of the way things could be. Something is blocking us or we are too close to the project. We need a second pair of eyes. We need a boost. Professional coaches start with where you are. They work with you, as a collaborator, to help you realize your goals. Frequently, they help you define and clarify your goals. Once your goals have been articulated, they then work with you to develop a plan of action for achieving those goals.

Coaching and Consulting

Consulting is a much more recent development. Industrial consulting developed after WWII followed by executive consulting and continued to evolve with the development of the human potentials movement in the 1970s. Business schools and schools of management incorporated executive consulting into their programs. Executive consultants assisted top-level managers in developing training programs, human resources, management skills, and organizational development.

Coaching is related to consulting; some consider coaching a subset of consulting. However, the consultant normally provides the consultation service for the period of the contract; once the consultant has completed the project, the relationship terminates. In personal coaching, the coach not only helps the client develop a plan of action to achieve a desired set of goals, the coach also stays with the client to help implement the changes and goals. With a consultant you pay for an expert's advice and opinion. A coach will help you explore options. A personal coach will assist you in discovering alternatives that fit *your* agenda, rather than tell what to do. A coach will empower you to find the answers to your questions and develop a strategy for your life that is consistent with your values and beliefs. Generally speaking, coaching goes beyond consulting to incorporate all areas of your life rather than the narrower focus commonly found in consulting.

Coaching and Psychotherapy

What is the difference between coaching and psychotherapy? *Coaching is not therapy.* Personal coaches don't work on "issues" or delve into the past. Nor do they deal much with understanding human behavior. Coaches neither focus on resolving past traumas that affect personality development nor do they try to change personality structures. Coaches do not attempt to ameliorate psychic pain, anxiety, depression, or sexual dysfunction. These are issues that are dealt with in psychotherapy.

A personal coach focuses on:

> Helping people set better goals.
> Asking their clients to do more than they would on their own.
> Helping their clients to focus better so as to product results more quickly.
> Providing clients with the tools, support, and structure to accomplish more.

Whereas psychotherapy focuses on the past and the present, *coaching focuses on the present and future.* The personal coach maintains a focus on the goals that the client decides she/he would like to achieve. The collaborative effort propels the individual to continually move toward the goal. In psychotherapy, the assumption is that there is something wrong that gets in the way of a person's functioning that needs fixing. In coaching, the assumption is that there is nothing wrong with the client, but the client wants an even better life. In psychotherapy, the main focus is on the client's internal world. In coaching, the focus is on the client's entire life including health, relationships, career, spirituality, etc., and how it all fits together.

Personal coaches help people develop a balanced life. They do this through strengthening their client's personal foundation. Part of one's personal foundation is recognizing and clarifying one's core values. Most of us seldom take the time to delineate and clarify our values, those beliefs that are at the center of our belief. Often, we act in ways that our contrary to our internalized values and we end up feeling uncomfortable, guilty, or even ashamed. Frequently, we are not aware of the causes for our disquietude. On exploration, we may find that we are acting in ways that are contrary to our own value system. A coach can help you explore your values and assist in developing a set of goals and actions that comport with this value system such that you feel in synch with yourself.

Coaches have no agenda but that of their clients. It is one of the few relationships where the client's agenda is the only agenda that matters. Personal coaches want to assist you in actualizing your agenda on your terms. The objective of the coach is to open new possibilities. The attention in coaching is solely on you and your agenda.

How Does Coaching Work?

Similar to psychotherapy, coaching works best when there are regular appointments. In order to maintain focus and honor commitments, continuity is necessary. However, coaching is not limited to face-to-face meetings. In fact, most personal coaching takes place over the telephone. Coaching is not limited to geographical location. One can be coached from any location. Coaching sessions are usually thirty minutes in length, with three or four sessions scheduled per month.

There are many variables that contribute to the effectiveness of coaching:

- Better goals are set, ones that naturally impel you forward.
- Synergy between the coach and client creates momentum.
- Accountability. Knowing that you have to report to someone on progress or completion of an assignment impels you to completion.
- Time limits and deadlines may set which mitigates procrastination.
- Prioritizing tasks with your coach makes it more likely that the tasks will be accomplished.

- Tasks are put into manageable pieces to avoid feeling overwhelmed with the enormity of the task.
- You can borrow your coach's belief in you, until you develop a belief in yourself.
- You have a partner in your coach; working with someone always feels more empowering than working alone.
- You develop new skills.
- When you have a coach, you tend to take yourself more seriously.
- You take more effective and focused actions immediately.
- You stop putting up with what is holding you back.
- You set better goals that are more in accord with what you want out of life.

Why is coaching becoming so popular?

Thomas Leonard, founder of Coach University, says that coaching is becoming so popular for several reasons:

> "Many people are tired of doing what they think they 'should' do and are ready to do something special and meaningful for the rest of their lives. One problem is that many can't see what this is or, if they can, they can't find a way to reorient their life around it. A coach can help them do both.
>
> *"People are realizing how simple it can be to accomplish something that several years ago might have felt out of reach or like a pipedream. A coach is not a miracle worker . . . but a coach does have a large tool kit to help the Big Idea become a Reality. Fortunately, people now have the time and resources to invest in themselves in this kind of growth.*
>
> *"Spirituality. If you track the phenomenal success of James Redfield's Celestine Prophecy on*

the New York Times *best-seller list back in 1994, you got a sense of just how many people are willing to look at, and consider, the notion of spirituality. Wow. Many coaches are spiritually based—even the ones who coach IBM or AT&T. America is growing more spiritual very quickly. [(My) working definition of spirituality? How connected you are with yourself and others?] The coach helps the clients to tune in better to themselves and to others. "*

How can I know whether I need a coach or a therapist?

Generally, people have turned to a psychotherapist when they experience psychological pain that interferes with the conduct of their everyday life. They may experience anxiety, depression, sexual dysfunction, dysphoria, low self-esteem, lack of identity, obsessions, compulsive rituals, or a feeling that they are not functioning to capacity. Many people have turned to psychologists and other psychotherapists when they want to enhance their life. They seek therapy for personal growth and greater self-understanding.

Coaching begins where psychotherapy leaves off. The coach assumes that the client is well-functioning and is facing a roadblock or finding it difficult to get over the next mountain to greater fulfillment. People turn to coaches when their life is going well. Usually, they are high-functioning people who want to expand their lives, their businesses, and their general outlook. They tend to be successful people who have a vision that they could go beyond where they are, but feel that they would like someone to work with them to achieve their goals. These are the same people who would seek a coach to improve their golf or tennis game, seek consultation in their business, or utilize a financial planner to assist with their finances. They seek a coach to accelerate their growth or maximize an opportunity. Some people choose a coach to help in the short-term for a specific task or project, while others engage a coach to restructure their life.

What training do coaches have?

Many coaches have a background in human behavior, psychology, or human development. A large number of coaches hold licenses in a psychological discipline, e.g., psychology, counseling, social work, etc. Others have a background in business, law, or consulting. These individuals usually have sought additional training in coaching. Most all coaches have had extensive personal experience.

Many coaches, like me, have found that coaching emerged naturally out of their clinical practice. After having been in practice for over 30 years, I have developed a body of experience. I have worked with individuals for years and watched them through their various life transitions. Many times people come back after being in therapy, seeking something different from their therapy experience. They are facing an obstacle to their progress and wanted a trusted professional with whom to discuss their situation. Whether it is a business decision, a life decision, or a wish to change their lifestyle, they want a different perspective. So they have turned to me. Over the years I have found this type of relationship very rewarding. Often, these people would jokingly refer to me as "coach." Little did I know that this title was to be prophetic. I am sure that many practitioners have found their way into coaching by a similar route.

People choose their coach on the basis of whether there is reason to believe that this person can help them to accomplish their goals. If they feel comfortable with their coach and believe progress is being made, they continue. Otherwise, they terminate the relationship. Coaching is not about "the doctor knows best" model. It is about what works for you.

29

CHOOSING YOUR RESPONSE

A teenage girls walks down the street on her way home from school. On the other side of the street a group of teenage boys are congregated. Boys being boys, they notice the girl walking across the street and begin to make various remarks, inaudible to the girl, but it is obvious that they are addressing her. They whistle, they laugh as she continues walking. She feels hurt, anxious; tears well in her eyes as she accelerates her pace; she cannot wait until she is home away from the boys. Ten minutes later her identical twin sister walks down the same street on her way home from school. The boys are still across the street. They make the same sounds, laughter, whistles, and shouts. The girl smiles, slows her pace, and meanders home feeling wonderful. What happened? Why the difference in reaction to the same information? We later learn that the first teenage girl interpreted the boys' reactions as poking fun at her. She believed that they did not like her and thought she was ugly. Her sister, on the other hand, believed that the boys were flirting with her, thinking that she was pretty, and wanted to get to know her. Which sister was right?

Without additional information, we don't know who made the correct interpretation of the boys' behavior. We only know that it was an interpretation based on each of the girl's perception and self-concept. This is not an uncommon occurrence. Most of us make interpretations of data and assume that our reactions are to the data rather than to our interpretations of the data.

Events that occur in our lives are merely data. Data does not change. A spouse says something to you that you do not like. You react by getting angry. Your spouse looks at you bewildered, wondering what she/he did to evoke your reaction. You are driving down the freeway and someone flips you the proverbial "bird." There are other cars around. You interpret their gesture as intended for you, personally. You roll down your window and shout something back at the person with the upturned middle finger. In each of these instances we have the following sequence: data (event), interpretation, and reaction.

In the first scenario, your partner says something that you do not like. The data is whatever words your partner uttered plus the tone in which she/he uttered them. You hear the words and the tone and interpret them as indicating that your spouse is criticizing you. You react to your interpretation by becoming hurt or defensive. It never occurs to you that there might be another interpretation. You can't imagine that anyone else in the same situation would interpret your partner's comment any differently than you. Not only do you believe that everyone would interpret the data similarly, you also believe that everyone would react the same as you did.

In the second scenario, you interpret the data (the flip-off) as intended toward you and react by becoming angry and retaliating. It does not occur to you that the gesture could have been toward someone else or a reaction to something else or even merely an arthritic middle finger being waved in the air. Or it may be that the driver is listening to a radio show and disagrees with the host. Or she/he just got fired from his/her job and is angry at the world.

Data, interpretation, reaction. We all want to believe that we are reacting to the world as it is and that other people perceive the world similarly to ourselves. We also want to believe that others would react similarly to ourselves in similar situations. Additionally, we would like to believe that we are able to control events around us or, at the very least, that we can influence events around us. Unfortunately, this is not the way things work.

A husband and a wife go to the movies. They sit next to each other sharing a bag of popcorn. They watch the movie. After the show the two people describe the movie that they have just seen to friends. The chances are that they will describe two different movies. Each of them brings a different history to the event and will interpret the event differently. And they each will have a different reaction. In some cases, they will have entirely different reactions to the same scene! Often, it may appear that they attended two different movies!

In hospitals we often see people who come in with minor injuries reacting as if death were imminent, while other people who have experienced major injuries are reacting with calmness, as if the injury were merely a splinter.

Let us take another example. On September 11 two planes hit the World Trade Center. At first, people interpreted that horrific event as a plane having gone off-course. As such, the public had one reaction. Soon thereafter, as we received more information, another interpretation arose, with an entirely different response. And even then, there was more than one response to the same interpretation. Even at the moment, some people reacted by running away in panic; others froze in their tracks, paralyzed, while others ran back into the inferno seeking to save those trapped. Subsequently, people had many different reactions and responses to the terrorism.

The only thing we have control over is how we interpret events and how we will react to those interpretations. Think about this; it is a very powerful truth. We can interpret events (data) in multiple ways. Every event has more than one interpretation. For most events, we do not have sufficient information to be absolutely certain of only one interpretation. In addition, there are many different responses we can choose to have to any given interpretation.

Frequently, however, we will choose an interpretation that makes us feel poorly; we choose interpretations that leave us angry, hurt, insulted, or some other way damaged. Then we react to that interpretation with depression, anger, the desire to retaliate, or other equally painful emotion or behavior. In a relationship, this process can escalate into an all-out war between the parties.

You are responsible for your interpretations and for your reactions or your responses. The data (event) does not change, though the spin you put on it might. You can choose how you wish to interpret the event. Let's say, for example, your partner says, "Where are you going to get the money to pay for that? . . ." You could interpret the inquiry in any number of ways. She/he could be simply asking a question, being critical of your spending habits, making a point about priorities, etc. Each of these interpretations could result in several different reactions. One could react with anger, indignation, hurt, calm, curiosity, frustration, defensiveness, etc. The initial question could lead to many different outcomes depending on how the responder chooses to interpret the question.

A word about reactions and responses. There is a difference between reactions and responses. Reactions tend to be knee-jerk. They are instantaneous, shoot-from-the-hip comments in reaction to an interpretation. A response, by contrast, is deliberate and thoughtful, based upon reflection. One chooses to first consider the interpretation to which one will respond and then chooses an appropriate response. Sometimes the response will be an inquiry to solicit additional information or clarification. Sometimes the response may be, "Let me think about how I wish to respond. I will get back to you on that." Most situations do not necessitate an immediate reaction; a considered response, more often than not, will suffice.

We have data or event, interpretation, and reaction or response. It seems to me that a great many arguments, personal hurts, and ill feelings could be averted if we were to follow this paradigm. We could avoid some situations and ameliorate others if we analyze our feelings either before we react or afterwards. We could raise the question when perceiving an event, "How many different ways could I interpret this event?" Then we could ask the question, "How many different ways might I choose to respond to these interpretations?"

This forces us to look at ourselves. Why am I choosing to interpret this event in this particular manner? And why am I choosing to respond in this particular way? What is the benefit to me to choose this interpretation or this response? How will this interpretation create a better relationship? What is my goal in responding this way? Too often we choose an interpretation or a response that does not serve us. The interpretation does not leave us feeling good, and the response leaves us feeling poorly as well.

Why do we choose the interpretations that we do, especially ones that leave us feeling poorly? Why do we choose the responses that we do, especially when they seem to create ill will? Wouldn't it be better to choose interpretations that leave us feeling good about ourselves?

Wouldn't it make more sense to choose a response that increases our sense of well-being and creates a connection with the other person in those instances when other people are involved? It seems to me, in the absence of clear evidence to the contrary, we could choose interpretations that leave us feeling good, just as the young girl in the anecdote mentioned at the beginning of this essay did. Her sister chose an interpretation that left her feeling badly about herself. She also chose a response (more of a reaction!) that left her feeling worse. Unless they confronted the boys directly, asking what they were saying, what they intended by the comments, and then believed their answers, we have no evidence to assure the correctness of either of the girl's interpretations. However, it would seem logical to assume that the interpretation that made the girl feel good was a better choice.

Some of you may think that it is Pollyanna-like to choose a positive interpretation. After all, you might later find out that the interpretation was wrong. The girl might find out later that her crying sister was right; the boys were in fact teasing her rather than complimenting her. What was lost? She has time enough for feeling badly. Whereas her sister, on finding out that the boys were being complimentary, won't be able to erase the bad feelings she put herself through.

People like Pollyanna look through an equally distorted lens as those who look at life through dark lenses. Neither pays attention to the data and neither sees how many different interpretations could be made that fit the data. Pollyanna just views everything through rose-colored glasses, while her counterpart looks at the world negatively. The latter group is never disappointed. Their life is always filled with dissatisfaction. Those who choose to interpret data in a positive manner may be disappointed from time to time as new data emerges. However, their world is more often filled with optimism and discovery.

It has been demonstrated that those who choose to look at the world optimistically tend to live happier, more fulfilling lives. They tend to have fewer illnesses and when they are ill, they tend to recover quicker. Even their hospital stays are shorter. These folks tend more quickly to see criticism as gifts encouraging them to reach their higher selves. They see hardships as challenges forcing them to look for new solutions and to strengthen their resolve. They see even the worst scenarios as opportunities to learn something new about their world and themselves. The difficulties they face challenge them to become better, to rise to a higher level, and to increase their resilience.

Let's take a look at some real-life situations to see exactly how this approach might work.

Example 1: A husband buys his wife a present of a set of luggage for their wedding anniversary. When he gives her the luggage, instead of being happy for the gift, she is hurt. He is befuddled by her reaction. Through her tears she tells him that the gift is not romantic and that she feels discounted by him. She says that being romantic is very important to her and that luggage is something that she would buy for herself. She accuses him of being thoughtless, saying that if he really knew her he would have known that this was not an appropriate gift for her. He is unable to console her. The husband is left feeling awful.

Let's examine what happened. The data was receiving an anniversary gift consisting of a set of luggage. The wife interpreted the gift through her own set of expectations and her own belief system. She was disappointed because the gift from her husband did not fit her expectations and was not on her list of what she considered appropriate, romantic gifts. She immediately assumed that he was not feeling romantic towards her, and that the gift was merely a practical gift that she could have purchased for herself. Having this interpretation, she then reacted to the internal hurt. She was not responding, but simply reacting, based on an inner experience predicated on her interpretation.

She could have just as soon had several other interpretations of the data. She could have thought it quite romantic because it implied that they would be going on a vacation. She could have thought it very considerate since she had been traveling for business a great deal and he wanted her to symbolically take a piece of him with her. She could have thought of it as demonstrating that indeed he was thinking specifically of her knowing that: (a) she was traveling a great deal, and (b) he knew that she liked to go on vacations to exotic places and the gift was making an implicit promise to make use of the luggage in that way.

Each of these interpretations could have led to a series of different responses in which case both husband and wife would have felt good about each other and themselves. Instead, by choosing the interpretation that she did and having the reaction that she had, they both ended up feeling badly.

Example 2: A man walks into a restaurant with a colleague. He notices his girlfriend of six months sitting at a table with a man he does not know. She is holding his hand, as they are engaged in what appears to be intimate dialogue. She does not notice her boyfriend and continues the conversation. Her boyfriend leaves the restaurant in a stew. He is hurt and angry and contemplates making a scene, but his colleague stops him. When he and his girlfriend get together he expresses his hurt, anger, and jealousy. He accuses her of having an affair, or at the very least, of flirting with the stranger.

Again, we see how he took the data, interpreted it, and then reacted to his interpretation. In retrospect, it is easy to see that there are a number of other interpretations that could have been made that would have accounted for the data. The stranger could have been a relative, an old school chum, or a co-worker. He could have been telling her that he just was fired, that his wife died, that he has cancer. Any of these would have accounted for their behavior. She could have been holding his hand as a way of offering comfort. The boyfriend could have chosen to respond in any number of ways to each of these interpretations. He could have chosen to simply state that he noticed her in the restaurant and that because she seemed to be involved in a serious conversation he did not want to interrupt. He could have gone over to the couple and introduced himself. He could have inquired about the conversation he observed, once they got together in the evening. Nothing about the situation required that he make the interpretation that he chose or to have the reaction he had.

These are but two of hundreds of examples that I could have used to illustrate the point of this essay. In each case, the reactor chose an interpretation that could only leave him or her feeling poorly. They set themselves up to feel miserable and subsequently made their partner miserable as well. It would have been easy to pause and ask themselves the question, "Given the available data, how can I interpret this event in such a way that I feel good?" How could I respond in a way that more closely resembles my ideal self?

The next time you are faced with a situation in which you find yourself interpreting the event in such a way as you end up feeling badly, ask yourself, "What is the data, how shall I interpret it, and how shall I choose to respond?" Remember, you are responsible for your interpretations and your responses. Hence, how you feel depends on you, not upon the circumstances in which you find yourself.

30

DESIGNING YOUR LIFE

If you were designing a custom home, your dream house, the house that you have always wanted, where how would you begin? Chances are that you would begin by contacting an architect who would help you put your ideas, your vision, on paper. The architect would ask you, "What kind of house did you have in mind? What did you envision?" The process would begin with an idea of what you wanted. You would literally see the house in your mind, whether it was a house openly connected to the outdoors or a formal house in which you felt secure. You would have some idea of how the rooms would be connected to each other and the areas of the house that you would use for entertainment, for sleeping, for eating, and so on. In short, you would have a concept of what you wanted the house to represent. From the preliminary conversations with the architect, to the sketches, to actual blueprints that would be sent out for bids by a contractor, you would see your ideas develop into a concrete plan. And this plan would guide the contractor to build your dream house. You would not be surprised if it took months to develop this plan or even years, depending upon the degree of complexity and the details that were to be included in the house. The more details, the less likely there will be problems along the way.

You would engage in a similar process if you were designing a business. You would have to develop a well thought-out business plan. You would begin with a vision. You would have an idea for the business you wanted to build and you would develop a plan for how you intended to develop this business. You would want to translate your vision into action. Each aspect of the business would have to be thought out in advance. You would want to know how much capital you would need, how many employees, what size facility, the cost of products, supplies, and personnel. You would have to figure how to market your business, where to advertise, and how to promote the business in general. You would figure out mark-ups, profit margins, projected sales, etc. Your business plan might take months or even years to develop. The better your business plan, the more likely you will be to succeed. And the plan must be in writing. No one would hire an architect or contractor to build a house who said, "I have the plans in my head." No bank would loan money to an entrepreneur who said, "I have my business plan in my head."

Yet, when it comes to building our lives, rarely do we hear people say that they have a "life plan." Most people spend little or no time developing a plan for their life. Fewer even consider writing a life plan. Most people's lives look like they have been developed without having a plan. People's lives look like they have been thrown together haphazardly in the hopes that they would work. People have lives that don't have architectural integrity; they don't hang together as a whole. Parts of their lives work, while other parts are falling apart. Much like a house that's built without a plan, the living room may work, but the kitchen doesn't seem to fit with the rest of the house. The rooms seem off, skewed, as if they were simply banged together like so many boxes.

Imagine what your life might look like if you actually designed it in the same manner as you would design your dream house.[14] Imagine if your life had the same attention to detail, the same integrity, and the same sense of craftsmanship as that custom-built house you would love to own and live in. Imagine how you would feel living that life, as you would feel living in your dream house.

The question is, "Are you willing to put in the time and effort to design, plan, and construct your dream life?" Henry David Thoreau declared that most people live lives of quiet desperation. There is no doubt that the folks to whom Thoreau was referring did not design their lives. The truth is that most of us simply fall into our lives. It sort of develops around us as we are pursuing our careers, motherhood, or other goal. We tend to operate in the world like a horse with blinders on. We pursue our careers with focus and dedication trying to get ahead, but we seldom look around us to see what effect our single-mindedness is having on the rest of our life. We decide to become parents almost as an end in itself, with little concern for what it will mean to the rest of our life or where it will take us in the future, or how children will fit into our life. Rather, we build our life around the children, with no thought to what will happen when they leave. For the most part we think only of the immediate and short-term, seldom looking down the road to see where our choices may lead us in the long term.

The closest many people ever come to having a life plan is, "I want to have a good job, a lovely/handsome wife/husband, nice house in the suburbs, a couple of children, and two cars." Not much of a plan. It would be like telling one's architect, "I want a nice house with four bedrooms, a big yard, and a two-car garage." Without a clear, well-defined, well-articulated, detailed plan, we run the risk of living a life that is bland or, at worst, unsatisfying. We use more imagination in preparing for an important dinner party or event than we do in planning our life.

We often admire other people's lives, homes, careers, events, etc. and think that we could not have anything that even resembled theirs. The only reason those "others" seem to have what we want is because they took the time to plan for it. They put in the energy to be creative. Regardless of how much money they had, they designed their situation with maximum attention to detail. One does not have to have the best that money can buy; one can have the best that one's circumstances permit, and perhaps a little more. It takes desire, time, commitment, energy, creativity, discipline and the motivation to make one's dreams come true. As Napoleon Hill proclaimed, "Conceive it, believe it, achieve it!"

I operate from the assumption that a life based on a well thought-out, detailed, and integrated plan will be more gratifying and fulfilling than one that is not. I further believe that having such a plan, in writing, and following it, while at the same making adjustments as needed, will be more rewarding and more balanced. If all of the parts of your life are integrated into a whole, you will experience an extraordinary sense of power. You will be able to reach a higher level of mastery over your world and realize more of your human potential. Clearly, some plans are better than others. A poor plan may be no better than no plan, and in some cases, may be worse. The quality of the plan matters in business, in houses, and in lives.

Remodeling vs. Building New

When we think about designing a home, we often have to confront the issue of whether we should remodel our current residence, buy another home, or build a new home. When it comes to our lives, however, few of us have the choice of whether to create a totally new life or remodel the life we have. We certainly cannot go out and buy another life . . . a life that someone else has already lived! Most of us cannot simply discard the life we have and start anew; we are already living a life. We cannot stay, "Stop the world; I want to get off so I can build a new life for myself." Therefore, most of us have to resort to remodeling the life we have.

Once we decide to remodel, we should do a thorough inspection and evaluation as a beginning step in the process. This inspection will help determine the vision and the plan for what we want to accomplish. The inspection includes an evaluation of the infrastructure and foundation. Similarly, in restructuring a life, we must examine our own foundation. We must examine our personality, our history, our beliefs, our values, our aspirations, our hopes, and so on. This personal inventory will significantly influence the life we construct. Sometimes, it is necessary to do some serious soul-searching; sometimes it may require that we call in a consultant to help us correct some psychological issues that affect our functioning. The point is, we cannot remodel our lives on a shaky foundation any more than we could remodel a home on a shaky foundation.

Once the foundation is supported, shored, or repaired, we can decide on what type of structure it can support. Just as we cannot build a two-story house on every foundation, we may not be able to construct an elaborate life on a foundation that cannot sustain it. Whether a life or a home, we must be realistic!

When remodeling, we must have a plan in mind, and it must be put in writing. Writing out the plan keeps us focused. It keeps us on track. We can make notes as we go along, correcting and modifying as needed. In architectural terms, these are called field changes, i.e., changes made in the field to take into account new information. Hence, flexibility is necessary. Similarly, in life, there are many contingencies that must be taken into account that were not predicted at the outset.

Fail to Plan = Plan to Fail

"If you fail to plan, you are planning to fail." This adage ordinarily applies to business, projects, and other activities that require planning. But it is also true for how we live our lives. As I have suggested previously, we plan for many things in our life—parties, vacations, home construction, weddings, and so on. But we don't plan our lives. We just live them. I suggested that we would not consider building a house without a well-thought-out plan, indicating all of the steps necessary for the desired outcome. When it comes to housing, businesses, vacations, or even weddings, we know what we want the outcome to look like. We have a vision and we develop a plan for achieving that vision. Yet, most of us do not have either a vision or a plan for our lives. And then we wonder why our lives seldom evolve in the way in which we had hoped. Our lives resemble a house that was built without a plan.

I recall when my children were just kids and they wanted to plant a vegetable garden in our backyard. I thought it would be a great idea for us as a family—a joint venture. I asked them what kinds of vegetables they wanted to plant and suggested that we sit down and plan out the limited space we had for the vegetable they wished to plant.

Well, as you might well imagine, they did not want to take the time to plan the garden. They wanted to just go out to buy the plants and get them into the ground. Not wanting a battle on my hands, I agreed. We went out and bought the plants: zucchini, watermelon, string beans, tomatoes, radishes, and carrots. The plants were very tiny in their individual containers.

The kids wanted six of each. We brought them home, cultivated the soil, and planted them, trying to give them as much space as the small plot of land would allow. My children had a great time planting. Now they had to wait for the plants grow. They were ready to harvest. And the plants did grow.

Over the next several weeks of summer, they grew and grew and grew. The zucchini and the watermelon grew huge; the string beans snaked throughout the garden, as did the tomatoes. The carrots and radishes didn't stand a chance. The other larger and more aggressive vegetables soon crowded them out. What started out as cute little plants all lined up in their freshly cultivated and fertilized rows ended up as a jungle, with each vegetable tangling with the others, fighting for the available nutrients. It was a big mess. Eventually, only the zucchini survived.

My children learned a valuable lesson, the value of planning. What looks cute and workable in the beginning may turn out to be quite ways off the mark when fully executed. When planning, one must think long-term. Slightly off at the beginning can lead to being way off months or years later. Just think of the trajectory of a bullet, slightly off as looked down the sight, will be way off as it approaches its mark.

A Life Vision

So now that we understand the concept, how do you begin designing your life? As with any other design, designing a life begins with a vision. If we are going to have a vision, the vision should be complete. It should cover all areas of your life, as you would like to live it. Your vision should be vivid, crisp, so much so that when you visualize yourself in your life, you can almost feel it as though it were real.

There is no sense visualizing a sloppy life. If you were visualizing yourself playing golf, you wouldn't visualize the bad shots. You would visualize yourself playing the perfect game. Every shot would be solid and true. Similarly, when you visualize your life, it should be solid and true. In order to visualize your life, you must know what goes into a well-balanced life.

A Well-Balanced Life

Most researchers agree that are eight areas that make for a balanced life. The data is derived from explorations of high-achieving individuals, studies in self-actualization, and research into what makes for highly effective individuals. These areas are:

* Personal growth
* Spirituality
* Recreation
* Health and fitness
* Community involvement
* Career
* Family and social life
* Financial security

Personal growth refers to activities that are geared toward developing the individual as a person. It is a combination of psychological, intellectual, and emotional development. Such activities as personal exploration through psychotherapy, self-reflection, educational activities, self-help groups, etc. would be included in this sector.

Spirituality includes, but is not limited, to religion. In fact, religious beliefs may or may not be included. Spirituality refers to activities that enhance one's experience of being part of something that is larger than one's self. It is a heightened state of consciousness that can be achieved through meditation, prayer, experiencing nature, pondering the imponderable questions as to the meaning of life, increasing one's understanding of the nature of the universe, and even through metaphysics. Spirituality is the indefinable experience that often occurs when we view a sunset or majestic mountain, or when we connect with another human being. It is a sense of renewal that comes from inside, from what might be called, our soul. Recent reports have indicated that there is a positive correlation between spirituality and recovery from illness, rapidity of healing, and longevity. Spirituality can be an attitude that one brings to an event. For example, many surfers and hikers have said that they have a spiritual experience when on the waves or in the hills, communing with nature and experiencing the vastness of the universe.

Recreational activities are those in which we participate on a regular basis, but not necessarily daily or weekly. These activities could be sports or hobbies that enhance our sense of well-being, give us respite from the everyday activities, and a chance to renew ourselves in a relaxed way without pressure. The activities may be physical and outdoors or sedentary and indoors. Such activities as golf, photography, collecting, climbing, hiking, biking, and sailing all fall into the recreational category. To be recreational, the activity would have to be regularly enjoyed rather than only once in a while.

Health and fitness concerns itself with how we eat, how we take care of our body and mind, and how we exercise. Food is the fuel that runs the machine that creates the life we want. People often take better care of their cars than they do of themselves. They would not think of putting cheap gas and oil in their Porsche Carerra, but they eat fast foods with high fat content. Exercise is an important component of a balanced life. Exercise stimulates the heart, brain, muscles, and lungs. All of these are essential for a balanced life. It is difficult to achieve harmony and balance when one is feeling poorly. There is abundant evidence indicating the positive affects of diet and exercise on emotional and physical well-being.

Community involvement is positively correlated with happiness and even with physical health. People who participate in some form of community activity, such as volunteering with non-profit agencies, being active on a city counsel, becoming involved in a political campaign, or other political or community involvement live happier, fuller, more rewarding lives, with fewer illnesses.

Career satisfaction plays an important part in one's overall feeling about one's self. We identify with our work and our profession. When we enjoy what we do for a living, and derive satisfaction from doing a job well, we feel better about ourselves. For most people, money is not the most important reason they work. Job satisfaction, feeling appreciated and valued, feeling competent, all rank higher than money. However, when these issues are not addressed, we often seek more money to make up for it. Of course, money is important. If we are not adequately compensated for our labors, we feel distressed and even angry. It permeates our life. If we feel trapped in a job that we do not like, despite the money, we feel distressed and discontent. People need to feel connected to what they do for a living. Hence, one's fulfillment with their work can affect their entire life.

Family and social life are major contributors to our sense of fulfillment, happiness, and satisfaction with our life. If one is lonely, unhappily married, or isolated from family and friends, it affects one's entire emotional state. Unhappy relationships affect our physical health, our productivity, our ability to concentrate, our feelings about ourselves, and even our very sense of self. The more content one feels in one's relationships and family, the more content and meaningful one's life will be experienced.

Financial security is another important factor contributing to one's sense of well-being. Finances are separate from one's career. You can love your career, but if you are not able to pay your bills, you will be very distraught. Similarly, one can feel very financially secure, but if you hate your job, you will be likewise distraught. Keeping one's financial house in order is extremely important for a sense of well-being, contentment, and happiness with one's life. Too many people live from day to day, paycheck to paycheck, living with a constant state of dread realizing that they are one step away from homelessness. Any tragedy, serious illness, or change in the economy can send them into a serious depression and perilous circumstance. More than one person ended his or her life because of financial ruin.

Designing Your House

These are the eight sectors (rooms, if you will) in a person's psychological house. Many people spend far too much time developing one sector, at the expense of the others. They live in a one-room apartment rather than an eight-room house. Or worse, they live in one room while the others decay from neglect. Men are notorious for doing this. They spend a great deal of time developing their careers, professional life, or business, often to the neglect of their families, their health, or any other area of their life.

There are inherent dangers to this approach. First, they may lose their families because their spouse may become dissatisfied and decide to dissolve the marriage. Second, if their health suffers, they are not able to continue their careers. Third, if they lose their jobs due to layoffs or economic changes, they have nothing to fall back upon. A person with a balanced life has seven other sectors to fall back upon in a time of crisis. The same could be said for any of the other sectors. A woman builds her life around her family. This is the only sector in which she spends her time. A tragedy strikes. Her husband dies, loses his job, or runs off with another woman. Or her children simply grow up; she is no longer needed as "supermom." What does she have left?

While everyone's life will have the same eight sectors, the sizes of the sectors will vary (just as all houses have similar rooms that vary in size). Some people will spend more time and energy in their health and fitness room or community sector, while others will spend more time in their career and finance sectors. The important thing is that all sectors must be furnished, however sparsely. Some basic activities (furniture) are required in each sector. For example, there should be at least daily exercise and health eating in the heath and fitness sector.

What kind of life do you want for yourself? What is the overall purpose of your life? What does it represent? Lives, like houses, come in all sizes, shapes, and styles. If we fail to design the life we want, we run the risk of ending up with a life that we don't find satisfying, rewarding, or meaningful. Hence, it is important that you think about what you want your life to represent. If you were designing a restaurant, you would not simply say that you want to serve food, nor would you say that you merely wanted to open an Italian restaurant. Rather, you would have a concept, such as a place where people can feel as though they were in an Italian home, as guests, eating with the family. This is a very different mission than saying a place where people can dine in an elegant, intimate atmosphere resembling what one would find in Northern Italy where people dine in quiet sophistication. These two restaurants have very different missions. Their respective missions would guide them as the underlying philosophy for pursuing their vision.

A Clear Vision

Now that you have an idea of what goes into a vision for your life, it is time to construct one for yourself. Begin with a series of statements that clearly represent the life that you want. Include in it statements about how you see yourself living that life. Your vision should allow you to actually "see" yourself, as you want to be, living the life you want to live. This vision serves as the blueprint for future action. You will have to ask yourself, "Am I doing all that I can do to make my vision a reality?" If you are not, then ask, "Why not?" Ask yourself what you are doing that moves you away from your vision and why are you doing it?

The following are examples of a vision statement:

1) *I picture myself well-groomed, muscular, healthy, vibrant, and vital. My high energy, articulate speech and self-confidence naturally attract people to me. I care about people and desire to enhance the lives of those with whom I come into contact. I can see myself as a good listener who is empathic with the feelings of others. I am focused and committed to making a difference in the lives of others, in my community, and in the world. I can see myself being comfortable in a corporate boardroom working with leaders, in an office working with individuals, and groups. I visualize myself serving on the board of directors developing policy that can help others achieve their potential. I envision myself as possessing a spiritual side that recognizes that all people are connected to one another and to the world around them. I see myself living in a beautiful home, tastefully furnished, where people feel comfortable and welcome. I visualize myself being financially secure, affluent, enjoying the good things in life, enjoying the fruits of my efforts. I see my family, wife, children, grandchildren, grandchildren, nephews, as well as my sisters, brother-in-laws and sister-in-laws around me, appreciating each other closely and being friendly. I have a picture of my life as fulfilling, exciting, loving, caring, and joyful, participating fully in my community, while achieving recognition, respect, and acknowledgement from those around me.*

2) *I see myself connected to nature. I imagine living in a home near*

or in the mountains or ocean, where the air is clean. I can see myself involved in environmental issues in my community. My home is rustic, utilizing natural elements as much as possible. I visualize myself focusing more on my family and community than on earning money. I imagine that I am working for an agency that concerns itself with protecting the environment or improving the quality of our environment. I can see myself teaching my children about the wonders of nature and the responsibility that we all have for protecting our natural gifts. I see myself married to a woman/man who shares my interest in the environment and who is a life partner. I see myself hiking and biking along the beach and through the hills, or even kayaking in the early morning hours appreciating the serenity and wonder of our planet. I can feel a spiritual sense of being part of a larger whole. All of my activities are directed toward a similar end of being connected to the world around me.

Once you have developed a vision of the life you want, then it is time to articulate a mission statement. Your mission statement should be derived from your vision.

Mission Statement

A mission statement for your life serves as an overarching principle that gives your life coherence and integrity. When you have a mission statement, you are able to ask yourself whether the decision you are about to make or the direction you are heading, honors your mission statement. Your mission statement becomes the acid test for all decisions and actions. If what you are about to do, how you are behaving, or the decision you are about to make, does not honor your mission statement, then you must ask yourself why you are doing it. Everything you do, every decision you make, should honor you personal mission statement.

A mission statement gives purpose and direction to your

life. It is based on principals and values that represent you. It is a declaration of your highest ideals, letting the world know what you stand for. A mission statement may be short or long. It does not have to be complex. However, it should be substantive enough to be meaningful and give direction to your life. Having a clearly stated mission statement can serve as a guide directing your life. The following are two examples of mission statements:

1. To live life with integrity, respect for the rights and dignity of others, with empathy and compassion for all human beings; make a contribution to society, my community, my country; earn the respect of my wife, children, and grandchildren; participate in the lives of my family members with love and generosity; be open to criticism, learn from my own mistakes, and to continuously strive to be a better person, husband, and father; earn sufficient income and achieve sufficient wealth such that I can enjoy the "good life" while working, and in retirement, have sufficient wealth to enable me to travel and care for the needs of my wife and myself.
2. To live an energetic life, focusing on accumulating and creating wealth through innovative ideas that benefit others, while being ethical and responsible; to make a difference in the world through political involvement and influence; to approach the world as filled with opportunity.

Making a Plan

Now that you have a clear vision, a mission, and an idea of what sectors are needed for a balanced life, it is time to draw the plans for your life. For each of the eight areas previously discussed, make a list of activities that you would include in each area. Think not only about the activities in which you are already engaged, but also of those activities in which you might wish to become engaged. Let your mind wander outside of the box. Do not think of practical constraints such as time, money, or skill. Look at the following examples:

> *Personal growth*: joining a self-help group; psychotherapy; taking classes at a local college; participating in a study group; learning meditation; reading non-fiction

> *Spirituality*: meditation; prayer; exploring nature; quiet contemplation; going to church or temple

> *Recreation*: hiking; biking; playing chess; collecting; tennis or golf; antique hunting; attending movies or plays; hobbies of any kind

> *Health and fitness*: going to the gym; jogging; biking; planning one's diet; avoiding toxins; yoga; participating in a regular fitness program

> *Community involvement*: local, state, or national politics; volunteering at a non-profit facility; participating on a committee to advance some social cause

> *Career*: working at a job that creates value; doing the job with integrity; gaining satisfaction from doing a job well; finding

right livelihood that enhances one's self-esteem; working with others cooperatively

Family and social life: participating in regular family activities; dinner with the family; recreation and vacations; participating in daily family life; family conversations

Financial security: planning one's finances carefully; keeping a budget; regular savings and investments; planning for retirement; living trust; having a will; having a living will; planning for your eventual death

Once you have listed some ideas for filling your life, you should go through the list again. This time, think about your vision; think about your mission. Each item listed in each of the eight categories should be tweaked so that it comports with both your vision and your mission. Each item should further your vision while honoring your mission. To the extent possible, try to have some items work in more than one category. For example, similar items may work in both recreation and family insofar as the recreational activities are done with your family.

You do not have to fill each area of your plan immediately. Quite the contrary. You should take your time. Spend time thinking about how you would like to furnish your life. Do some reading. Collect information. Try a few things on; similar to bringing home a piece of furniture or a painting, you want to see how it looks in your home before purchasing it. Just as designing your life takes time, furnishing it takes time as well. It is a work in progress. The important thing is to maintain a consciousness about your life. Reflect upon yourself and the life you're building. Think about what you are doing and ask whether the action moves you in the direction of honoring your vision and respecting your mission. In time, with discipline, dedication, patience, and consciousness you will have designed the life you want.

The 8-Week Cycle

Buy a loose-leaf notebook and divide it into ten sections labeling them: vision, mission, financial, spiritual, recreational, career, personal growth, health and fitness, community, and family and social.

Once you have your notebook set up, and place at least one sheet of paper into each section. On the sheet in the section labeled "Vision," write down your vision statement. On the sheet in the section labeled "Mission," write down your mission statement. In each subsequent section, indicate some of the activities, projects, ideas, etc. that you are already doing and that you have thought about from time to time.

For instance, in the financial sector, many people have thought about preparing a will or opening a family trust, or starting a savings plan, but have not yet gotten around to doing it. These items should be listed on the sheet. If you have these items, write them down anyway. If they need to be modified, indicate that as well. Write down any thoughts you may have as to how you might improve your financial condition.

Your notebook is a work in progress. It is your brainstorming vehicle. A worksheet, if you will, from which a specific, goal-oriented plan will be developed later.

From this point onward, the 8-week cycle begins. The plan will help you flesh out each of the sectors over time. The way it works is, for the first week of the plan you will only think about and work on one sector. During the course of the week your focus will be on this sector. You are not expected to complete the room in one week. You are just going to think about it, or perhaps investigate areas that you might consider putting in the room.

On week two, pick another area and do the same thing with it. On week three, do it again with another area. After eight weeks, you start all over again. With each eight-week cycle you are to add to each sector until it becomes more complete. A room is done when you feel satisfied with the activities that you have placed in it. For example, if we look at the health and fitness area, it may be complete when you have changed your diet so that you are eating healthier, have begun you exercise program, and have made these activities an integral part of your life. Once you have completed each area, the task becomes one of maintenance, making sure that you are vigilant about keeping on track with your life.

As you proceed in designing your life, regularly refer to your vision and mission statements to guide you in choosing activities that bring you closer to your vision while honoring your mission. Work toward having each of the sectors of your life support and sustain other sectors. This will give more power to your life. For instance, when choosing a community activity, you might think about how this activity might support your career. Try having your spiritual life support you social life as well as your psychological growth. When all areas are synchronized as much as possible with each other, your life takes on a synergy that will propel you forward. Try to avoid activities that are in conflict with your mission or with other areas of your life. When all areas of your life are lined up in synch with one another, you will experience a harmonious state; a state of balance. This is our goal. It is not easy to achieve. Hence, it is always a work in progress. It is something to strive toward rather than an end in itself.

SUGGESTED READINGS

Belliveau, Fred and Lin Richter, *Understanding Human Sexual Inadequacy*, New York: Bantom Books, 1970.

Bly, Robert, *Iron John*, New York: Addison-Wesley, 1990.

Bradshaw, John, *Healing the Shame that Binds You*, Florida: Health Communications, Inc., 1988.

Bruch, Hoilde, *Conversations with Anorexics*, New York: Jason Aronson, 1995.

Cousins, Norman, *Anatomy of an Illness*, Bantam Doubleday Dell, 1991.

Dreyfus, Edward A., *Someone Right For You*, New York: TAB/ McGraw-Hill, 1992.

Dreyfus, Edward A. *Someone Right for You: 21st Century Strategies for Finding Your Special Someone*, Philadelphia: Xlibris, 2003.

Erikson, Erik H., *Childhood and Society*, New York: Norton, 1950.

Hall, Lindsey and Leigh Cohn, *Bulimia: A Guide to Recovery*, New York: Gurze Designs & Books, 1992.

Hartman, William and Marilyn Fithian, *Treatment of Sexual Dysfunction*, New York: Jason Aronson Publishers, 1974.

Hite, Shere, *The Hite Report*, New York: MacMillan Publishers, 1976.

Kaplan, Helen Singer, *The New Sex Therapy*, New York: Times

Books, 1974.

Karen, Robert, *Becoming Attached,*

Keen, Sam, *Fire in the Belly,* New York: Bantam Books, 1991.

Mallinger, Allan E., *Too Perfect: When Being in Control Gets Out of Control,* New York: Fawcett Books, 1993.

May, Rollo, *Existence,* New York: Basic Books, 1958.

Menninger, Karl, *The Vital Balance,* New York: Viking Press, 1963.

Moyer, Bill, *Healing the Mind,* Main Street Book, 1995.

Roth, Geneen, *Feeding the Hungry Heart,* New York: Plume, 1993.

Roth, Geneen, *Breaking Free From Compulsive Eating,* New York: Plume, 1993.

Sandbek, Terence, *The Deadly Diet: Recovering from Anorexia & Bulimia,* New York: New Harbinger, 1993.

Szasz, Thomas, *The Myth of Mental Illness,* New York: Hoeber-Harper, 1961.

Wheelis, Allen, *How People Change,* New York: Harper & Row, 1975.

Endnotes

1   Thomas Szasz, *The Myth of Mental Illness*, New York: Hoeber-Harper, 1961.

2   Karl Menninger, *The Vital Balance*, New York: Viking Press, 1963.

3   *Substance Abuse: The Nation's Number One Health Problem*, by the Robert Wood Johnson Foundation

4   Edward A. Dreyfus, *Someone Right For You*, New York: TAB/ McGraw-Hill, 1992.

5   A highly recommended book by Robert Karen, Ph.D., entitled *Becoming Attached*, was the source of much of the data cited in this chapter.

6   Based in part on *Couples Psychotherapy from an Attachment Perspective* by Sondra Goldman, Ph.D. and Susan Thau, Ph.D.

7   Sam Keen, *Fire in the Belly*, New York: Bantam Books, 1991.

8   Robert Bly, *Iron John*, New York: Addison-Wesley, 1990.

9   May Rollo, *Existence*, New York: Basic Books, 1958.

10 This article was based on information provided by the National Institute of Health

11 Bill Moyer, *Healing the Mind*, Main Street Book, 1995.

12 Norman Cousins, *Anatomy of an Illness*, Bantam Doubleday Dell, 1991.

[13] Allen Wheelis, M.D., *How People Change*, New York: Harper & Row, 1975.

[14] Throughout this chapter I will be comparing building or remodeling a house to the process of designing and creating a life for yourself. This is a convenient analogy. I recognize that while there are many similarities between home building or remodeling to building and planning a life, there are many significant differences as well. A home is static, while a life is dynamic. There are many forces influencing the development of a life that are not present in building a house. Just as there are many contingencies that may come up while remodeling or building a home that have to dealt with as they come up, there are even more that come up when designing and creating a life. However, the concept of planning, designing, building a life is analogous to building a home. In both instances one must plan; one must be conscious. All of the parts must work together in order to have a well-constructed life or home.

www.ingramcontent.com/pod-product-compliance
Lightning Source LLC
Chambersburg PA
CBHW071149290526
45788CB00001BA/66